BABYSENSE

Written by Frances Wells Burck
With the help of over 500 parents

BABY SENSE

A Practical and Supportive Guide
to Baby Care

St. Martin's Press / New York

Manufactured in the United States of America
Library of Congress Catalog Card Number: 79-2476

Design by Lynn Braswell

Library of Congress Cataloging in Publication Data

Burck, Frances Wells.
  Babysense: a practical and supportive guide to baby care.

  1. Infants—Care and hygiene. I. Title.
RJ61.B948   649'.122   79-2476
ISBN 0-312-06457-8
ISBN 0-312-06458-6 pbk.

ACKNOWLEDGMENTS

The Roots of Love. Copyright © 1977 by Helen S. Arnstein. Reprinted by permission of Bobbs-Merrill Co., Inc., New York.

The Mother Person. Copyright © 1977 by Virginia Barber and Merrill Maguire Skaggs. Reprinted by permission of Bobbs-Merrill Co., Inc., New York.

The Well-Body Book. Copyright © 1973 by Hal Bennett and Michael Samuels. Reprinted by permission of Random House, Inc., New York.

Our Bodies, Ourselves. Copyright © 1972 by Boston Women's Health Book Collective, Inc. Reprinted by permission of Boston Women's Health Book Collective, Inc., W. Somerville, Massachussetts.

Infants and Mothers: Individual Differences in Development. Copyright © 1969 by T. Berry Brazelton. Reprinted by permission of Delacorte Press, New York.

The Cesarean Birth Experience. Copyright © 1977 by Bonnie Donovan. Reprinted by permission of Beacon Press, Boston, Massachussetts.

Distress and Comfort. Copyright © 1977 by Judy Dunn. Reprinted by permission of Harvard University Press, Cambridge, Massachussetts.

The Complete Book of Breast Feeding. Copyright © 1973 by Marvin S. Eiger and Sally Wendkos Olds. Reprinted by permission of Workman Publishing, Inc., New York.

The Magic Years. Copyright © 1959 by Selma Fraiberg. Reprinted by permission of Charles Scribner's Sons, New York.

The Womanly Art of Breastfeeding. Copyright © 1974 by La Leche League International. Reprinted by permission of La Leche League International, Franklin Park, Illinois.

Babyhood: Infant Development from Birth to Two Years. Copyright © 1974 by Penelope Leach. Reprinted by permission of Alfred A. Knopf, Inc., New York.

Now That You've Had Your Baby. Copyright © 1976 by Gideon G. Panter and Shirley Motter Linde. Reprinted by permission of David McKay Co., Inc., New York.

Don't Risk Your Child's Life. Copyright © 1971 by Physicians for Automotive Safety. Reprinted by permission of Physicians for Automotive Safety, Irvington, New Jersey.

The First Five Years. Copyright © 1973 by Virginia E. Pomeranz and Dodi Schultz. Reprinted by permission of Doubleday & Co., New York.

The Mother's Medical Encyclopedia. Copyright © 1972 by Virginia E. Pomeranz and Dodi Schultz. Reprinted by permission of The New American Library, Inc., New York.

Sylvia Porter's Money Book. Copyright © 1977 by Sylvia Porter. Reprinted by permission of Doubleday & Co., New York.

Preparing for Parenthood. Copyright © 1974 by Lee Salk. Reprinted by permission of David McKay Co., Inc., New York.

Baby and Child Care. Copyright © 1945, 1946, 1957, 1968 by Benjamin Spock, M.D. Reprinted by permission of Simon & Schuster, New York.

The First Three Years of Life. Copyright © 1975 by Burton L. White. Reprinted by permission of Prentice-Hall, Inc., Englewood Cliffs, New Jersey.

Contents

For Caitlin

Acknowledgments

Everyone who contributed ideas, information, experiences, and feelings is thanked in the back of this book. But I want to thank some people at least twice for being particularly helpful. They are Charlie Burck, my husband, for his support and enthusiasm, his experience and perception as a writer—and his help with child care; David Outerbridge for helping me in myriad ways to organize and translate a foggy idea into a reality; Joanne Michaels and Barbara Anderson for editing and making many useful suggestions; Joan MacNamara for assisting with some of the research and creating designs and instructions; Dr. Irwin Rappaport for answering many questions; Phyllis Silverman for welcoming me into her discussion group; and Mel Layton for typing the manuscript.

A special thanks to my parents, Frances and George Wells, and my friends Carolyn Curran and Meredith Hughes for listening so thoughtfully to me talk about the book. I also want to thank my special "mother friends"—Rosalie Austin, Harriette Heller, Pud Houstoun, Bette Lacina, Lisa McMullin, and Carol Morse—for all their ideas, encouragement, and useful criticism. And, of course, without the help of Mildred Burck and Gilbert Burck, Lila Pais, Mary Jo Martin, and Judy Brown, who so lovingly shared Caitlin's care, the writing of this book would not have been possible.

Introduction

I hope *Babysense* is the book I needed three years ago when our first child was born—a book that is practical as well as supportive. I say "hope" rather tentatively because I will never again be a first-time parent, and though I have tried very hard not to forget how that felt, those early months are only a memory, a pastiche of highs and lows, joys, discoveries, great tenderness—and some horrors. I am no longer in that state. But it's more than likely that you are, with a baby who is either in your arms or in your thoughts during most of your waking hours. Each baby brings his or her joys and challenges, but never again will one be so totally new, quite so nerve-wracking, consuming, or as exciting as the first.

When I look back over the first year of our child Caitlin's life, I realize there is a great deal I know now that I wish I'd known before. This is true of all of us. Much of parenting in our complex world is an art that can be learned only through experience. We do not know from instinct.

Some mastery of the practical and the logistical—learning how to bathe a newborn, prepare a day's supply of formula, find and assess good medical care, and so on, are essential both to the baby and the parent on the most basic physical level. Knowing that you are not alone in your feelings can truly make a difference in terms of psychological survival. For it is both these types of knowledge, about our babies' needs and our own, that free us to enjoy our babies, know them, love them, help them learn, and learn from them without the distortions fostered by feelings of inadequacy.

My husband and I spent a lot of time reinventing the wheel—working out solutions to problems that had been worked out before by millions of other parents. We were just too isolated to know any better. This is the biggest problem most new parents face. A lucky few will have a friend with a baby a couple of months older who has already lived through a particular growth stage and has some suggestions. More frequently we found that our friends had children already walking and talking, or they had no children at all. The few parents we knew had forgotten the moment of getting their newborn to burp, or keeping the eight-month-old from slumping in the high chair. They had forgotten the true agony of coping with colic for three months, and the terror of the first high fever. So, instead of turning to friends for advice and support, we had to rely on books and on our busy pediatrician.

A generation or two ago a new parent was not quite so alone as we were in the beginning. Many women—aunts, cousins, grandmothers—former schoolmates, the large family living next door, and perhaps a general practitioner who knew all the family members well made up a kind of extended family or network. They supplied the information and expertise and the much needed extra pair of arms to give direction and help to a new mother. Most of us today have moved from the places we grew up in and can't rely on this informal grapevine to tell us whether the baby is too hot, too cold, or suffering from prickly heat and not roseola. Many of us have also had to adjust to smaller budgets after we had a baby, and to living in cramped spaces. We can afford to buy and store only a few of the most essential pieces of equipment, and to make matters worse, there is more aggressive marketing of such equipment than ever before.

We have new concerns, too—ones that did not exist in the past. One is the women's movement, which has raised our consciousness. Many of us are older than our mothers were when they gave birth to their first child. Many of us have worked for several years or have established ourselves in careers. Roles within marriages have changed. We feel we must structure our time and share chores with our husbands in order to experience baby care without being swallowed up by it. Equally intimidating is the sophisticated new knowledge on infancy, the myriad theories, and the "expert" opinions, which often complicate our lives by forcing us to make more choices.

The more we know, the more responsibility we feel we must assume for the well-being of our children. While my grandmother dealt with the cruel reality of infant mortality, for example, she did not have to worry about the quantity of additives in commercial baby food or fret about the safest car seat and how to in-stall it. She certainly never considered the logistics of taking a baby on a business trip, nor did she regard my grandfather as competent and able to enjoy taking care of any of their babies' physical needs. She didn't know (though she may well have intuited) that within five hours after birth, the newborn begins to show a preference for increasingly complex visual stimuli.

Babysense explores these concerns. Above all, it is a practical book. The practical side of baby care is presented as simply as possible. Our babies must be well nourished, healthy and comfortable. The book covers feeding, from making the decision to breast- or bottle-feed and the basics of nutrition to helping the baby toward independence through the mastery of the cup and spoon. It deals broadly with health. Although this is not a medical manual, it covers discovering and understanding what goes into good health care, finding a pediatrician, knowing when to call, what to have on hand for emergencies, elementary first aid, and how to cope with minor problems like diaper rash. The book contains information on making the baby comfortable, how to deal with crying, sleep, and mealtimes as well as bathing and dressing the baby in easy-to-care-for clothing. *Babysense* also has a comprehensive section on travel and creating a safe environment at home.

Any parent with a baby has to evaluate the vast amount of equipment on the market. This book will help to do so in terms of both the baby's and parents' needs, their budgets, and space limitations. There is also a section with lots of money-saving suggestions. At the end of many of the chapters is a resource section of further readings for those who are interested and materials that can be ordered by mail.

Beyond the purely practical, this book is about how babies grow and learn. As the baby progresses from reaching, turning over, creeping, and sitting to crawling, standing, and walking, there are many challenges and rewards as well as frustrations for the infant and the parents. *Babysense* offers parents worried about understimulating their babies an array of toys to make, and book suggestions. It is also reassuring to know that despite parental feelings of incompetence and inexperience, babies flourish simply by being cared for by a loving and interested mother or father.

Unlike most baby-care books, *Babysense* is about new parents as well as their babies. Living with a baby involves many physical, emotional, and financial adjustments. Most of us start with misconceptions—or no conception—about what these changes in our lives will be. Caring for a baby makes tremendous demands on our time, our relationships, and our own interests. This book recognizes and identifies these changes and provides support and practical suggestions whenever possible. There are just as many how-to's for parents as there are for babies.

The most important thing to me about the book is that it is largely the product of people who live with babies. When I did begin to meet other parents, mainly mothers with whom I could share my experiences, discoveries, questions, and feelings, my life became much easier. Other parents are an invaluable source of information and support. Knowing them has been a tremendously reassuring and valuable experience for me, and it is what made me decide to write this book. I have tried to convey much of this "grapevine" information. Though we couldn't be without the experts, and I rely on them heavily—the pediatricians, infant researchers and psychologists, nutritionists, manufacturers of baby-care products, and their consumer advocates—parents are experts in their own right. They have to be because they are the ones who are truly responsible for and make that tremendous emotional investment in their babies. There is certainly no more knowledgeable group when it comes to the day-in-day-out care of a baby or providing a realistic picture of what life with a baby is truly like.

To reach many of my parent contributors, I developed an embarrassingly long questionnaire covering some fifty topics. The last question was, "Do you know anyone with a baby who might be willing to fill out this questionnaire?" The answers led me to many, many more parents. The completed questionnaire, as well as my participation in a mother-infant group for several months, is the backbone of my material. (A copy of the actual questionnaire begins on page 241.) Many of the quotes in this book come from tapes of those weekly discussions. I also talked to everyone I met with a baby on the street, in the park, in restaurants, on airplanes, in stores, and at my pediatrician's office. There isn't anyone I talked to who didn't make a contribution to this book. I should add that I interviewed and quoted myself and husband as well. I did not change our names.

Also, I've made an effort to refer to the baby as "she" as well as "he" throughout the book.

Having bought many baby-care books when Caitlin was an infant, but having had little time to read all of them, I realized how important it was to have one book that is practical and supportive rather than prescriptive. I also wanted a book which portrayed parents as real people rather than the shadowy composites that hover in the background in much of the literature on infancy.

If you wish, you can make *Babysense* more personal and fun to read by using the baby record-keeping section in the back. It seems appropriate, in a book written largely by parents, that there should be a place for you to make notes about your baby's early life as well as record your feelings.

Frances Wells Burck,
New York

Part I

WAITING

Waiting

You're in your last month and weigh more than you ever have in your entire life. From your amplitude, it's apparent to everyone that you are on the verge of becoming someone's mother. You may notice other women staring at you and smiling at you warmly. You sense that they want to talk to you, and sometimes they do. They want to know, "Is this your first baby?" They wish you luck. Even though they are strangers, they share your excitement. They haven't forgotten what a luxurious abstraction that yet-to-be-born baby is, or the miracle she or he will soon become. Maybe that's why they smile so knowingly.

People who have children have asked, "Are you ready?" They may have also tactfully hinted that your life will change dramatically. They make what sound to you like ridiculous, bizarre suggestions: "Go out to dinner at all the best restaurants in town." "Go to every movie you have ever wanted to see in your life." "Waste an entire afternoon window-shopping." "Take a joyride at midnight."

"Read novels." "Stay in bed until noon." "Take a two-hour bubble bath." "Daydream." "Do nothing." "Do everything." "Get your husband to sign a child-care–household division-of-responsibilities contract!"

But there's hardly room in your stomach for an expensive dinner, and you're not sure you're up to snails in garlic sauce. Can you sit through a two-and-a-half-hour movie without making six trips to the ladies' room? Window-shopping might be fun, but your back and feet hurt. As for staying in bed until noon and taking a two-hour bath, these things are just too self-indulgent and boring. Reading novels is a possibility, but the house is so dirty. You suddenly can't tolerate dirt or disorder. And you wouldn't consider asking your husband what his intentions are regarding child care. Together you made this decision to have a child, and together you will stand by it.

The one thing you are able to do is daydream—about the birth itself, once months away, now only weeks, or days

that can be counted. What will they do to me in the hospital? What will childbirth be like? Will it hurt? What will the baby be, a boy or a girl? And will the baby be okay? You try to imagine what it will be like to actually care for a baby, but you can't.

Then, too, birth is a lot easier to imagine than the reality of a living, breathing infant of your own. Though everyone else is absolutely positive that you will give birth to a baby, you won't believe it until you have one. And, one discovers, there's no such thing as being absolutely ready. Until this point, the idea of buying baby things, not to mention packing your suitcase, has made you feel a little foolish and very superstitious. So you return to the birth, an event that is so much more concrete and immediate. You will deal with what comes next—the baby—later.

But those parents giving all that strange-sounding advice are trying to tell you something: Having a baby is going to change your life, and the most immediate and direct effect will be on your time. To put it bluntly, there won't be much of it, at least during the first few weeks and months. The people who say "Indulge yourself now" are only remembering how they yearned for self-indulgent opportunities during their early parenthood. Within a month of your baby's birth, you'll realize that staying in bed is not an indulgence, but rather a luxury that ranks right up there with drifting through the Vale of Kashmir on a houseboat.

So force yourself to pursue the luxuries. At the same time, it's never too early to start dealing with the necessities of the near future. One of the reasons that you will not have much time is that the logistics of child care impinge more broadly on your life than you'd ever think possible. The difficulty of the early weeks in particular seems to mount in inverse proportion to parents' preparedness. This means both parents. You may not need a written contract with your husband, but you surely need to discuss the demands that will be made on his time, because you're going to need all the support you can get.

In myriad other ways you need to organize yourself. You need things for the baby. You need services, and you need to make arrangements for them. You need to rise above superstition, make a slight fool of yourself, and prepare for the possibility that there *may* indeed be a baby. And so you begin to get organized.

GOODS AND SERVICES TO OBTAIN AND ARRANGE FOR BEFORE YOU GIVE BIRTH

While some of the suggestions that follow may strike you as rather elaborate, you won't regret doing as many as make sense to you. Life with a newborn can be a surprisingly rigorous initiation into parenthood. Not having what you need, be it as major as a good, compatible pediatrician or as seemingly minor as the right bottle brush, can complicate your life tremendously.

WHAT YOU NEED FOR THE BABY

☐ First and foremost, a good, compatible pediatrician or clinic before the baby is born! See pages 203–206 for suggestions.

☐ Enough baby clothing so that you need only do the laundry every other day. See pages 93–96. If you don't have your own washer and dryer and will be using coin-operated machines, you should have a full week's worth of baby clothes, since leaving the home to do laundry can be an absolutely horrendous chore, especially at first.

☐ Diapers. Four to six dozen if you plan to use your own cloth diapers. See page 96 for suggestions on diapers and supplies.

☐ Diaper pail.

☐ If you plan to use a diaper service, contact those in your area for the best prices and choose one.

☐ At least one or two boxes of newborn-size disposable diapers, whether or not you use cloth diapers.

☐ A place to store clothing, and a changing table. See page 100.

☐ A place for the baby to sleep and some bedding. See page 86.

☐ Bottle-feeding equipment if you will bottle-feed. See page 40. One or two bottles if you plan to breast-feed, as well as a bottle brush and a nipple brush.

☐ Two pacifiers. See pages 43 and 74.

☐ A rectal thermometer (but wait to see if the hospital supplies you with one).

☐ Toiletries for the baby. Powder, lotion, something for diaper rash, and nail scissors.

☐ A car seat if you drive. See page 171.

☐ Interesting things for the baby to look at. See page 232 for making a simple mobile. A music box is nice, too.

☐ A lamp with a low-wattage bulb for the baby's room is useful for night feedings.

☐ A rocking chair or hammock are useful options for soothing the baby and relaxing a parent.

- [ ] A sling or front carrier are optional but useful. See page 168 for suggestions.

- [ ] An infant seat is also useful. See page 167 for suggestions.

WHAT YOU NEED TO DO FOR YOURSELF

- [ ] Preregister at the hospital. Private rooms are obviously the most expensive accommodations and wards the least expensive. Many women enjoy the company of a semiprivate room. It's very interesting to see just how unique each baby and mother is. It's also vital to be able to fulfill the tremendously healthy need to talk about the labor and delivery. Some women end up keeping in touch once they are home. As far as I'm concerned, every new mother needs at least one friend who is in the same boat.

  If your hospital provides rooming-in, an arrangement where you can have the baby with you most of the day except during visiting hours, do take advantage of it. You gain confidence about caring for your baby only by doing it. Though rooming-in will mean somewhat more work on your part, you will get to know your baby better by holding him, feeding him, changing and soothing him as

much as you can from the very beginning. Your husband will also have more opportunities to participate.

- [ ] Take a tour of the hospital where you will give birth. It's very reassuring to know where you will be admitted and what a labor room, a delivery room, and a newborn nursery look like. You may also be able to see the newborns.

- [ ] *Help!* Have ready either a husband, relative, friend, or paid worker to help at home so that you can concentrate on taking care of your baby.

- [ ] If you plan to breast-feed, you'll need two or three comfortable nursing bras, plus a box of nursing pads. Be sure to look over the breast-feeding section of this book for suggestions on buying bras and preparing your nipples in advance (page 30).

- [ ] Some comfortable, attractive clothing which is suitable for breast-feeding, with front openings. If you don't plan to breast-feed, some comfortable, attractive clothing that will tide you over until you get your shape back.

- [ ] A system for doing the laundry. If you are considering a washing machine and don't own one yet, buy it immediately! Babies are often born earlier than planned.

- [ ] Have enough staples in the house to last for at least two weeks. If you are

really organized, you can prepare meals in advance and freeze them. (Even if your husband cooks, he'll be as tired or busy as you are.) Have plenty of high-protein convenience foods on hand and plenty of juices for you to drink.

- [ ] Think about the services in your community which can be helpful, such as a grocery or drugstore that delivers.

- [ ] Most of the preparations we make before the baby is born have to do with goods and services. If you have never stayed at home before, scout out your community for other mothers. Friends are one of the most important parts of motherhood. Once you have a baby it may be several weeks or months before you will have time to be "outgoing." But these early weeks and months are the time when you need contacts most.

HOW TO ARRANGE FOR HELP

Husbands can be ideal helpers in the early weeks, but if yours isn't able to, do not be too proud to arrange for some kind of household help for the first week or two after your return from the hospital. You will need to have another presence to hold down the fort while you rest and take care of your baby.

Whether you hire a baby nurse—a rare breed of woman in white uniform who does nothing but take care of newborns—is an individual matter. The right person, who is neither obtrusive nor domineering, can inspire all sorts of confidence. The tasks she will be doing, such as bathing, changing, and feeding the baby at night, or bringing the baby to you so that you can feed him, are all things you will have to get used to doing eventually yourself. Baby nurses don't cook or run errands, and they need clean sheets.

If you can splurge on paid help, a part-time household helper is really ideal. A sink full of dirty dishes, unemptied wastebaskets, and piles of laundry can contribute to postpartum depression just as much as the hormonal imbalance in your weary body. A new mother really needs some nurturing herself. A new father does, too.

The most important quality in any helper, be it a husband, relative, friend, neighbor, or paid employee, is that she or he be someone who will not get on your nerves. If you are relying on a stranger for help, it's best to interview in advance and to go over—to the letter–what the person's responsibilities will be.

PACKING YOUR SUITCASE

Take a larger suitcase than you think you will need. You'll need extra room to bring home the gifts as well as the following:

- [ ] Two or three short nightgowns, with long front openings if you plan to nurse.
- [ ] A robe.
- [ ] Slippers.
- [ ] Six pairs of underpants.
- [ ] A sanitary belt.
- [ ] Two or three nursing bras if you plan to nurse.
- [ ] Toothbrush, toothpaste, and other toiletries.
- [ ] Address/phone book.
- [ ] Stationery, stamps, birth announcements, envelopes.
- [ ] Something to wear home in which you feel thin and elegant (a smock-type dress with sash is ideal).
- [ ] Something for the baby to wear home.
- [ ] A receiving blanket.
- [ ] Your favorite magazines or a good book.

If you have taken childbirth preparation classes, your instructor may have suggested that you bring along a "Lamaze Bag" containing such things as Chapstick, lollipops, tennis balls, and ice packs to make your labor easier. These

should not go in your suitcase, which gets put away in a locker, but in a separate bag you take to the labor room.

Question: *What made your return from the hospital particularly pleasant or unpleasant?*

Answer: *Just being home was a delicious feeling after the hospital experience. The hospital routines were very sanitary and cold. My husband had the baby's room completely ready. The clothes were in the drawers, the sheets on the bassinet, and flowers on the dresser. Everything looked so beautiful, and colorful and alive. That day is still so clear in my mind.*

A: *It was very important to me to have a little time at home with just my baby and my husband before my mother came to help. I suppose I felt I wanted to work things out my way so that my*

A: My homecoming was a little strange. I remember thinking people were behaving a little gingerly toward me. I also found that my husband, who was being incredibly supportive, needed some care too. Everyone had forgotten about him. My mother came from out of town, which was wonderful. Our time together was too fragile and short, though. I cried one of my rare deluges when she left.

A: Coming home with a baby was terribly exciting. We were a family! Walter had taken care of things at home very well while I was in the hospital, and my sister was coming to help out in a few days. She has three children, and is a pro with babies. She had cautioned me against inviting Mom, who is a wreck around newborns. So my mother went to take care of my sister's kids instead. I hardly ever get to see my sister. She understood exactly how I was feeling—like laughing and crying at the same time.

A: I was really up. We had no help and made a lot of jokes about postpartum depression because there was none. I jumped in full force immediately, up and down the steps, etc., the day I came home. Four days later I was in the hospital emergency room with a temperature of 105, a splitting headache, and the shakes.

A: Our baby was born at home on a Friday night. Over the weekend I was still high from the experience. On Monday everyone was off to work and back to school, and after about two days, I was so totally exhausted that I just started crying and couldn't stop. I asked some-

mother wouldn't take over. I also wanted it to be a special private time for the three of us. When my mother did come four or five days later, I enjoyed it very much. She was tremendously helpful.

A. My only unpleasant experience was the fact that I had hired a nurse who was much too old for the job. She slept more than I did, and this made me very nervous. After two days, I paid her and asked her to leave. From that point on my son and husband and I did very well together.

A: My mother was visiting. On the one hand I wanted her to magically make everything better, but in reality I was terribly critical of anything she tried to do for Toby. I was bone tired, but got angry if she picked up before I did. She didn't hold her right. She wrapped her up too tight. She let the pacifier fall out. Her nervousness gave Toby hiccups. She talked too loud. In short, I wanted help, but I couldn't accept it. It sounds crazy, but I feel this ambivalence is normal.

A: It was wonderful being home. We stayed in the hospital for ten days. Eliot was almost two months early and had to stay longer than usual. I wasn't about to leave without him. I did nothing for several days. Our neighbors had fixed casseroles for us, so I didn't have to cook. People were also wonderful about not visiting for too long, and I had lots of time to get to know my baby. After a week or two everything seemed to begin to come together and settle into place.

one to please stay home with me because I couldn't care for both the baby and myself.

A: We came home on the coldest day of the year and were beset by phone calls and people dropping in. It was ghastly. It was also a Sunday and nobody had anything else to do. I would never do it again. Never on a Sunday!

A: I took my sister's advice, and tried to spread my visitors out over the first couple of weeks. After Kim went back to work, I really enjoyed some company for a little while every day. My sister had said that after the first week, she was totally alone, and this is when she began to get depressed.

A: The first week was a disaster. The baby cried nonstop, and so did I. I didn't want help. I wanted out. A live-in pediatrician would have helped.

A: I hired a woman to come in three hours a day to cook dinner, buy the groceries, keep the house in order, and do the laundry. This was the perfect solution. I didn't want someone there all day because I wanted to be alone with the baby, but I was happy to have her company and help for part of the day.

A: I had too much help. My mother as well as my mother-in-law. Too many houseguests at the same time. Too many cooks!

A: My parents gave us a present of a baby nurse for two weeks, but we ended up letting her go after a week, mainly because I felt she was irritating. Having to deal with her was causing *me a great deal of emotional tension, which I didn't need. I really wanted to be taking care of Birch myself. She was not helpful as far as the cooking and the laundry went. She ate dinner with us, which made dinners unpleasant because she was a nonstop talker and had opinions on everything from the Common Market to the price of beans.*

Ostensibly, she supported breast-feeding, but kept pushing a schedule. Kim also overheard her baby-talking one evening referring to a formula relief bottle as the "good stuff." All she did was to change him, to burp him, and to keep him in her room at night—which made me anxious. I didn't feel free to check on him—you know, to see if he was still breathing.

I will say it was helpful having someone around who knew what to do with babies. She did show me how to put on a double diaper, and seemed to know about dressing him, so that he was neither too warm nor too cold, and administered honey in a demitasse spoon which cured his hiccups. But all in all, I would rather have had a book for this information and a daily housekeeper sort of person to keep the house clean.

A: *The baby nurse we had for Andrew was fantastic. She only came in during the day, and was more than happy to answer the door, make coffee for my visitors, and soothe the baby when he was fussy so I could sleep. I was breast-feeding and she was a font of practical information on this. The most important quality in helpers is that they be pleasant to be around.*

YOUR RIGHTS AS AN OBSTETRIC PATIENT

In recent years hospitals have become more and more supportive of the needs of the new mother, the new father, and the baby. It never hurts, however, to know in advance that as an obstetric patient, you do have certain rights. The following have been drawn up by the American Hospital Association.

The pregnant patient has the right to participate in decisions involving her well-being and that of her unborn child, unless there is a clear-cut medical emergency that prevents her participation. The pregnant patient, because she represents TWO patients rather than one, should be recognized as having the additional rights below.

1. The pregnant patient has the right, prior to the administration of any drug or procedure, to be informed by the health professional caring for her of any potential direct or indirect effects, risks or hazards to herself or her unborn or newborn infant which may result from the use of a drug or procedure prescribed for or administered to her during pregnancy, labor, birth or lactation.

2. The pregnant patient has the right, prior to the administration of any drug, to be informed of the brand name and generic name of the drug in order that she may advise the health professional of any past adverse reaction to the drug.

3. The pregnant patient has the right to determine for herself, without pressure from her attendant, whether she will accept the risks inherent in the proposed therapy or refuse a drug or procedure.

4. [She] has the right to know the name and qualifications of the individual administering medication or procedure to her during labor or birth.

5. She has the right to be informed, prior to the administration of any procedure, whether that procedure is being administered to her for her or her baby's benefit (medically indicated) or as an elective procedure (for convenience, teaching purposes or research).

6. She has the right to be accompanied during the stress of labor and birth by someone she cares for, and to whom she looks for emotional comfort and encouragement.

7. She has the right to have her baby cared for by her bedside if her baby is normal, and to feed her baby according to her baby's needs rather than according to the hospital's regimen.

8. She has the right to be informed if there is any known or indicated aspect of her or her baby's care or condition which may cause her or her baby later difficulty or problems.

9. She has the right to have her baby's hospital medical records complete, accurate and legible and to have their records, including nurses' notes, and to receive a copy upon payment of a reasonable fee and without incurring the expense of retaining an attorney.

Part II
FEEDING

-1-
Breast-Feeding

THE BIG QUESTION: TO BREAST-FEED OR NOT?

How you plan to feed *your* baby, with breast or bottle, shouldn't be anyone's business but yours. But you will find that it is, from practically the moment of conception on. Some people can be very dogmatic on the pros of breast-feeding. They stress the psychological and physical benefits to the baby to the point that you may begin to feel that breast-feeding is a must, a test of your worth as a woman/mother, rather than the choice that it truly is.

There is little argument that mother's milk does have an edge over infant formulas. And if we were to make choices on a strictly rational, factual basis, breast-feeding probably would be the preferred method in most cases. But people don't work this way, especially during one of the most vulnerable periods in their lives, the early days and/or weeks after the birth of the first child. We make decisions based on all sorts of things—on feelings and attitudes that come from our unique histories, how we feel at the moment, how we think the baby is doing, how we plan to share the care of the baby, and how available we can be to feed him. In the midst of the breast vs. bottle controversy, the most forgotten fact can be that the whole purpose of feeding is to benefit the baby and promote a loving relationship between the parents and the child.

Eating is everything to a newborn baby whose world is limited. Besides providing her with the nutrients she needs and eliminating the very real discomfort that hunger causes, feeding means contact, love, and stimulation. As the baby sucks, swallows, tastes, looks, touches, and listens, all of her senses come into play. The times you feed the baby are the times you come to know each other. For the baby's sake and the mother's, mealtimes ought to be relaxed and pleasant.

A woman who is feeling comfortable and relaxed when she is breast-feeding—that is, because she wants to nurse, is not in great pain or overly exhausted, and is *reasonably* sure that the baby is getting enough to eat—can provide the baby with all the nourishment and sensual comforts that he needs very conveniently. But a bottle-feeding mother can provide them just as well, with a little extra time and a lot more paraphernalia.

If you are repelled by the idea of breast-feeding, you probably shouldn't do it. If you are the least bit interested, though, it's a good idea to prepare yourself in advance, read about how it works, and clear up any misconceptions you may have. The best preparation of all, however, is to actually see and talk to a woman who is nursing her baby. She can discuss her experience, and perhaps offer suggestions for some of the basic how-to's, and simply be encouraging. While breast-feeding is a growing phenomenon in this country, it still remains a fact that many of us have never even seen a nursing mother before we set out to nurse our own babies. Lack of information and support are probably the biggest reasons many women don't breast-feed in the first place or give it up in the early weeks after birth.

COMMON MISCONCEPTIONS ABOUT BREAST-FEEDING

Successful breast-feeding depends on the size and shape of the breast and nipple. Untrue. The size of your breasts has nothing to do with the amount of milk you produce. The shape of your nipple is not a problem unless it is inverted or retracted. A rubber breast shield, available through the La Leche League, can help solve this problem, particularly if you wear it while you are still pregnant.

Breast milk may contain PCBs, potentially toxic compounds used in industry which have been found to have contaminated soil, water, air, and food. So far there is absolutely no evidence of PCB toxicity reported in a human baby. Fresh-water fish are the chief nutritional sources of PCBs—bass, whitefish, trout, pike, carp, catfish, and pickerel—but those which are marketed commercially must be within the Food and Drug Administration guidelines for safety.

Breast-feeding changes the shape of

HOW DOES BREAST MILK DIFFER FROM MOST COMMERCIAL INFANT-FORMULA PREPARATIONS?

Human milk may not look like much—it's thin, watery, and on the whole rather insubstantial looking—but it is a highly complex, subtle substance. Well over one hundred different elements have been discovered in it, and there may well be many more yet to be isolated. Some of the elements are duplicatable by formula manufacturers and some aren't. But many of the comparisons between breast milk and plain cow's milk that one reads in pro-breast-feeding literature are rather unfairly drawn—they do not take into consideration the modifications that formula manufacturers have made. Infants are not switched to plain cow's milk until it is felt by a pediatrician that the baby's system is capable of handling it. Until then the similarities between human milk and modern infant formulas generally outweigh the differences.

Broadly speaking, formula is cow's milk in which the protein and mineral content has been lowered, the carbohydrate content increased, and the butterfat replaced by vegetable oils which are more easily absorbed and utilized by the baby. More specific differences, summarized from *Consumer Reports*, follow.

Colostrum: All babies receive some protective antibodies from their mothers. These cross over the placenta to the fetus before birth. It is thought that this protection lasts for the first few months only, but that it may be supplemented by a number of protective elements in colostrum, the yellowish, protein-rich, premilk fluid secreted from the breasts before the mature milk comes in one to three days after the birth. Included in colostrum are any number of antibodies against bacteria and viruses, including *E. coli,* a common cause of infection in newborns, and polio, mumps, and influenza viruses. So far, there is no manufactured substitute for colostrum.

Protein content: Human milk contains about one-third of the amount of protein as plain cow's milk, for the obvious reason that babies don't grow nearly as quickly as cows and remain dependent on their mothers much longer. The level of protein in infant formulas has been reduced to approximate that in human milk; however, there is a difference in the type of protein present. Human milk protein is mainly lactalbumin, or whey protein, which is highly digestible. Formulas contain casein, which forms a harder curd in the stomach, and thus takes longer and is somewhat more difficult to digest.

All proteins must be broken down into amino acids before they can be of use to the body. Breast milk contains combinations of amino acids different from those in formulas. Cysteine and taurine, for instance, much of which appears in breast milk and is thought to play an important role in the development of the nervous system and the brain and in visual perception, appear in smaller quantities in infant formulas. Human milk also contains a greater number of nucleotides, factors that enable the body to make proteins. In addition, very small amounts of the proteins in a nursing mother's food also reach her milk unaltered and thus go to the baby. It has been suggested that this may result in the baby's being acclimatized in advance to the household diet that she will receive when she is older and eating solid foods. It is thought that this early acclimatization may be what helps a nursing baby avoid some food allergies. (This is still only hypothesis, however.)

Fat: Human milk and formulas have about the same amount of fat, an important energy source for the baby. Besides the replacement of butterfat by vegetable oils in formulas, there is one other primary difference between human milk and formulas. Human milk has more cholesterol. Though there is no conclusive evidence yet, it is thought that this may be important in helping the baby deal better with cholesterol later in life.

Carbohydrates: Infant formulas and breast milk contain the same kind of carbohydrates—a sugar called lactose, an important source of energy for the baby. Lactose, the least sweet of the sugars, helps to create an acid environment in the intestinal tract. This helps ward off harmful bacteria.

Vitamins and minerals: Breast milk contains all the important minerals, but in fewer quantities than infant formulas. Human milk contains very little iron, but it is felt that this iron is fully and easily absorbed by the baby and is adequate for the first four to six months while the baby is using up iron stores that he was born with (see Introducing Solid Foods, Chapter 3). Infant formulas contain more calcium and phosphorus than breast milk, but it is by no means clear that they need to. The formula-fed baby tends not to absorb all the extra minerals. Because she excretes them, her immature kidneys are put under more of a load.

The vitamin content of human milk depends on the mother's diet. Many pediatricians recommend a supplement of vitamins A, C, and D until the baby is eating a balanced diet of solids, just in case the mother's breast milk does not meet recommended daily allowances (RDAs). Infant formulas are fortified to meet RDAs.

your breasts. Any changes that your breasts undergo are the result of pregnancy, not breast-feeding. Exercises before as well as after the birth will also help (see Chapter 11, Postpartum).

Breast-feeding will restore your svelte figure. If you breast-feed, your uterus will contract more quickly during the postpartum period, due to the release of hormones that trigger the let-down reflex than if you don't. But beyond that, it requires just as much discipline, exercise, and "reasonable eating" to regain your shape when you nurse as it does when you are bottle-feeding. When you are nursing, it's very easy to rationalize that you are eating for two.

Breast-feeding will tie you down. This is all in the way you look at it. All new mothers are tied down during the early weeks after their baby's birth. It is true that breast-fed babies tend to eat more often in the beginning than bottle-fed babies, because it takes a while for your milk supply to be established, and since breast milk is more easily digested and passes through the baby's system more quickly than formula. In this sense you may be needed every two or three hours instead of every three or four hours. It is also true that frequent feedings are important in the early weeks to establish an adequate milk supply. However, if you do miss a feeding, you can hand-express your milk or pump your breasts with a small hand-operated breast pump that can fit in your pocketbook. Once you feel confident about breast-feeding, usually after the first month or two, it's not difficult to work out a very successful part-time breast-feeding arrangement.

Breast-feeding is a reliable form of birth control. Untrue. Don't believe it. Theoretically, women do not ovulate for the first couple of months during lactation. But how can you ever know for sure? Do not take birth-control pills while you are lactating, however. These will decrease your milk supply.

PREPARATIONS FOR BREAST-FEEDING

Bad Advice: Some people recommend various nipple exercises to prepare for breast-feeding, but these are actually unnecessary. Breast-feeding is a natural phenomenon and the breasts are ready at the time of birth, even if the child is born early.

Good advice (from a parent): Please urge the women who read your book to make some preparations for breast-feed-

ing, even if they have not decided with great conviction that they want to breast-feed. No one told me that it can hurt at first! I have very fair skin and developed a classic case of cracked and bleeding nipples primarily because I didn't know I should toughen up my nipples in advance. If early feedings are painful, a vicious cycle can be established. You feel tense and miserable, and this affects the flow of the milk. The baby is hungry and when he does suck, he pulls even more vigorously on the breast. Rather than enjoying the experience, I watched my digital clock counting the minutes until the feeding ended. I did get through this—but feel it was unnecessary.

PREPARING YOUR BREASTS IN ADVANCE

Following are a few routines you can choose from to toughen up your nipples before the baby is born. The last trimester is a good time to start, *but any amount of preparation is better than none—particularly if you are fair-skinned!*

1. Avoid using soap or any other drying agent (such as powder) on your nipples. These things dry up the natural oils that soften and protect your nipples.

2. When you shower or bathe, gently

but firmly rub your nipples with a washcloth every day.

3. Go braless as often as possible, if this is comfortable for you, or cut holes in the end of your regular bra. The friction of your clothing will help toughen your nipples and you won't even have to think about it.

4. Expose your nipples to air and sunlight (with caution) whenever possible. If you do sunbathe, lubricate your nipples with Massé cream or pure lanolin afterward.

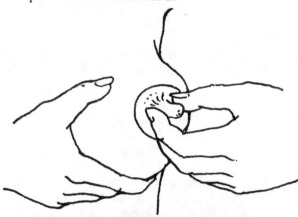

Nipple Rolling Exercise
Take the nipple between your thumb and forefinger and pull it out firmly—enough so that you feel some pressure, but not so much that it hurts. Roll the nipple between your fingers for a minute or two. When you're finished, apply a mild cream such as pure lanolin, vitamin A & D ointment, or cocoa butter to the areola and the sides of the nipple, but not over the tip where the duct openings are located.

Breast Shield
The breast shield, worn during pregnancy, applies gentle pressure to help draw out inverted nipples.

5. You can also do the nipple-rolling exercise two or three minutes a day (see page 30).

6. During pregnancy check to see if your nipples are inverted. The tip of an inverted nipple is flat or folded in like a slit. Take your breast between your thumb and forefinger and squeeze gently around the dark area, the areola. If the tip recedes, the nipple is inverted. The nipple will often work itself out during pregnancy, but you can aid this by doing exercise #5 or by wearing rubber breast shields, which put suction pressure on the breast. These can be ordered through the La Leche League (see page 38).

7. Besides these simple measures, the most helpful preparation is talking to women who have breast-fed their babies and enjoyed the experience.

THE RIGHT BRA

The last month of pregnancy is a good time to buy two or three nursing bras. Your size won't change significantly after the baby is born. The bra must offer enough support so that you feel comfortable, but if it is too tight problems can arise. You might also want to buy a bra extender, a piece of elastic with hooks and eyes on it, at a notions department, just in case you are much bigger than calculated.

The most convenient kind of bra has snaps or Velcro strips that can be operated with one hand while you hold onto the baby with the other. Avoid bras with plastic liners. The plastic traps moisture, which can irritate your nipples.

Should you not be able to get to the store to buy your own bras for some reason, here are some guidelines from the La Leche League for determining your correct size.

1. The inch part of your bra size is determined by your chest measurement, that is, the distance around your back and under your arms and across your chest (under the breasts).

2. The cup size is the actual bust measurement—across the nipples and around your back—minus the chest measurement. If the difference is . . .

one inch, you take	A	cup
two inches, you take	B	cup
three inches, you take	C	cup
four inches, you take	D	cup
five inches, you take	DD	cup
five to six inches, you take	E	cup

You will also need comfortable clothing that opens conveniently down the front for nursing. Start thinking about this now, so you won't feel like a frump later!

HOW-TO'S FOR BREAST-FEEDING

Question: How does breast-feeding work?

Answer: The breast has a truly elegant design. When the baby nurses, he is not sucking as much as squeezing or jawing on the areola, the dark area surrounding the very tip of the nipple (see illustration). This pressure exerted on the areola sends messages to the pituitary gland, which in turn releases two hormones. The first, prolactin, stimulates the milk production in the alveoli (see illustration). The second hormone, oxytocin, is responsible for causing the cells in the ducts attached to the alveoli to contract and move the milk forward and out to the baby.

This movement forward is the key to successful nursing. The pituitary gland is connected to the hypothalamus, the "seat of the emotions," and its output is dependent to some degree on emotional state. A mother who is an emotional

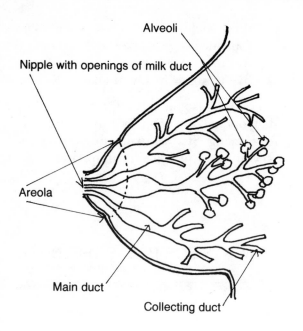

How the Breast Works to Produce Milk

wreck from fatigue or tension may produce plenty of milk, but not be able to get it to the baby. In short, you can see why it is important to be rested and relaxed.

If you are breast-feeding for the first time, the following procedure will help you make a successful start:

1. Wash your hands, and if possible have something to drink before you begin. This is a good habit to get into from the very beginning. You need three extra quarts of fluid a day during postpartum, whether you are nursing or not. If you are nursing, you will continue to need extra fluids throughout lactation.

2. The first time you feed the baby, you might find it more comfortable to lie down. Place the baby on the bed next to you on his side with his feet close to you and his head slightly away at an angle. Later you will be able to sit up in a chair with a pillow under the baby, and eventually talk on the phone, read, write, or even cook (one-handed), but this takes practice. Do not feel bad if you are awkward. We all are.

3. With your free hand, cup your breast and use the index finger and thumb to help form the nipple. Take it and touch the baby's cheek. This will stimulate what is called the rooting reflex, the instinctive oral search for the nipple. This gentle stroking will also make the nipple more erect and easier for the baby to grasp.

4. Contact of the nipple with the roof of the baby's mouth is what makes her suck. So tip the nipple slightly upward when you insert it into the baby's mouth. It is very important to get as much of the areola into her mouth as possible, so you almost have to stuff it in. If the baby gets only the tip, nursing can be very painful. It also means that she is not putting pressure onto the pools that empty into the ducts. This is frustrating and infuriating to the hungry baby. If the baby doesn't get enough of the areola, remove her from the breast by inserting your little finger between her mouth and the breast to break the suction. Then start over. Incidentally, this finger-in-the-mouth tactic also works to dislodge an energetic feeder who just won't stop nursing.

5. *Allow breathing space for the baby!* This is crucial. The first time you feed your baby, your breasts are likely to be rather full. Be sure to compress your breast beneath the baby's nose. If he can't breathe easily, he may shake his head back and forth, scream, and refuse to nurse. "Fighting at the breast" can quickly become a conditioned response, and this is very discouraging for the new mother, to say the least.

6. Use both breasts at each feeding, burping the baby between breasts at least once. The baby may not drain the second breast as thoroughly as the first. So, at the next feeding, start with the breast you used last. You can help yourself remember which one it was by pinning a safety pin onto your nursing bra on the side last used.

7. Nurse your baby often. If you have

rooming-in, this is no problem. Otherwise ask that your baby be brought to you whenever she's hungry, or every two to three hours.

8. To avoid soreness, a very common problem during the early weeks, it's important to start out gradually. Following is a timetable recommended by New York Lying-in Hospital.

first day .... five minutes on each breast per feeding

second day ...... seven minutes on each breast per feeding

third day .... ten minutes on each breast per feeding

fourth day ...... ten minutes on each breast per feeding

fifth day .... fifteen to twenty minutes on each breast per feeding

from then on .... twenty minutes per breast is said to provide the baby with a healthy supply of milk and give him all the sucking he needs. The length of feeding will depend on the baby and the mother, of course. But in the beginning it's advisable to let the baby suck all he needs to, as long as your nipples are not tender.

Question: *What did you find to be the most useful information when you started breast-feeding your baby?*

Answer: *Because I had a great deal of soreness when I first started, I was very comforted by knowing that the baby more or less emptied the breast during the first seven to ten minutes of nursing. Until I got over this problem, which took about two weeks of carefully air-drying my nipples, an aspirin to reduce the discomfort every four hours on my doctor's suggestion, heat-lamp treatments, and rubbing my nipples with Massé cream after each feeding, I felt very reassured that the baby was getting enough to eat, even if he wasn't sucking for as long as he ideally should have. We used a pacifier in between.*

A: *Oxytocin Spray helped with my slow let-down reflex. I was assured that I probably was producing enough milk, but that it wasn't getting to the baby, and was glad that I knew to ask for the spray in the hospital. I would not have known if I hadn't read two good books on breast-feeding, though.*

A: *I never saw a drop of my milk. It did not squirt across the room the way my roommate's in the hospital did. This is perfectly normal, but I suppose I expected that it would come pouring out and was a little worried when it didn't. Knowing that it takes a couple of weeks to really get going smoothly helped me over those first anxious weeks. Also knowing that breast-fed*

babies eat quite frequently in the beginning helped me a lot with the worry that I wasn't providing Jerehme with enough milk.

A: *I was very grateful to the La Leche League for providing me with a Woolwich breast shield because one of my nipples was inverted. My doctor, who didn't know the first thing about breast-feeding, suggested that I simply nurse the baby on one side indefinitely, or stop.*

A: *My sister gave me the best piece of advice. She told me not to worry about anything that has to do with housework, and not to entertain or be sociable after nine o'clock at night until after your postpartum checkup. If you are just managing to nurse your baby frequently during the first six weeks, you are doing plenty, and you're doing fine!*

A: *If you need help getting started in the hospital, don't be intimidated by busy nurses. I got no help whatsoever until I demanded to see the head nurse. She took the time to spend an entire feeding with me, showed me how to put the baby to my breast without suffocating him, and how to take him off the breast so that it didn't hurt. You only learn by doing, but sometimes the best way is to have someone who knows about breast-feeding watching and encouraging you.*

A: *I think everyone should be prepared for the possibility that her experience will not be typical. I had no problems in the beginning, and it appeared that I had plenty of milk, but after two weeks at home with a baby who cried almost all the time, I finally had to face the fact that she* was hungry. When I took her to the doctor, she had lost weight. I had to give her small amounts of formula every two hours and pump my breasts because the doctor felt that her stomach had probably shrunk. I don't need to tell you how incredibly awful I felt. The doctor was very sensitive and supportive. He said that in 98 percent of the cases where supplements have to be used because the baby isn't getting enough or isn't gaining, they are eliminated as soon as the baby starts gaining steadily and the woman is then able to return to full-time nursing as long as her confidence isn't shot.

My state of mind improved considerably knowing that Jessie was no longer crying from hunger all the time. I went to see the pediatrician every week on his request so that the baby could be weighed, and this helped, too. When he suggested stopping the supplemental feedings, I went back to the doctor the next week, and she had gained as much as she had in the previous weeks. After this very rocky beginning, I had a very positive experience. I guess what I'm trying to say is that the early weeks didn't have anything in common with the later months—it's just getting past the beginning.

A: Knowing how to hand-express milk was a lifesaver to me. I went back to work part-time when Lisa was six weeks old. My job involves traveling from Los Angeles to San Francisco once a week, overnight—which does not make for what you would call a regular feeding schedule.

A: My pediatrician had told me to forget about

schedules in the beginning, and to feed the baby every two hours or two and a half hours if necessary.

A: I regarded the whole thing as an experiment. I had some problems in the beginning due to lack of encouragement as well as soreness. I kept telling myself, if this doesn't work out, I can bottle-feed the baby. But I was not the least bit calm about it in the beginning. I was tired. I was nervous. I was sure that my body could not come through. I had read that you had to be very calm, and this made me even more nervous. The only motherly instinct I had was to jump three feet into the air every time Salina cried, and to feel like a klutz every time her diaper fell off. Somehow I defied my self-image as a totally unphysical person. I fed her, and she grew. I still regard the whole thing as a miracle. By the way, don't listen to your in-laws. Grandmothers worry incessantly about whether or not you are starving their grandchildren.

A: I knew nothing. When I was checking out of the hospital, the resident pediatrician came by to give me a full report on Matthew. His parting words were, "Have your husband offer the baby a bottle-feeding every few days so that you can get a full night's sleep, because you will need it." We followed this suggestion and neither the baby nor my milk supply seemed to suffer. I have since read that this isn't standard advice, but in my case, I guess, ignorance was bliss.

A: The most important and useful piece of information I can pass on is that babies cry a lot

in the early weeks and it isn't always because they are hungry. My obstetrician had told me that women breast-feeding for the first time in this uptight, technological, advice-oriented society were notoriously insecure about being able to produce enough milk, and that they were much harder on themselves than bottle-feeding mothers, particularly if they intellectualized about it. Since I tend to intellectualize about almost everything, this was the biggest hurdle—doing, rather than thinking.

A: I hadn't known that there are times during the day, like late afternoon and early evening, when you produce less milk. The baby may be hungrier then. You should also know that babies have growth spurts at about two or three weeks, at about three months, and at about six months. The baby may be hungrier around these times, too. Feeding the baby more often will help build up your milk supply to meet those needs.

A: As a father, I think it's important to give your wife as much support in the beginning as possible. You can also help comfort the baby between feedings, rather than handing the baby back to the mother for the tit all the time.

A: Something people don't talk about! My vagina was dry when I was nursing, which made lovemaking pretty uncomfortable. This is quite common, and has to do with the hormonal changes in your body. This does not mean you are suddenly frigid. K-Y jelly helps a lot.

A: I felt tired a good deal of the time when I

was nursing. But maybe all mothers are tired, I don't know.

A: I made the mistake of offering formula after a feeding because I was afraid she wasn't getting enough. When she chugged it down so quickly, I was really discouraged. I don't think you should do what I did unless the pediatrician confirms that the baby isn't gaining enough weight, even though it's very tempting when the baby is screaming her head off.

A: I'm afraid I had no information. I just did it, and it worked!

The Big Question: *How do you know that the baby is getting enough to eat? (See also Chapter 6, Crying.)*

Answer: *You can satisfy yourself about the adequacy of your baby's rations in several ways. If he seems contented, sleeps well and cries for feedings at fairly well-spaced intervals, you can be confident that he is getting enough to eat. But most of us don't have such perfect babies. All babies cry—and some cry after every feeding. How can you tell whether a baby who cries a lot is crying from hunger?*

One way is by checking his weight gain. Be careful not to fall into a common trap. We live in a competitive society where the biggest is often considered the best. It is often hard for the new mother to avoid comparing her baby's weight gain with that of the baby next door. Your breastfed baby, though, is almost certain to gain more slowly than a bottle-fed baby, and he may

even gain more slowly than another breastfed infant. The fact is that rapid weight gain is no guarantee of health. In fact, doctors are now investigating the possibility that our methods of feeding babies over the past couple of generations have stimulated excessive weight gain that may lead to obesity and heart trouble in later life.

The average breastfed baby gains from four to six ounces a week in the first month and between six and eight ounces a week during the next three months. This gain is likely to vary considerably from week to week, ranging from an ounce or two in one week to a whopping seven or eight ounces the next. Since these weekly fluctuations are so great, it's best to wait for your regular checkups at the doctor's office to weigh the baby. If you buy your own scales, you will be tempted to weigh your baby much too frequently and then worry unnecessarily. If you're really anxious and your doctor's not too far away, you can probably take the baby in for an occasional weighing. And remember, just like adults, babies don't eat the same amount of food at every feeding or the same every day.

Meanwhile, you can judge whether your baby's taking in enough food by checking his diapers to see what comes out. If he has six or more wet diapers a day with pale yellow urine and regular bowel movements (either frequent small ones or less frequent large ones), he is getting enough to eat. (If he's drinking a lot of water, however, the diaper test is not a reliable indication.)

Other signs of a well-fed baby are bright eyes,

an alert manner and good skin tone.

Note: do not try to test for hunger by offering the baby a bottle after nursing. The typical infant has such a strong urge to suck that he will usually take some milk from a bottle even if he isn't hungry.

—MARVIN S. EIGER, M.D., and
SALLY WENDKOS OLDS,
The Complete Book of Breastfeeding

EXPRESSING MILK

To express milk you can use your hands, use a small pump which looks like Clarabelle's horn, or rent an electric breast pump (the latter is recommended only if you must keep up your milk supply over a long period of time).

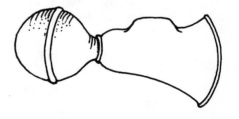

Breast Pump

Hand expression is certainly the most convenient method. You will need a sterile bowl, funnel, and container with a lid.

- [ ] Wash your hands.
- [ ] Massage your breast by circling the breast with the fingers and thumbs of both hands. Then draw the hands together gently but firmly—first about ten times around the outer area, and then about ten times midway between the outer area and the areola.
- [ ] Cup the breast in one hand and place your forefinger below the nipple on the dark edge of the areola, your thumb above the nipple.
- [ ] Squeeze fingers together, being careful not to pinch the nipple.
- [ ] It might take a while for something to happen, so keep trying.
- [ ] Rotate your hand around the areola to have contact with all the milk ducts.
- [ ] Do this for three to five minutes.
- [ ] Switch to the second breast.
- [ ] Go back to the first breast and repeat the process with both breasts.

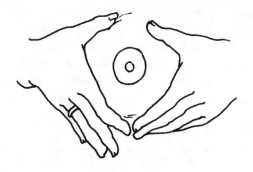

Breast Massage

Manual Expression

A MOTHER ELABORATES

I never could understand the how-to's of hand-expressing milk from reading about it. It sounds easy, but the fact of the matter is you have to fiddle around yourself before you get the knack of it. Here are some suggestions.

1. *I found it helpful to massage the breast being emptied with the free hand, applying pressure on the firm areas and moving toward the nipple.*

2. *I always had to lean way over the bottle to get the milk to spray into it, thus breaking my back. I suggest finding the most comfortable height surface.*

3. *Hand-expressing is probably hard to do in the first six weeks, since the milk supply is trying hard to keep up with the baby's appetite.*

4. *Also, if you are attempting to collect milk, it's easier to take one or two ounces before each feeding begins, when the breasts are very full.*

FREEZING AND STORING

Breast milk can be kept in an airtight, lidded, sterile container and can be refrigerated for up to forty-eight hours. It can be frozen for several months without losing any of its important properties. When you defrost breast milk, first put it into the refrigerator for a few hours, then run it under tap water (lukewarm, not hot) and shake it up so that the cream spreads evenly though it.

COMMON PROBLEMS

All breast-feeding literature is supportive and encouraging, as it should be. Nursing a baby can be a wonderfully close and satisfying experience, with as many benefits for the mother as there are for the baby.

But there can be a dark side, which falls into the category called common problems. Here there are usually many good, practical suggestions that work more often than not. But little mention is made about the mother who is heavily invested in the notion of "successful breast-feeding," and how terribly vulnerable she can feel if her experience is fraught with "common problems." One suspects that if these problems did not coincide with the initial shock of new parenthood and the demands of newborn care, the problems would not seem so great, and we would be better equipped to handle them. But, alas, they usually come in the beginning.

Engorgement. This swelling of the breasts is very common when the milk first comes in. The breasts feel hard and warm, and they hurt. Check to make sure your bra isn't too tight but is giving you adequate support. Try heat (warm showers or hot-water bottles) or cold (ice pack) treatments. *Feed the baby frequently,* perhaps hand-expressing some milk before you start, to get the milk flowing. This truly is a temporary problem. If it persists, ask your doctor about the temporary use of Oxytocin Spray to speed the let-down reflex, or get in touch with the La Leche League.

Soreness. The treatment for soreness is similar to preparing your breasts for nursing in the first place: do not use drying agents such as soap; use soothing creams such as lanolin or Massé cream; give careful heat treatments with a reading lamp; and also keep the flaps of your nursing bra open most or all of the time to air your nipples. *Frequent, short feedings,* in which you offer the less sore breast first, so that the milk will have already let down when you offer the sore breast, also help. Ask your doctor if he thinks the temporary use of Oxytocin Spray will help speed the let-down reflex. Some women find temporary relief by using a plastic nipple shield, but this cannot go on indefinitely or the breasts will not be stimulated sufficiently to produce enough milk. If you make little progress on your own, get in touch with your doctor or the La Leche League, who have dealt with this problem thousands of times.

Insufficiency of milk. See Some Suggestions for Building Up and Maintaining a Healthy Milk Supply, below, if you're doubtful.

Breast Infections. Get in touch with your doctor. Infection does not by any means imply that you have to stop nursing. Get in touch with the La Leche League to back you up, offer encouragement, and other suggestions.

SOME SUGGESTIONS FOR BUILDING UP AND MAINTAINING A HEALTHY MILK SUPPLY— ESPECIALLY IF YOU'RE IN DOUBT

1. Rest.
2. Relax.
3. Go to bed early.
4. Forget about housework.
5. Indulge yourself. If your doctor approves, have a glass of wine at that difficult time of day when the sun is setting and dinner may still be uncooked.

6. Drink plenty of fluids—three quarts a day during postpartum.

7. Take vitamins, as well as iron, particularly during postpartum.

8. Eat a well-balanced diet, high in protein.

9. Don't listen to people who are critical of breast-feeding.

10. Remember that as the day wears on, you produce somewhat less milk than you do in the morning.

11. Remember that babies go through growth spurts, and their demands may be greater during those periods.

12. Be in touch with your pediatrician often when you are concerned about the baby's well-being.

13. Make use of the La Leche League. You do not have to share their entire philosophy if it doesn't agree with your own. Their goal is to be supportive, helpful, and informative. They are all mothers themselves, who tend to understand how you are feeling.

P.S.: Sometimes it takes courage to decide to persevere—or not to persevere—and feel okay about your decision, or to work out a system somewhere in between that involves both breast and bottle. There are many women who do this, but they usually have no place in breast-feeding literature.

Should you decide that you want to stop breast-feeding the baby, don't dwell on the past. Any amount of nursing is beneficial and to have tried is to have had a new and unique experience. Nursing can be lovely, but it is not synonymous with good mothering. Again, it is only one facet of a relationship that goes on for a lifetime.

RELIEF BOTTLES—INSURANCE

The time to decide whether you are going to be a breast-feeding purist is right in the beginning. While many breast-feeding advocates say, "Don't let a bottle in your house," I disagree with this approach.

You simply don't know how you will feel about full-time nursing when your baby is six or eight months old. Unless the baby has already become used to the rubber nipple in the first three months or so, he may balk. If he's not yet able to drink from a cup, you'll need to be there to feed him when he's hungry. If you offer a biweekly or weekly relief bottle consistently, and don't get lazy about it, you will have the insurance of having an alternate feeding method should you have to be away.

I breast-fed totally, but now feel it would have been better to offer Lucy an occasional bottle of formula. When I did try this at about six months, she wouldn't touch the rubber nipple. I really needed some time away by then—not a couple of hours, but an entire afternoon—but I was stuck and didn't feel I could leave her happily with anyone else, which would have expanded her social experience and mine.

It was my job to give Caitlin her relief bottle, after she was a few weeks old, so that Franny could sleep through the two A.M. feeding. Appalling as the idea of getting up from a warm bed was, it seemed the least I could do—Franny, after all, had to get up at the cold light of dawn. In fact, after the first couple of times, these feedings grew into moments of incredible tenderness and affection. They got me intimately involved with Caitlin and were my first hints of the joy of parenthood.

BURPING THE BABY

Some babies need to burp more than others. You'll soon find out what kind of baby yours is. Start out burping her at least twice during a feeding. You can ei-ther place her over your shoulder or across your knees. A third method is sitting the baby on your lap with her body leaning forward over your forearm. Then pat gently. A good rule of thumb is to work on the burp for about a minute. If nothing happens, then give up and don't worry about it.

If your baby is the kind who sucks very strongly and tightly on the nipple, the air bubbles that she swallows will be very small. It may take up to an hour for the bubbles to collect into one large one, and there may be some milk on top of the bubble. If and when the baby does finally burp, some milk or spit-up may come up. This is not the same as vomiting, and it usually looks like a lot more than it really is. So again, don't worry.

I found that Patsey was fussy for about half an hour after every feeding—even though I'd burped her, or tried to, after she'd taken each breast. My pediatrician suggested that in her case I try to get the air up every five minutes during a feeding. This meant at least eight burpings, which was rather tiresome, but if I didn't do it we'd both suffer a lot more. At night I gave the job to Neal. After about eight weeks all this burping wasn't necessary, but until then I felt like my life was centered around getting air out of the baby.

RESOURCES

Breast-Feeding

Eiger, Marvin S., M.D., and Olds, Sally Wendkos, *The Complete Book of Breastfeeding*, Bantam, New York, 1973.

Pryor, Karen, *Nursing Your Baby,* Harper & Row, New York, 1973.

Lact-Aid Kit
An ingenious device, to help nonlactating mothers relactate, by which baby nurses on breast and receives a formula supplement at the same time.
Write to: Lact-Aid
      Box 6861
      Denver, Co., 80206

-2-
Bottle-Feeding

Bottle-feeding is a perfectly fine way to nourish a baby. Many parents decide to bottle-feed their babies, and there certainly are some advantages to this method. Any member of the family can help feed and comfort the baby, and this, of course, can give a mother far more freedom in terms of leaving the baby with other people if she wants or needs to be away. Also, by bottle-feeding, your husband and family can really share in one of the most pleasurable aspects of baby care.

Sharing the feeding of the baby means that a new father can be involved and that a new mother has a chance to sleep the night through during postpartum, when she needs it the most. Her own health, state of fatigue and of mind, her diet, and any medications she is taking, will also not affect the baby's meals. And because she can actually see what goes into the baby, a mother is far less likely to worry, as many first-time breast-feeders do, whether or not the baby is getting enough to eat. If anything, there is a slight risk of overfeeding a bottle-fed baby. You have to be careful not to nudge the baby to take the very last drop.

Modern commercial infant formulas have made preparation very simple. If you buy a six-pack of prebottled formula, you only need to add a sterile nipple and collar. This is the luxury route, however. Concentrated formulas, to which you add

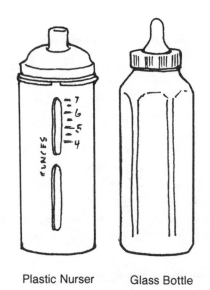

Plastic Nurser   Glass Bottle

water, are more expensive than powder-based equivalents (which usually must be bought at a drugstore rather than at the supermarket, and which are the least expensive of all—next to formula you brew yourself).

Even if you breast-feed, it's a good idea to give the baby an occasional bottle, so that he becomes used to taking milk from another source. Following is some information about what you need for bottle-feeding, sterilizing, and storing formula, as well as some other suggestions.

USEFUL EQUIPMENT

- ☐ 6 to 8 glass or plastic bottles or a nurser set (either 4-oz. or 8-oz. size) with nipple collars, caps or discs, and covers (optional, to keep the milk from spilling if you travel)

- ☐ At least a dozen nipples (see box on Nuk nipples, page 43)

- [ ] A sturdy bottle brush and nipple brush
- [ ] A quart measuring cup (heat resistant) with a spout
- [ ] A long-handled spoon
- [ ] A sterilizer with a rack; or a large spaghetti pot with a tight-fitting lid and a pie plate with holes poked in it and turned upside down for a rack (a towel may also be used as a rack)
- [ ] Tongs for lifting hot bottles
- [ ] A can opener
- [ ] A small jar with a screw-top lid with holes punched in the top if you use the aseptic sterilization method
- [ ] Another small glass jar with a screw-top lid (no holes) for storing sterile nipples
- [ ] A timer (optional)

STERILIZING BOTTLES

If you are using plastic-frame nursers with disposable bags, follow the directions on the package for keeping the equipment germ-free. For regular plastic or glass bottles, there are two methods of sterilization. One is called the *terminal method*, and the other the *aseptic* or *presterilization method*. The terminal method is quite simple. You mix up the formula and fill the bottles, then sterilize everything at once. With the aseptic method, you boil the utensils and the formula separately, then fill the bottles. Either method works well for a single bottle preparation. If you have a dishwasher, you can forget about these two methods. It will automatically sterilize your bottles. Once you read through the procedures, which tend to sound more complicated than they really are, you may be tempted to ask the following question:

Question: How old should the baby be before you can stop sterilizing bottles?

Answer: Every pediatrician differs on this. Dr. Virginia Pomeranz, author of The First Five Years, *feels that sterilization is unnecessary, and that a thorough washing and scrubbing of bottles in hot soapy water will do perfectly well. The standard advice however, is to sterilize for two to three months.*

THE TERMINAL METHOD

With this method, the prepared formula is sterilized along with the bottles and the nipples. But start early, at least two and a half hours before you'll need a bottle.

1. Wash all your equipment with hot, soapy water. Rinse well and drain dry.

2. Either mix the formula base and water in individual bottles or make one large batch in a measuring cup or pitcher. In either case, use cold water from the tap. The formula will be sterilized along with the bottles in step #5.

3. Fill the bottles. Place a clean nipple, inverted, in the neck of each bottle. (The nipple should not go into the formula.)

4. Put rings and caps on loosely so that the steam can pass under them.

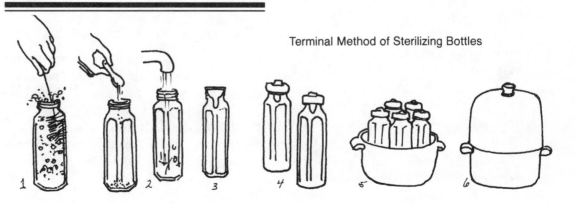

Terminal Method of Sterilizing Bottles

5. Place the bottles upright in three inches of water in a spaghetti pot or sterilizer. Make sure the bottles are close enough together that they can't fall over. Cover and boil for twenty-five minutes.

6. Let the sterilizer cool with the lid on for about two hours. This gradual cooling will prevent a skin from forming on the top of the milk.

7. Remove bottles, seal the caps tightly, and store in the refrigerator immediately.

THE ASEPTIC METHOD

The aseptic method of sterilization requires that all equipment (bottles, nipples, caps, rings, discs, spoons, funnels, tongs, measuring cups, etc.) be sterilized before you fill the bottles with sterile formula (either powder or concentrate mixed with water that has been boiled and then cooled).

Aseptic Method of Sterilizing Bottles

1. Before you even begin to sterilize your equipment, start preparing the water that you will need to mix with the formula plus an extra half ounce for evaporation. Bring the water to a boil for three minutes, then set aside to cool.

2. To sterilize equipment, boil it for twenty-five minutes in a sterilizer, a covered saucepan, or a spaghetti pot.

3. After sterilizing your equipment, mix the formula. The formula base and sterile cooled water can be mixed either directly in each individual bottle, or in one large batch. In the latter case, use an oversized measuring cup and a long-handled spoon. A funnel will help you get the formula into the bottles without spills.

4. After you have mixed the formula and filled the bottles, place inverted nipples on the bottles. Be careful to touch only the outer rims of the nipples.

5. To store, tightly screw caps or discs on the bottles and refrigerate immediately.

OTHER EQUIPMENT

The Nuk Nipple and Exerciser

The Nuk nipple is recommended by many pediatricians and hospitals because it conforms to the shape of the baby's palate more readily than the traditionally shaped nipple. It collapses and expands easily and allows the baby to control the rate of the flow of milk with less tongue-thrusting. The flat passage also encourages the baby to close his lips entirely around the nipple and breathe through his nose rather than his mouth. The nipple fits all standard bottles. Nuk also makes a pacifier called

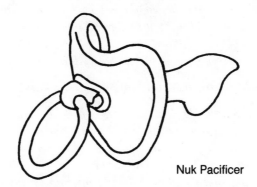

Nuk Pacificer

the Orthodontic Exerciser. This pacifier, similar to the nipple in design, has advantages over the traditional pacifier, and if your baby accepts it, it is also less likely to fall out of his mouth every two minutes.

Bottle Straws

When your baby is old enough to hold his own bottle, a bottle straw is a great boon. It allows the baby to sit up and drink, which is particularly helpful if he gets thirsty in the stroller or the car seat. There are two brands of sit-up straws. Essentially they consist of a tube and a valve. One brand is molded plastic in one unit. The other has a tube which

Nuk Nipple

separates from the straw. Both get filled with milk and juice deposits and, as you can imagine, the straw that comes apart can be cleaned much more easily and has a longer life. Sit-up straws do not fit with Nuk nipples, so you will need to use a standard nipple with the straw.

Besides being convenient, these bottle straws have other advantages. If the baby becomes used to sitting up and drinking, he is less likely to demand a bottle at bedtime. One bedtime bottle is fine, but several can really cause damage to the teeth, and perhaps the ears as well if he is lying down.

Bottle Straw

COMMON QUESTIONS ABOUT BOTTLE-FEEDING

Question: How do I get the right-sized hole in the nipple?

Answer: To make a small hole larger, heat the sharp point of a fine needle over a flame. Stick the needle into the nipple and quickly pull it out. Repeat this procedure until the hole, when tested, allows the milk to drop out in a steady flow of drops. To make a large hole smaller is somewhat chancier. Try boiling the nipple for three minutes.

The butterfat in milk causes the rubber to deteriorate. It is a good idea to at least rinse nipples before you actually wash them or sterilize them. A pinch of salt in the nipple cuts the butterfat and opens any clogged holes. Shake the salt down inside the wet nipple to form a paste. Then squeeze and roll the nipple between your fingers to force the paste through the hole.

Also, as soon as the baby is finished with a bottle, fill it with cold water until you have time to get back to it. A tablespoon of vinegar in the water will dissolve the filmy deposits on bottles which have been sterilized in hard water.

A: I spent hours adjusting nipple holes so that the orange juice would flow through. If the needle is too hot, the hole will instantly become too big, with burned rubber around it. On the other hand, it's impossible to get the needle into the same hole twice before the needle cools off. I forgot about needles and put a wood toothpick into the hole and boiled the nipple for about five minutes. When I got tired of all this rigamarole, I bought regular Evenflo nipples, strained my orange juice, and left the holes alone.

Question: Is it necessary to warm bottles?

Answer: No. Several years ago Bellevue Hospital performed a study with premature babies to see whether warming their bottles affected the babies' well-being. Half were fed warmed formula and the other half cold formula (straight from the refrigerator). The results: There was no significant difference in spitting up, diarrhea, cramps, or weight gain between the two groups.

If you do warm a bottle, a simple way to do so is to place the bottle in a coffee can containing hot water from the tap, rather than investing in an elaborate electric bottle-warmer.

Question: How long can you store leftover formula?

Answer: The cans of formula base (including evaporated milk) come in the correct size for making single batches of formula. If you do have any left over, you can store it safely in the refrigerator for forty-eight hours, but be sure to cover it tightly with a plastic bag or plastic wrap. Bottled formula also can be kept safely in the refrigerator for two days. A bottle can stand out at room temperature for an hour without spoiling. If the baby has taken none of it, it can go back into the refrigerator. But if the baby has taken some from the bottle, the remainder should not be kept for more than an hour, and only a half-hour in hot weather. Then it should be thrown away.

SOME GENERAL DO'S AND DON'T'S WHEN YOU BOTTLE-FEED

DO'S

Cuddle your baby and change his position from side to side the way a nursing mother does. This will give him a change of perspective.

When you mix up formula, follow the doctor's instructions or the instructions on the commercial formula to the letter.

Do check the size of the nipple hole. The milk should drip out in a steady series of drops. Ideally it should take twenty minutes for each feeding. If the hole is too small, the baby will tire easily and swallow too much air. If the hole is too large, the milk will come too fast. Besides not getting enough sucking, the baby will thrust his tongue forward to try to slow the flow. Tongue thrusting is a bad habit to get into. It can affect the placement of the baby's teeth when they come in as well as later speech development. Nuk nipples are recommended (see box, page 43).

Make sure that the neck of the bottle is always filled with milk. This way the baby will swallow less air.

DON'T'S

Don't prop bottles—not so much because the baby may choke, but because the baby needs cuddling and love while she eats.

Don't feed the baby lying flat on his back. It's hard to swallow this way. It is thought that babies fed in this position are more susceptible to inner-ear infections. It is theorized that this happens because the milk is forced into the inner canals when the baby swallows in a horizontal position.

Don't keep a bottle warming for later use. Give it to the baby immediately. Bacteria multiply rapidly in a warm environment.

Don't urge the baby to finish her bottle if she has stopped sucking. Offer a pacifier between feedings if the baby likes it and seems to want additional sucking.

RESOURCES

Bottle-Feeding

If you have difficulty finding Nuk nipples or bottle straws in your area, write to:

Nuk Nipples
Reliance Products Co.
108 Mason Street
Woonsocket, R.I. 02895

Sit'n Sip
Medi Inc.
P.O. Box 325
27 Maple Avenue
Holbrook, Mass. 02343

-3-
Introducing Solid Foods

WHEN AND WHY TO ADD SOLIDS

Just when you are beginning to settle in with your new baby, and he has demonstrated that you can both sleep for five glorious hours in a row (maybe), you may begin to feel some pressures from concerned, well-meaning people to start offering solid, "real" or "grown-up" foods.

Some babies eat cereal at one month, fruits and vegetables at three, and meats at four, but these foods are neither necessary nor particularly good at such an early age. One forgets that both breast milk and formula are "real" foods, supplying the right balance of protein, fat, and carbohydrates in the easiest-to-digest form. They also supply the vitamins and most of the minerals that an infant needs (see pages 52–53).

The only crucial nutrient which neither supplies enough of is iron, necessary for the production of the hemoglobin that carries oxygen from the lungs to all the cells in the body. But babies are born with enough iron stored in their livers to last until they are between four and six months old. When a baby is around this age, the pediatrician usually performs a routine blood test for anemia and may or may not suggest introducing some foods rich in iron, changing to an iron-fortified formula, or adding iron drops.

Interestingly enough, the period between four and six months coincides with the time the baby's most intense desire to suck begins to taper off. The pacifier might be rejected (seemingly mysteriously), and nursing periods may shorten. By this age, too, the muscles used for swallowing are strong from all the sucking. Also, the baby's interest in the world around her has increased tremendously. She may enjoy sitting up for longer periods of time; she will reach out and grab for objects, hold them, and try to bring them to her mouth. She's begun to vocalize and socialize, to wiggle and kick and roll, and is generally feeling rather curious and experimental. And her parents are feeling more relaxed and experimental, too.

But introducing solids to the younger baby can interfere with his desire to suck. This can decrease a nursing mother's milk supply just enough to confirm her worries that the baby is not getting enough. Solids may also crowd out room for milk without making up for its nutritional loss. Until a baby is at least three months old, these more complex foods pass, along with their vitamins and minerals, largely undigested through his system. And in the meantime his immature kidneys have worked much harder to process out the wastes than they do for milk. Many experts also believe that delaying some of the more allergenic foods (egg whites, citrus fruits, and wheat) until six months will minimize the likelihood of allergy.

Just as important, the early breast- and bottle-feedings provide the kind of closeness, holding, and cuddling the baby needs. As soon as spoons and dishes are introduced, feeding becomes, in addition to more work for parents, somewhat less personal.

MYTHS AND REALITIES

Myths	*Realities*
"I introduced cereal at a month because I'd been told it would help weigh the baby down like cement so that he would sleep longer."	Alas, such a tempting theory! Who isn't susceptible? But, as the Child Research Council of the University of Colorado School of Medicine has shown, there is no connection between feeding of solids and sleeping through the night.
A fat baby is a healthy, happy baby!	There is growing evidence that overfeeding in the first half-year actually increases the number of fat cells by programming an increase in the production of insulin and growth hormones. An adult who has been overweight since infancy or early childhood can diet to reduce the size of individual fat cells, but

never the number. The tendency to take on weight easily will always be there.

Moreover, a fat baby can't move around as easily as a thin baby. This can be very frustrating. There is always a tendency to feed a frustrated baby to quiet him, and thus the vicious cycle perpetuates itself.

FIRST SOLID FOODS

I first tried to get Birch to eat some cereal when he was five months old. I was getting a little nervous about being the sole source of his diet, even though he was doing fine on breast milk alone. I gave him a demitasse spoon full of cereal and milk, and he spit it out and cried. I waited a couple of days and tried again. He still hated it. I tried altering the consistency. No luck. I tried applesauce. No luck. Then I tried bananas. No luck again. I had visions of never being able to wean him. After a week of experimenting, I finally said the hell with it. Two weeks later Kim casually offered him a spoonful

of his yogurt. He loved it. It's been smooth sailing ever since.

I gave her cereal at a month, hoping it would help her sleep through the night. Ha! The next day she had a bright green bowel movement. I panicked. The pediatrician said it was nothing to worry about. But it didn't seem right to me anyway. I backed off until she was four and a half months old. She had a green bowel movement then, ioo, but I was more prepared to handle it, less nervous about everything, I suppose.

It does not matter which simple food you start your baby out with. Pediatricians all have their own approaches. Some favor the commercial baby cereals because they are fortified with iron. Others feel that the first food ought to taste good, and suggest fruit and yogurt. And some, noting that babies are notorious for disliking vegetables, may suggest that you take the plunge—start out with vegetables in order to get the baby used to them before she becomes too opinionated or totally hooked on bananas (see quotes above).

Feed the baby his first solids after he's had his milk—not when he's dying of hunger. This way he is most likely to be in a good mood. It's important to remember that these first feedings should be relaxed experiments—not ways of getting "good nutritional stuff" into the baby. He has to get used to the spoon and learn to coordinate his swallowing muscles first. If he isn't interested, try again a few days later. After he has gotten used to one food, wait at least three to five days before introducing the next one. This way, if the baby does have an allergic reaction, you will be able to isolate the culprit. And do not confuse very strange bowel movements with allergic reactions (see page 215).

Question: What causes green bowel movements?

Answer: Stool color is a source of concern to caretakers of babies. The green often seen in them is due to bile from the upper part of the gastrointestinal tract. As it passes through the lower tract, it changes to yellow, orange, and then brown. Greenish-black is also undigested bile. The color, then, reflects the speed with which it comes along this pathway.

Fluid is absorbed from the stool in the large intestine, or colon, and hence a liquid movement also means a rapid movement through it. A loose, wet, and green movement simply implies this rapid transit. Breast milk commonly is laxative in its action on the infant's intestinal tract. Sugars are laxative. New solids are also responsible for loose, greenish stools until the digestive system becomes accustomed to them . . .

—T. Berry Brazelton, M.D., *Infants and Mothers*

SOME OF THE BASICS OF NUTRITION

There is nothing like a baby in the family to make parents concerned about nutrition. Once the baby has become used to a variety of solids, we start to become concerned about getting the right balance of foods. Good nutrition is, after all, one of the most important factors in your baby's life. A healthy diet is the best form of preventive medicine and the foundation for future eating habits. Food is also the raw material for growth. In the first year the baby does more growing proportionally than he will ever do again and expends tremendous amounts of energy absorbing information and striving to reach, turn, creep, sit, stand, crawl, and finally walk. One of the many bonuses of becoming concerned about a baby's diet is that we usually become more aware of our own nutritional habits and needs as well. We tend to shop, cook, and eat more carefully.

We have all been schooled in the basics of the balanced diet, and our natural instinct is to try to provide such a diet for our babies. But we soon come up against the reality that babies, like adults, have likes and dislikes and their own styles of eating. One learns quickly that a baby doesn't necessarily embrace the notion of a balanced meal. It's good to keep in mind that there is a lot of flexibility in balancing foods. In the oft-quoted experiment by Dr. Clara Davis, year-old babies were allowed to choose freely from a sampling of natural foods. With no adult interference, the babies selected what they wanted. Taken on a day-to-day basis their diets were lopsided, but over the course of a month their diets were very well rounded. Those likes and dislikes, therefore, will almost always add up to a diet that is right for the baby.

One useful guideline comes from Dr. Myron Winick, head of Columbia University's Institute of Human Nutrition. He suggests that, by the second half of the baby's first year, parents aim to create a varied diet in which about 30 percent of the calories come from protein, another 30 percent come from carbohydrates, and the rest come from fats.

The best way to make sure your baby receives a balanced supply of nutrients is to offer him a wide variety of dairy products, meats or meat substitutes, grains, fruits and vegetables (see table of nutrients, their functions and sources, on page 52).

Proteins, carbohydrates, fats, vitamins, and minerals, along with water and oxygen, constitute the raw materials for growth. Of these, only two—vitamins and minerals—are ready for immediate use. The other foods must be chemically broken down into simpler components before cells can utilize them. Digestion, starting in the mouth, but doing the bulk of its work in the stomach and small intestine, transforms these large nutrients into usable small units. Proteins are broken down into amino acids, carbohydrates into simple sugars, and fats into fatty acids and glycerol. From the digestive sites in the alimentary canal, the processed chemicals, as well as the unprocessed vitamins and minerals, are absorbed into the bloodstream or the lymph system and carried to the cells. In the cells the amino acids, fatty acids, glycerol, and minerals will be assembled into new compounds that will form structural components such as cell membrane. The sugar in the diet will be used mainly to supply the energy for this complex assembly process. And the vitamins serve as catalysts to speed up the synthesis of the new compounds.

PROTEINS

Proteins are the body-builders and maintainers, and the most important group of compounds in the body. Besides being the body's main structural elements, they form the enzymes which control and create the thousands of chemical reactions and help convert food into compounds the cells can use. For example, they preside over each step in the complex process by which sugars are broken down to give energy. Proteins also form antibodies to fight infection and form the hemoglobin which carries oxygen to all the cells in the body.

The greatest amounts of protein are needed when the body is building new tissues—during pregnancy, during lactation, and especially during infancy. Unlike some other nutrients, protein is not stored in the body in large quantities for very long. This is why it is so important that a baby receive an adequate amount every day.

The Quality of Protein. In order to be of use to the body, protein foods are broken down by digestion into amino acids and then absorbed into the blood. These amino acids (there are twenty-two in all) are then used as building blocks in all cells to form replicas of themselves. Of the amino acids, fourteen are created by our metabolisms and are called nonessentials. The remaining eight are called essentials, and are the ones to be most concerned about because they must be gotten from food.

Foods which provide all the essential amino acids in the right proportions are known as complete or high-quality protein foods. High-quality proteins are found in breast milk, infant formulas, cow's milk, eggs, cheese, yogurt, meats, poultry, and fish. Milk is probably the most common high-protein food in a baby's diet during its first year. To add variety to the baby's diet, use the following chart to substitute milk products for milk.

Useful Milk Equivalents

1-inch cube cheddar-type cheese	= ½ cup milk
½ cup yogurt	= ½ cup milk
½ cup cottage cheese	= ⅓ cup milk
2 tablespoons cream cheese	= 1 tablespoon milk
½ cup ice cream or ice milk	= ⅓ cup milk

An incomplete or low quality protein is either missing one or more of the essential amino acids or has an incorrect proportion of them. Low-quality proteins are found in some vegetables, seeds, and grains. By combining two complementary sources of lower-quality protein, you can add variety to a baby's diet and increase usable protein. But you must be careful to choose foods which complement each other correctly. Also remember that these foods must be served together at the same meal. For example, 1¼ ounces of cheese, when served with ¾ cup cooked rice, yields 20 percent more usable protein than when it is served alone. Other good combinations of lower-quality proteins are grains with milk or dairy products (cereal with milk, pasta with cheese, grilled cheese sandwich, French toast, rice and milk pudding), grains and legumes (rice with beans or lentils, peanut butter on bread, cornmeal with beans, baked beans with

THE JOYS OF YOGURT

Yogurt is one of the healthiest, most versatile, and most convenient foods for babies. It has a protein value almost as high as milk and is rich in B vitamins and in certain healthy bacteria which fight off infections. Milk kept warm over a period of hours produces two bacteria or bacilli (lactobacillus bulgaricus and streptococcus thermophilus) which convert milk sugar or lactose into lactic acid. The lactic acid gives yogurt its tart taste and creates an environment in which many harmful bacteria in the intestinal tract cannot survive—for instance, those that cause dysentery.

Yogurt also introduces protective bacteria to fight off constipation, diarrhea, and perhaps colic. Because it is predigested by the bacteria, yogurt is easily digested and assimilated into the system in about an hour. Milk takes three or four hours.

Yogurt stores well in the refrigerator and can be served at any meal; it can be used as a base for cereals, fruits, or vegetables, a thinner for pureed meats, or a base for drinks. And what the baby doesn't eat, you can eat. It's also great for travel.

MAKE YOUR OWN YOGURT

1 quart milk

¼ cup commercial plain yogurt (unpasteurized brand)

1. Bring milk to a boil and remove from heat. Let milk stand until it is at room temperature.

2. Combine yogurt with about a quarter-cup of milk and stir until blended.

3. Stir this into the remaining milk and pour mixture into a clean glass bowl. Cover with plastic wrap, then cover with a towel and let stand at 70 degrees (either in your oven, which has previously been warmed and then turned off, or on the floor at the exhaust of your refrigerator if this is convenient).

4. If you want yogurt on the sweetish side, let it stand for twelve hours. If you want it on the sourish side, leave for eighteen hours.

Yield: About 1 quart

brown bread), and seeds with legumes (sesame or sunflower seeds with legumes).

CARBOHYDRATES

Carbohydrates are the starches and sugars the body needs to supply energy for protein synthesis, and the fibers or roughage necessary for proper digestion and elimination. Many important functions depend on carbohydrates as their primary fuel. The brain, for example, relies on sugar glucose, which comes primarily from the starch in the diet.

Like all other forms of energy used by people, the energy we receive from our diets originally comes from the sun; it is stored in seeds, grains, roots, tubers, and fruits. With the exception of table sugar, carbohydrate foods supply many of the essential vitamins and minerals, such as iron, calcium, B vitamins, vitamin A, and vitamin C, that a baby needs.

Carbohydrates can be thought of as protein conservers. If too few energy foods are consumed each day, valuable protein will be converted to carbohydrates for fuel instead of being used for the growth and repair of tissues. Proteins and carbohydrates should normally be eaten together at the same meal to keep this protein-sparing action working efficiently—though, once again, as long as the baby is drinking milk, this will occur automatically. The baby's first carbohydrates are sugars called lactose, found in breast milk or infant formulas. Later his carbohydrate needs can be met by fresh fruits, whole grains, vegetables, cereals, and breads.

Enriched vs. Whole-Grain Products. Whenever possible, buy whole-grain products. Most breads and pastas available today are enriched, which means that about one-third of the iron, vitamin B, and niacin is removed in the process of refining the flour and then replaced. But many of the other nutrients, such as calcium, potassium, and magnesium, are not totally restored. In addition, the protein of the wheat germ, rich in essential amino acids and B vitamins, is discarded in the making of white bread and pastas.

The difference between the nutritional value of white and brown rice is also astonishing. Brown rice has almost four times the protein and calcium value of white enriched rice and over twice the iron content.

Another excellent whole-grain product is wheat germ. The embryo (germ) of the wheat kernel is the most nutritionally superior part of the plant. It is rich in B-complex vitamins and is the best known source of vitamin E, as well as a good source of complete protein. Wheat germ must be stored in the refrigerator, or oxygen will combine with the oils in it that contain vitamin E, and it will turn rancid. Add it to cereals, yogurt, meat loaves, stews, pancakes, and so on. However, if your baby has an allergic reaction to wheat products, as some do, wheat germ should be avoided.

Sugar. A preference for sweet foods appears to be inborn in almost all of us. But try to stick to the natural sweeteners in fruits and vegetables (such as yams and carrots). Table sugar is one of the few foods that supplies no vitamins or minerals—only calories that can crowd out room for other nutrients, destroy the appetite, cause cavities, and make a baby fat. It may also increase the body's need for thiamin (a B vitamin) and the trace mineral chromium. There is also growing evidence that the consumption of refined carbohydrates may be related to hyperactivity. Anyway, there is much more nutritional value in a fresh peach than there is in the peach cobbler found in the baby-food section of your local supermarket.

Several of the baby-food cookbooks suggest substituting honey, molasses, or brown or "raw" sugar for regular table sugar in various recipes. It has recently been suggested that raw honey may contain botulism spores, which under some conditions produce the poison that sometimes causes the deadly botulism infection. The Sioux Honey Association, made up of the world's largest honey-producing cooperatives, believes that feeding raw honey to infants under twenty-six weeks of age has caused some cases of crib death. Apparently older children and adults are not susceptible. While molasses does contain some nutrients, the nutritional value really is negligible. The important thing in any diet is not what kind of sweetener (excluding raw honey), but how much.

FATS

Fats are part of every cell in our bodies. They supply a concentrated source of energy—twice as much, in fact, as either proteins or carbohydrates. They also carry the fat-soluble vitamins A, E, and K as well as linoleic acid, needed in small quantities for the development of healthy skin. Fat is necessary to cushion the vital organs, and to insulate the body from loss of heat. Premature babies have not had time to lay down a protective layer of fat; that is why such care must be taken to keep them warm.

Babies need some fat in their diets, and it is supplied by breast milk, formulas, cow's milk, other dairy products, and meats. It is not recommended that you give your baby skim milk unless your doctor prescribes it. The fat in milk is needed for the proper absorption of calcium. Though fats are an important ele-

NUTRIENTS: THEIR FUNCTIONS AND SOURCES

NUTRIENT	CHIEF FUNCTIONS	IMPORTANT SOURCES
Vitamin A (fat-soluble) Extra vitamin A is stored in the liver—that is why animal livers are such a good source.	Helps prevent infection. Helps eyes adjust to changes from bright to dim light (prevents night blindness). Needed for healthy skin and certain tissues, such as the lining of eyes and lungs.	Liver, whole milk, fortified margarine (A is added), butter, most cheeses (especially Swiss and cheddar), egg yolks, dark-green and yellow vegetables (especially carrots, parsley, kale, and orange squash), apricots.
Vitamin D (fat-soluble)	Needed for strong bones and teeth (regulates calcium and phosphorus in bone formation). Essential for calcium absorption from the blood.	Sunlight shining on bare skin, vitamin D fortified milk, fish-liver oil, sardines, canned tuna.
Vitamin E (fat-soluble)	Helps preserve some vitamins and unsaturated fatty acids (acts as an antioxidant). Helps stabilize biological membranes.	Plant oils (especially wheat-germ oil and soybean oil), wheat germ, navy beans, eggs, brown rice.
Vitamin C or ascorbic acid (water-soluble) C is easily destroyed by air and heat. Like many other water-soluble vitamins, it is *not* stored in the body, so we need some every day.	Needed for healthy collagen (a protein that holds cells together). Helps wounds to heal. Needed for normal blood-clotting and healthy blood vessels. Needed for iron absorption. Spares or protects vitamins A and E and several B vitamins. Needed for strong teeth and bones.	Citrus fruits, green and red peppers, green leafy vegetables, parsley, tomatoes, potatoes, strawberries, cantaloupe, bean sprouts (especially mung beans and soybeans).
B vitamins (water-soluble) include thiamine (B_1), riboflavin (B_2), niacin, pyridoxine, folic acid, cobalamin (B_{12}), cholene, etc. Folic-acid deficiency is common during pregnancy. It may also be caused by birth control pills. Riboflavin is destroyed by sunlight, so use milk containers that keep out light.	Needed for steady nerves, alertness, good digestion, energy production, healthy skin and eyes, certain enzymes involved in amino-acid synthesis, maintenance of blood.	Whole-grain breads and cereals, liver, wheat germ, nutritional yeast, green leafy vegetables, lean meats, milk, molasses, peanuts, dried peas and beans.

NUTRIENTS: THEIR FUNCTIONS AND SOURCES

NUTRIENT	CHIEF FUNCTIONS	IMPORTANT SOURCES
Fatigue, tension, depression are often signs of a B deficiency.		
Calcium Calcium is more easily digested when eaten with acid foods (such as yogurt or sour milk).	Needed for building bones and teeth, for blood clotting, for regulating nerve and muscle activity, for absorbing iron.	Whole and skim milk, buttermilk, cheese, yogurt, green vegetables, egg yolk, bone-meal powder, blackstrap molasses.
Phosphorus	Needed to transform protein, fats and carbohydrates into energy in the body. Makes up part of all the body's cells. Needed for building bones and teeth.	Milk, cheeses, lean meats, egg yolks.
Iron Daily intake is important. Children, teenagers, pregnant and menstruating women are especially likely to have iron deficiencies.	Makes up an important part of hemoglobin, the compound in blood that carries oxygen from the lungs to the body cells.	Lean meat, liver, egg yolk, green leafy vegetables, nutritional yeast, wheat germ, whole-grain and enriched breads and cereals, soybean flour, raisins, blackstrap molasses.
Iodine	An important part of thyroxine; helps the thyroid gland regulate the rate at which our bodies use energy. Affects growth, water balances, nervous system, muscular system, and circulatory system.	Iodized salt, seafood, plant foods grown in soil near the sea.
Magnesium	Required for certain enzyme activity. Helps in bone formation.	Grains, vegetables, cereals, fruits, milk, nuts.
Potassium	Needed for healthy nerves and muscles.	Seafood, milk, vegetables, fruits.
Sodium, chlorine, fluorine and other trace minerals Most of our diets now contain too much sodium, largely because of sodium compounds used in processed foods and excessive use of table salt.	Varying functions, many of them not well understood.	Meat, cheese, eggs, seafood, green leafy vegetables, fluoridated water, sea salt.

ment in the diet, the type of fat has been a consideration in the past several years. Eating too much saturated fat—animal fat or fat that hardens at room temperature—and too little polyunsaturated fat—found in vegetable oils—can raise the blood levels of cholesterol.

Cholesterol is a controversial subject nowadays. Some cholesterol is important to the body's metabolism. It forms the raw material from which vitamin D, bile salt, and sex and adrenal hormones are made. But new data has shown that cholesterol is transported through the bloodstream by different kinds of lipoproteins, or blood fats. High levels of high-density lipoproteins (HDLs) mean less chance of heart disease or stroke. High levels of low-density lipoproteins (LDLs), on the other hand, may lead to an increase in the chance of coronary disease. Only a blood test for HDLs and LDLs can determine whether you need to modify your diet or your baby's for cholesterol control. If cholesterol is a problem in your family, by all means ask your pediatrician about this test. In the meantime, many nutritionists and pediatricians continue to advise that egg yolks, which are particularly high in cholesterol, should be limited to two or three a week.

VITAMINS AND MINERALS

People cannot manufacture vitamins in their bodies and must get them from a variety of foods or from synthetic sources. Vitamins help the body utilize nutrients and promote normal growth of tissues, and they are essential for the proper functioning of nerves and muscles. They are also part of the reproductive and digestive processes, and they may well help the body resist infections. Minerals are important because they give strength and rigidity to certain body tissues and assist with a number of other bodily functions. Vitamins and minerals work with each other in many combinations. Though each is described below as having a rather specific function, they seldom act independently.

Vitamin supplementation with A, C, and D is important for the breast-fed baby. Infant formulas are fortified in adequate amounts to meet RDAs, and additional vitamin supplements are unnecessary. After the breast-fed baby is eating a varied diet of solids, these supplements are usually discontinued, but check with your pediatrician.

On the previous two pages is a table adapted from *Our Bodies, Ourselves* by the Boston Women's Health Collective.

-4-
Making Your Own Baby Food

There is nothing mysterious or complicated about making your own baby food, and there are many advantages in doing so. You can leave out the unnecessary sugar, salt, and fillers, such as water and cornstarch, found in commercial baby foods. You can also save a great deal of money. You'll need a few standard kitchen implements (which you may own anyway) and/or an inexpensive pocketbook-size baby-food grinder, which can be bought at a department store. And you will need some time. If you cook in bulk and freeze portions, or grind up a portion of your own dinner before you add the seasonings, you will save a great deal of time.

There are no recipes included here. Everyone knows how to mash a banana and to thin it with liquid if it seems too bulky for the baby. No baby particularly profits from elaborate puddings—eggs and milk fortified with molasses and honey (instead of sugar) for dessert—unless you enjoy cooking these things and have the time. Many of the foods you

eat, such as stews and soups, can be pureed to become "combination" dinners. Scrambled eggs, cottage cheese, and yogurt are excellent vehicles for vegetables if the baby is horrified at the sight of a spoonful of string beans.

The number of months that a baby will allow the parent to be in control of her feeding—that is, putting pureed foods into her mouth with a spoon—are very few, especially if you encourage self-feeding as soon as the baby shows signs of being able to pick up anything and everything and putting it in her mouth. For this reason it's not recommended that you spend a great deal of money on elaborate electric baby-food grinders and special cookbooks.

USEFUL ITEMS FOR COOKING

☐ A blender, food mill (which will separate out skins and seeds), food processor, or small hand-operated

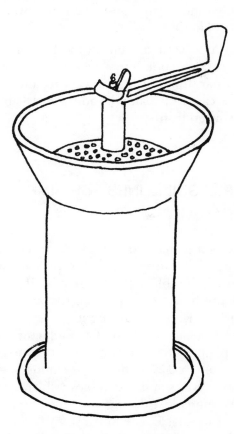

Portable Baby Food Grinder

baby-food grinder for pureeing, and/or a sieve to put blended or milled foods through as a final step if a smoother consistency is desired.

☐ A small vegetable steamer, colander, or sieve for steaming rather than boiling vegetables and fruits. (Many vegetables and fruits contain vitamins C and A, which are water-soluble and easily destroyed by overcooking.)

☐ A pot with a well-fitting lid, or a pressure cooker to save time, and/or a pan for braising or stewing meats (a cast-iron pan will add a little absorbed iron).

SIMPLE GUIDELINES FOR SIMPLE FOODS

Make sure that you work with clean hands, clean utensils, and especially a clean butcher block if you use one. If you taste the food, don't put the spoon back in the pot without washing it.

For thinning: Baby-food manufacturers add plain water for the proper consistency, but you can add the steaming water from fruits and vegetables (which has the vitamins lost during cooking), breast milk, formula, cow's milk, yogurt, meat broths, vegetable broths, soup liquids, stew juices, tomato juice, or, to sweeten, apple or orange juice.

For thickening: Baby-food manufacturers add modified starch or cornstarch, neither of which is particularly well digested by infants. You can add arrowroot, wheat germ, whole-grain cereals, cottage cheese, farmer cheese, cooked egg yolks, yogurt, soy grits, or mashed white or sweet potatoes.

FRUITS

Bananas are often the first fruit that a baby eats. Choose ones with brown spots on the skins, because these are the ripest. Simply mash with a fork, and thin or thicken as desired. All other fruits should be peeled, cut up into small pieces, steamed until just soft, then pureed, adding liquids or fillers as needed.

VEGETABLES

Try carrots, zucchini, peas, beans, and sweet potatoes first. You can bake the potatoes. Cut the other vegetables into small pieces and steam them over one or two inches of water in a tightly covered pot. Use this water or other thinners when pureeing vegetables. The approximate ratio of vegetables to liquid is 2 cups of fresh vegetables to between 1/3 and 1/2 cup of liquid. Offer spinach and beets less often because they can contain an excess of nitrates from the soil. Cabbage, broccoli, and cauliflower may produce gas in the baby, but you never know until you try. Corn is hard to digest, so wait on this until you have a toddler.

MEATS

These can be baked, broiled, poached, stewed, or braised—but not fried. Chicken is a good meat to start with because it is so easy to digest. Chicken livers are also one of the great inexpensive convenience foods for babies. They are easy to portion, very easy to puree, and cook quickly. It's quite difficult, as well as unnecessary, to approximate the lumpless consistency of commercial baby-food meats. In most cases you will need to add some liquid. If you use a baby-food grinder first or a food mill as a first step, and a blender or a sieve as a second step, you can get the texture quite smooth.

TO WARM UP THE BABY'S FOOD

You can place the food in one or two small Pyrex dishes in a pan of water on the burner of your stove, in a multiple egg poacher, or (more expensive) in an electric warming dish.

GENERAL COOKING TIPS

1. Don't cook in pots with copper on the inside. This metal acts as a catalyst to break down vitamin C.

2. Don't cook acidic foods, such as tomatoes, in aluminum pans.

3. Handle fruits and vegetables gently. Crushing or bruising releases an enzyme which destroys vitamin C.

4. Canned foods need only a little heating. Don't cook them for too long or vitamins will be destroyed.

5. Vitamin-rich foods should be cooked covered, not in an open pot.

6. When you can, cook fruits and vegetables in their skins, which contain nutrients and fiber. Skins also help keep soluble nutrients from dissolving in the cooking water.

7. Don't add baking soda to green vegetables to improve their color. This destroys vitamins.

8. Vitamins A and B are destroyed by light. Keep milk or formula in its carton or can, not in a glass jar or pitcher. Dried beans also need lightproof storage.

9. Don't soak or boil dried legumes for long periods of time because the vitamins will be destroyed. Instead, boil them for two minutes and let stand for an hour. This is equivalent to fifteen hours of soaking. Don't rinse after soaking.

10. Bake grain products to a light brown crust and avoid vitamin loss.

STORING, FREEZING, AND THAWING

1. After preparing the baby food, cool it quickly in the refrigerator; there is less chance for bacteria to form in a cool environment.

2. To store pureed foods, try one or two pop-out ice-cube trays, each section of which holds about 1½ ounces, or use squares of aluminum foil for wrapping up small globs.

3. Seal ice-cube trays and aluminum-foil packages in plastic bags which are dated and labeled.

4. Food stored in the freezer is good for a month. A small amount of vitamins C and A are lost in the freezing process, but this is far less than what is lost by storing baby food in the refrigerator over a period of a few days.

5. When thawing, never leave food uncovered on the kitchen counter. Thaw in the refrigerator. Room temperature allows bacteria to grow. If you are in a hurry, you can thaw by submerging a cube in a plastic bag in cold water.

SUGGESTIONS FOR USING COMMERCIAL BABY FOODS

1. Look carefully at the list of ingredients before you buy. Ingredients are listed in the order of the quantities in which they exist in the food. If possible, avoid those with salt, sugar, and modified starches. Don't buy anything with water listed first.

2. Meats and vegetables are the best buys, the fruit juices and mixed dinners the worst buys (mixed dinners are usually full of fillers). If you want a mixed dinner, you are better off combining plain meats and plain vegetables.

3. Check to make sure that the "safety button" on the lid is concave, which means the jar is vacuum-sealed. If it isn't, the jar may be contaminated.

4. If you are warming foods, do not do so in the jars. They are not heat resistant. Moreover, if all of the food in a jar is heated and not eaten, the remaining food is very susceptible to bacteria.

5. Don't feed the baby from the jar,

unless he is going to eat the whole jar. The enzymes from his saliva will spoil the leftover food.

6. Store jars in the refrigerator no more than two days. If the food is not eaten by then, throw it away.

I am a purist. I make all of Sebastian's food from foods I buy at the health-food store; organic bananas, apples, and pears; stone-ground, whole-grain baby cereals; meat from cows that aren't full of hormones, and "raw" certified milk that hasn't had all the nutrients boiled out of it. No fish. The mercury content is too high. Well, yes, we are spending more on his diet than our own. The three of us can't afford to eat this way.

I make most of Andrew's food from scratch from fresh foods that I buy at the supermarket. I try to read labels carefully if I use processed foods, but I must say, it is confusing. And I do keep a supply of commercial baby foods on hand which have no salt or sugar added. I use them when I'm just too tired to think about what to feed him or too tired to make it. Now, do you really think, looking at him, that he is suffering?

A FEW WORDS ON FOOD ADDITIVES

Over three thousand additives are used in the manufacture of the foods we eat. No one can agree, even the experts, on what is safe and what is necessary. Some additives are necessary and even beneficial, such as the vitamins used for enrichments.

However, there are some additives, which are controversial and which are thought to be potentially dangerous, that have not been eliminated from many of the foods we buy. These tend to appear in such foods as ice cream, soft drinks, gelatin desserts, cereals, puddings, some bakery products, cooking oils, and particularly prepared meats like hot dogs, sausage, and bologna. After reading some of the selections from such pamphlets as the *Consumer's Guide to Food Additives* prepared by the City of New York, Consumer Affairs Department, 80 Lafayette St., New York, N.Y. 10013, you may well want to eliminate some of the products you ordinarily buy—particularly if you are using any of them to feed your baby as part of a solid diet or if you are nursing.

Synthetic Food Colorings. Be leery of anything containing artificial food coloring. Food colorings are not listed by name on labels, so there is no way of knowing if you're eating one of the suspect additives that follow.

Red dye #40 is a synthetic color which replaced Red #2 in many foods; it is added to soft drinks, ice cream, cherries, candy, and cake frosting. An all-purpose red dye whose only function is to color the food, it is used to color foods that are not only red, but brown, purple, and orange. Red #40 was shown to cause tumors in mice in preliminary results of a study prepared for the Allied Chemical Co., the manufacturer of the dye.

Yellow dye #5 is the most widely used color additive. It is used in beverages, desserts, candy, cereal, ice cream, baked goods, and snack foods; and it also is used in prescription drugs, pain relievers, and antihistamines. It can cause allergic reactions, wheezing, asthmatic symptoms, and hives. Individuals who are allergic to aspirin seem to be allergic to this additive as well.

Blue dyes #1 and #2 are brilliant blue, coal-tar derivatives, used in coloring for soft drinks, gelatin desserts, ice cream, ices, dry drink powders, candies, cereal, pudding, and bakery products. They may cause allergic reactions; tests have shown they produced malignant tumors in rats, but they are on the FDA's permanent list of acceptable color additives.

Bromine. This is a heavy, volatile, corrosive, nonmetallic liquid element added to vegetable oils or other oils that are blended with low-density essential oils to make them easier to emulsify in soft drinks, citrus-flavored beverages, ice cream, ices, and baked goods. Bromine has been shown to cause ill effects when released in the system at certain levels. However, it is permitted for limited use in flavoring oil and in fruit-flavored beverages.

Caffeine. Found naturally in coffee, cola, maté leaves, tea, and kola nuts, caffeine is a stimulant of the heart and nervous system. The dosage and effect varies with each individual, but in excess it has been shown to cause nervousness, insomnia, and irregular heartbeat. High doses can cause convulsions. It can cross the placental barrier and can affect the quality of breast milk.

BHA. An antioxidant preservative which prevents fats and oils from turning rancid, it is used in cake mixes, shortening, potato chips, dry breakfast cereals, gelatin desserts, candy, pudding and pie-filling mixes, and bakery products. BHA can cause allergic reactions, and an advisory panel has recommended that further studies be conducted by the FDA.

BHT. Another antioxidant used in many foods such as potato flakes, enriched rice, and shortening containing animal fats, it is also used as an antioxidant to retard rancidity in frozen and fresh pork sausage and freeze-dried meats. It can cause allergic reactions. Experiments on mice have shown the offspring frequently had chemical changes in their brains and subsequent abnormal behavior patterns.

Glycerides. Mono- and di-glycerides are used to maintain softness in bakery products, beverages, ice cream, ice milk, lard, chewing-gum base, shortening, oleomargarine, sweet chocolate, and whipped toppings. In large quantities, they are suspected of causing reproductive problems and malformations.

MSG (Monosodium Glutamate). Recently removed from commercial baby foods, this flavor-enhancer is used in canned and frozen foods, prepared meats, pickles, soups, candy, baked goods, mayonnaise, Chinese food, and Accent, which is 100 percent MSG. MSG can cause symptoms of dizziness, numbness in the area of the mouth, headaches, and general ill effects.

Sodium Nitrites. Previously used in commercial baby foods, these are now used for curing meats like bacon, hot dogs, and bologna and other luncheon meats. They help keep the pink color, hold flavor, and—most important—destroy botulism. Most nitrites are excreted in the urine. But what isn't excreted converts the hemoglobin in the blood cells to methemoglobin, which can't carry oxygen. Infants are much more susceptible to methemoglobinemia than adults, both because an enzyme that converts methemoglobin back to hemoglobin is in short supply in infants, and because the less acidic environment in the stomach and small intestine of infants favors the multiplication of nitrite-producing bacteria. The infant outgrows this in a year, but many parents have permanently eliminated meats containing nitrites from their diets.

HIGH CHAIRS AND FEEDING TABLES

Your lap or an infant seat are good places to feed the baby until she has developed strong enough back muscles to sit comfortably in a high chair or feeding table.

THE PROS AND CONS OF HIGH CHAIRS

The most important features in a high chair are safety, comfort, and cleanability. Many accidents have been caused by babies falling out of high chairs or pulling them over on top of themselves. As a result, some parents prefer to use feeding tables which are lower to the ground and designed to be tip-proof. A high chair, however, is less expensive, is much easier to store, and without the tray can be used at the table when your child is older. Following are some points to consider when you choose one:

High Chair

1. Look for a strong, adjustable, easy-to-operate safety belt and crotch strap. The crotch strap is essential for keeping the baby from sliding totally out of the chair. Another suggestion to keep the baby from sliding and/or slumping is to put a piece of foam under the baby for traction. Bathtub stickers work quite well, too.

2. Most modern high chairs have removable trays. This is essential so that you can thoroughly clean them in the sink. Look for a lip on the tray, so that spills don't reach the floor so quickly. Make sure that the latches holding the tray are easy to operate—by feeling, rather than having to bend down to see what you are doing. Also make sure that there are no parts on the latches that could pinch the baby.

3. If you are considering a collapsible or folding high chair, make sure that the locking device is strong and reliable.

4. For overall stability, the base must be wider than the seat of the chair. Different models vary tremendously. Shake the chair to test it.

5. Make sure the backrest is high enough to support the baby's head, and that the footrest is adjustable.

THE PROS AND CONS OF FEEDING TABLES

Feeding tables are much safer than high chairs, but they are generally harder to get the baby in and out of, take up considerably more room, and are more expensive. Do not let a salesperson sell you one on the grounds that it will be a good place for your toddler to sit and do arts and crafts or read quietly alone. No toddler in his right mind will sit in such a confined place for more than two minutes, and toddlers don't do arts and crafts. If you buy one, look for general stability, an adjustable seat, crotch and safety belts, as well as a strong, adjustable footrest.

Feeding Table

SELF-FEEDING—FROM HAND TO MOUTH

Your baby will probably let you know when he is ready to try to feed himself before you start wondering when to encourage him to do so. He may flatly refuse to let you put a spoonful of pureed peas into his mouth by clamping his jaw and shaking his head. Alternately, he may simply grab the spoon out of your hand—or he may gradually express an interest in feeding himself over a period of months.

A baby's signs of readiness usually coincide with his newly found mobility and dexterity at doing such things as creeping, crawling, and picking up anything and everything from the floor and putting it into his mouth. If babies only worked as hard at feeding themselves as they do at cleaning floors, there probably wouldn't be as many high-chair battleground horror stories as there are.

Self-feeding is a great stride forward in the baby's independence, as well as in the coordination of his eyes, hands, and mouth, and it should be encouraged. Let the baby try to feed himself with a few bits of soft food when he's six or seven months old, but be patient. It does take some getting used to on everyone's part. For the first months mealtimes are relatively efficient, with parents shoveling spoonfuls of food into an open mouth with a minimum of mess. It can be disconcerting for parents (often rather abruptly) to be no longer in control of what goes into the baby's mouth.

It will be several months before the baby is very good at feeding himself and before food is no longer a toy or a cosmetic rubbed onto the face and into the hair. It also takes some imagination to select a balance of good finger foods—and a lot more patience and humor to watch most of it land on the floor.

Meals will be much happier if you remind yourself that the baby's need for food and his growth do not increase proportionally with age. At some point, growth has to slow down. Also, don't present the baby with too much food. Place one or two pieces on the high-chair tray, and don't turn your back on these early experiments at self-feeding, since the baby could start to choke.

Question: *When will the baby be able to feed himself with a spoon?*

Answer: *Give the baby a spoon to hold so that he can practice. It will take many, many months, however, until he becomes good at it. Many toddlers can use a spoon efficiently by the time they are sixteen months old, but some need a lot more time.*

GOOD FINGER FOODS

PROTEIN FOODS

- [ ] Cheese, milk-and-egg custards cooked to firm consistency
- [ ] Small chunks of soft cheese
- [ ] Large-curd cottage cheese
- [ ] Farmer cheese or pot cheese
- [ ] Small, frozen yogurt bits
- [ ] Macaroni and cheese
- [ ] Grilled cheese on whole wheat bread
- [ ] Chicken livers
- [ ] Small ground beef, lamb, or veal balls
- [ ] Crumbled hamburger
- [ ] Crumbled meat loaf
- [ ] Stewed beef, chicken, veal, lamb, etc.
- [ ] Sole or salmon or any soft, well-boned fish
- [ ] French toast
- [ ] Whole wheat pancakes made with eggs and milk
- [ ] Hard-boiled eggs, scrambled eggs
- [ ] Peanut butter on whole wheat bread

FRUITS AND VEGETABLES

- [ ] Slightly steamed and softened apples, pears, peaches, etc.
- [ ] Banana
- [ ] Avocado
- [ ] Tomato with skin and seeds removed
- [ ] Mashed potatoes
- [ ] Bean curd
- [ ] Cooked zucchini, carrot, potato, etc.
- [ ] Lima beans, peas with pods removed

GRAINS

- [ ] Well-cooked rice, moistened so that it holds together in little balls
- [ ] Whole-grain breads or toast
- [ ] French toast
- [ ] Small bits of sugarless dried cereal

FRUSTRATIONS AND VARIATIONS ON THE BALANCED DIET

Molly's repertoire got smaller and smaller. Finally she would eat only pureed chicken and bananas and, of course, teething biscuits. I did give her vitamins, but stopped offering her a lot of the other foods out of pure frustration. When we left her with my mother for a day, she reported that Molly had gone on a vegetable binge. I felt so guilty.

Mildred Fischer, the great food writer, suggests balancing the day, rather than the meal. With our baby I found that it wasn't so much a matter of balancing the day as it was of balancing the week.

I finally learned that a meal can be only one food or even none. A baby doesn't have to get all the nutrients from each meal each day the way food charts would have us believe. I kept seeing those brightly colored four basic areas of nutrition—the bright, shiny eggs next to neat slices of white rather than whole wheat bread and those beautiful fresh fruits! If I didn't get a fresh fruit in, I was in a state of near-panic. If she concentrated on vegetables, I would push the meat. I could never just be happy letting her eat what she wanted to eat. I've finally come to realize that Anna will get all she needs in her own way even if she seems to eat several meals in a row of all carbohydrates. Letting go of this controlling urge is difficult. I wanted to be a "good mother" and provide good food. I had trouble accepting that offering it was where my job as a "good mother" ends.

Besides eating practically nothing and dropping most of it on the floor, she won't stay sitting down in the high chair. She stands up. I'm ready to throw both of them out the window!

It is always so easy for me to talk about the fifth baby, when I know how I felt with the first. I really didn't think he would survive without three solid meals a day on a set schedule. I sang and danced and wheedled and coaxed. Meals were really tense, and I was reluctant to feed Jason between meals because I wanted him to be hungry at the next meal. With each baby I have become more and more flexible. I feed them healthy snacks, or parts of the meals they didn't eat at various times during the day. Maybe I'm just worn out from motherhood, but I don't worry anymore. I spread **The New York Times** *out in several layers in a five-foot radius around the high chair, and throw a layer away at each meal. When he stands up in the high chair, I take him out rather than arguing.*

CONSOLATIONS RE: THE BALANCED DIET

No one needs to create a feeding problem to-day. We have too many substitutes for foods that a child needs. The substitutes make it possible for a mother to stay out of her child's feeding conflicts. His nutritional needs are completely met by (1) a pint of milk or its equivalent in cheese, ice cream, or calcium substitute (one tsp. is equivalent to eight ounces of milk); (2) an ounce of fresh fruit juice or one piece of fruit; (3) two ounces of iron-containing protein, such as one egg or two ounces of meat (one half jar of baby-food meat or a small hamburger); and (4) a multi-vitamin preparation. (This last may even be unnecessary, but it makes me feel one can forget whether a child has eaten green, yellow, or any vegetables.) With these four requirements a child will grow and gain weight normally. No more is necessary.

—T. BERRY BRAZELTON, M.D.,
Infants and Mothers

RESOURCES

Nutrition

Ashley, Richard and Duggal, Heidi, *The Dictionary of Nutrition,* St. Martin's Press, New York, 1975.

Davis, Adele, *Let's Have Healthy Children,* New American Library, New York, 1972.

Lappé, Frances Moore, *Diet for a Small Planet,* Ballantine, New York, 1975.

Eater's Digest: The Consumer's Fact Book of Food Additives, Anchor Press/Doubleday, Garden City, N.Y., 1976.

Nutrition Labeling, How it Can Work for You, The National Nutrition Consortium, Inc., with Ronald M. Deutsch

Write to:
The National Nutrition Consortium, Inc.
9650 Rockville Pike
Bethesda, Md. 20014

Chemical Cuisine (A poster covering dangerous and safe additives)

Send $1.75 to:
Nutrition Action
Center for Science in the Public Interest
1755 S Street, N.W.
Washington, D.C., 20009

-5-
Weaning

Breast-feeding is such an emotion-laden subject! The question when you are pregnant is, Are you going to do it? Once the baby is born, it becomes, When are you going to stop? One discovers that any answer (including indecision, recommended as the safest approach) is bound to evoke an opinion.

The only real truth is that any amount of breast-feeding is good, and the advantages of breast-feeding do not cease at any definite time. You are neither a failure if you nurse for a very short time, nor a weirdo if you nurse until your baby weans himself sometime after his first birthday. There is no evidence to suggest that prolonged nursing produces dependent people, or that no nursing or only a little nursing produces psychologically damaged people.

How you wean the baby is more important than when or why. Try to cut down a little each day, and don't impose rigid goals or timetables if you can help it. You may have to slow down if the baby has a cold or is getting a tooth. It is important, too, to remember that the older baby who has relied on the breast for food as well as comfort for several months and has not yet weaned himself may be a little angry. He will need more attention, additional cuddling, and other forms of soothing. This can make you feel rather ambivalent or even guilty, but as one authority says, weaning "includes the gradual process of disillusionment, which is part of the parents' task."

Some mothers, particularly if nursing has been very positive, experience a mild depression or sadness when they wean their babies. This may be caused by the hormonal changes that the body undergoes when the demand for milk is lessened. But it's just as likely that the sadness occurs because a very complex, indefinable, close part of the relationship with the baby comes to an end with weaning. These feelings usually don't last too long, especially if you accept them and are not frightened by them.

DIFFERENT POINTS OF VIEW ON WEANING

. . . For the most part, in the United States and some other western countries, mothers plan to wean their babies from the breast at some time between six and nine months.

There are some good reasons for the popularity of this weaning time. At six months of age, the baby in a modern industrialized society can meet his nutritional needs through cow's milk and a wide variety of solid foods. . . . After nine months, a nursing mother usually produces less milk and her let-down reflex takes longer to operate. The anthropologist Ashley Montagu theorizes that human babies are born only half done, that half of their gestation takes place in the womb and the other half outside it. This extra-uterine gestation comes to an end at about nine months of age, when a baby can crawl around after food, has several teeth to chew it with and has the intestinal maturity to handle a diversity of foodstuffs. . . . The emotional benefits that a mother and baby derive from breast-feeding are just as valid, however, at nine months or a year or even later.

—MARVIN S. EIGER AND SALLY WENDKOS OLDS, *The Complete Book of Breastfeeding*

There are at least three lags in interest in breastfeeding that originate in the infant. The first is at four or five months and is associated with the sudden widening of interest in his surroundings. The second accompanies the tremendous motor spurt at seven months. The third occurs between nine and twelve months in most babies. A few never lose interest and probably have to be pushed away. When a baby begins to lose interest after nine months, it seems appropriate to me to take him up on it. He has had enough nutritional sucking and I do not find that many need much more extra nutritional sucking after they have had nine months at the breast. The spurt of motor development and independence that will be coming around a year is geared to a natural separation from the mother, and weaning seems indicated by then.

—T. BERRY BRAZELTON, M.D., *Infants and Mothers*

There are lots of mothers who either aren't able or don't want to nurse until a baby is ready to be weaned to the cup at about five or six months.... The physical advantages of breast milk, its purity, its easy digestibility, are most valuable to the baby at first. But there is no age at which they suddenly become of no benefit. The emotional advantages of breast feeding will not cease at any definite period, either. One sensible time to wean to the bottle is at about three months. By this age, the baby's digestive system will have settled down. She will be about over any tendency to colic. She will be pretty husky and still gaining rapidly. But if a mother would like to stop at one or two months, those are satisfactory times to wean, too. It is a little safer not to wean in very hot weather.

—BENJAMIN SPOCK, M.D., *Baby and Child Care*

So our suggestion is—let the baby do it. In this, as in everything else, you release, but you do not reject. You will, of course, be helping him along. Once he is eating a variety of solid foods you will find him losing interest in nursing one feeding at a time. Taking his cue, just skip that nursing, next time around, unless he has clearly changed his mind. In other words, you don't refuse the breast, but you don't offer it at the feeding either, unless the baby asks for it or your breast is uncomfortably full.

—LA LECHE LEAGUE, *Womanly Art of Breastfeeding*

PARENTS ON WEANING— DIFFERENT POINTS OF VIEW

I have four children, and breast-fed each of them for only a month, a rather maverick approach nowadays. My theory is that this first month is the most important in terms of health benefits for the infant and the mother.

I had planned to breast-feed Anna for six months, but I ended up nursing her for eighteen. By that point, I was beginning to feel like a human pacifier and decided enough is enough. We discussed it—she talked quite well—and then we stopped.

I had breast-fed Kim for six months, and had wanted to start weaning her then. She was down to three feedings a day at that point. I had hoped to continue with one nursing a day, but by the time she was seven months old, she would only nurse for five minutes. I didn't seem to have enough milk for one feeding and stopped. I did feel a little depressed, and a little at sea. She was fine, however. Her father had to give her the bottle at first. She wouldn't take it from me.

My nipples were so sore that I gave up after a month. I dropped a feeding every three days and took aspirin for the pain in my breasts. I offered a bottle after each feeding, when I sensed my milk was really tapering off.

I nursed Caroline for a month, then I stopped because I was feeling so tired and overwhelmed.

I thought the nursing contributed to this. I was still tired and overwhelmed, however, when I stopped, and then I also felt guilty. I guess, though, that every new mother is entitled to the luxury of saying, "I'd do things differently with a second child," and that's what I say. I am perfectly aware that it is stupid to feel guilty, by the way.

I tried to wean Ann at five and a half months, but she wouldn't take a bottle. I tried everything—putting my own milk into the bottle, using different kinds of nipples, juice, having her father give her the bottle. I also tried sweetening the nipple with honey. She simply refused. She'd laugh, and then scream and cry. We were having a real battle, and I remember spending an entire afternoon indoors trying to dribble four ounces of milk into her. I was frantic. Finally a friend said, "Is it worth it? The baby is obviously just as stubborn as you are. You've had such a good breast-feeding experience, why end it with a battle?" I gave up. I waited a few weeks. One day I just handed her the bottle to play with. She put it in her mouth just like she puts everything else in her mouth. Once I knew she'd take a bottle I wasn't nearly as uptight about weaning her, and nursed her for two more months, offering bottles a couple of times a week.

Rachael has been nursing part-time since I went back to work when she was five months old. I haven't thought of this as weaning. At fourteen months she now nurses only in the morning or takes a few sips throughout the day if she's having a bad day.

I tried to wean Molly from the breast to the bottle when she was six months old. We'd gotten very lax about relief bottles, and every time I put a bottle in her mouth, she cried. Talk about guilt. She did finally take the bottle, when I made her a milk shake as a last resort (bananas, orange juice, yogurt, and milk). When she was ten months old, she threw the bottle away. I took the hint. I guess she never was a bottle baby.

Max gave it up when he was getting his first tooth. He just didn't seem to want to suck then. By nine months he was pretty good with the cup, though I must say that I did worry about him getting enough fluids. He survived though.

It felt very conflicted about weaning Andrew because he loved nursing and I loved nursing him so much. It was so simple and easy. This may sound crazy, but I didn't want to overprotect him the way my husband's mother had done with Adam. Somehow, extended nursing reminded me and Adam of this overprotectiveness. But on the other hand I really wanted to keep on nursing because I kept thinking, what if we only have one child and this is the only time in my life that I'll have this experience. When Andrew was thirteen months old, he'd really become interested in having sips of orange juice from our glasses at breakfast. Adam kept saying, why don't you get him one of those tip-proof cups? I did, and Andrew hated the training cup I bought him. He'd knock it on the floor every time I put it in front of him. I must admit that this made me feel a little gratified. Then Adam decided that Andrew wanted a glass, not a cup.

He got out one of those plastic champagne glasses which was very easy to hold. The baby was so thrilled. He was really in charge, sitting there with his own glass. He was ready to go on to something new. When I realized this, I felt okay about ending nursing. I think I had been looking at weaning him as depriving him of something he deserved—and which I of course enjoyed, when in reality, something new and exciting, the control he had over that plastic glass and the fun he had with it, was taking its place. Isn't it incredible what we can put ourselves through when we become parents? On the one hand I laugh at myself a lot for being so silly about so many things. But then I also say, so what, you're entitled to have doubts and needs yourself. We're all only human after all.

FROM BREAST OR BOTTLE TO THE CUP

Many parents want to wean their babies directly from the breast to the cup. This way you can avoid bottles altogether, which is a mixed blessing. There certainly aren't many two-, three- and four-year-olds carrying cups as security objects, and you will never be accused of prolonging your baby's "infantilism." Though toilet training is and ought to be a distant prospect when you have a baby, a cup-drinking two-year-old is easier to help along than a child who carries a bottle and nips at it all day. There are other advantages as well: If you forget a bottle, you are sunk. A cup is replaceable, and a small thermos very portable. A baby who is used to a bottle, however, may not take the cup very seriously.

No matter at what age you start introducing cups, it will require more involvement and patience on your part than the bottle. You can begin to offer the baby small sips as early as five months, but it will be several more months before she can handle the cup efficiently. One concern that plagues all of us is how the baby will get enough milk from a cup. Over the course of a day, try to give the baby twelve to sixteen ounces of milk. If this seems like a discouragingly large amount, see page 48 for milk equivalents.

The cup is a ridiculous status symbol with some mothers. My child was two and still drinking from a bottle, and we both encountered some gratuitous comments from busybodies. Can you imagine an adult trying to make a child feel badly about her bottle by telling her she's a baby?

Two-handled Training Cup

Part III
COMFORTS

-6-
Crying

How I wish there was a "magical force" that would penetrate the baby and make her stop crying!

There is nothing quite like the sound of your own baby crying! Poignant, insistent, unnerving, and, to be honest, infuriating if it goes on for more than a few minutes. A baby's cry is designed to make us respond. And it works. There are few parents who can or who would want to ignore their baby's distress. Most of us have been roused from deep sleep, through closed doors, when we are rooms or even floors away. In fact we become so tuned to the signal, we sometimes "hear" the baby crying even if we've left him at home and have gone out for the evening.

INTERPRETING THE BABY'S CRIES

Though a baby can almost always make her demands heard, she can't always make them understood. If you don't know why your newborn is crying each time she cries, you are not unusual, nor do you fall into the "parent without instincts" category. Common parent mythology has it that by instinct we are supposed to be able to distinguish a hungry cry from a tired one, or a cry of pain from one of apprehension in a mere three weeks, according to some authorities. Though there is certainly some truth to this for all of us *eventually*, we must simply rely on plenty of trial and error and logic as we wait for the instinct to develop.

Sensing how to meet a baby's needs works two ways. With each day his behavior becomes slightly more organized, and his cues clearer as he adjusts to life outside the womb. And with each day a parent becomes more skilled at reading the baby's cues and more relaxed.

In the meantime, it should be comforting to know that even if you take the "wrong" approach in your attempt to sooth the baby—should you diaper her when what she really needs is sleep, or burp her when she's starving—just making the attempt makes a difference. Answering a baby's cries promptly and consistently and not leaving her to "cry it out" gives her a sense that she is not alone and that you care.

I called the pediatrician almost daily for the first two months. He finally lost his patience one day and said, "I don't know any better why your baby is crying than you do. Sometimes they just cry because life is tough!"

Every time she cried I became frightened and panicky. I had read that mothers could tell the difference between different kinds of cries. As I could never tell, I felt terribly inadequate.

YOU WON'T SPOIL THE BABY

A study done by Mary Ainsworth and

Sylvia Bell at Johns Hopkins University confirms that babies who are tended to quickly will cry less frequently and for a shorter duration than those who aren't. The researchers also noticed that by the end of the first year, the babies who had been "spoiled" by some people's standards were more independent and better at communicating and at getting adult attention through means other than crying.

Question: Can you spoil a baby if you pick him up each time he cries?

Answer: You will find when your baby cries, you will have a strong desire to pick up the baby, find out what is causing him to cry, and make him happy. This is a perfectly normal and natural desire, probably an inborn behavior pattern that helped the species survive. Wait and see what happens when you exercise this natural tendency! You are sure to find someone saying, "Uh-uh, uh-uh, don't pick up that baby. You'll spoil it!" . . . The advice not to pick up your crying baby, in effect, says, "Your baby will be better off being unhappy than if you pick him up and make him happy." If you look at it this way, the recommendation will seem as foolish as it is.

— LEE SALK, M.D.,
Preparing for Parenthood

But the truth of the matter is that a baby under the age of four or five months or so has not acquired the necessary mental equipment to figure out how to run the lives of others; his "whims" (wants) are still his needs; he cannot yet rely on himself; picking up the baby when he needs solace or some response has nothing to do with spoiling.

—HELEN S. ARNSTEIN,
The Roots of Love

I don't think you need to worry much about spoiling in the first month or even the first three. . . . Even if you decide later that he has been somewhat spoiled from an early age, you can usually undo the harm in a few days, in the first four or five months.

—BENJAMIN SPOCK, M.D.,
Baby and Child Care

During the first month you'll probably spend a good deal of time wondering why the baby is crying. Perhaps the following will provide some clues to the mystery.

IS THE BABY CRYING BECAUSE HE IS HUNGRY?

Question: How does the baby feel when he is hungry?

Answer: His hunger is a ravenous hunger, the tensions it produces are intolerable, and the satisfaction of this hunger is imperative.

—SELMA FRAIBERG,
The Magic Years

There are many reasons a baby cries, but the one we tend to think of first is hunger. If a baby is hungry, a pacifier, sugar water, or fun and games will not fulfill his need. Few of us ever experience true hunger pains, but when a baby does, it is excruciating.

None of us would think twice about feeding a baby who wanted to eat, if we *really* knew she was hungry. The notion of schedules, particularly hospital schedules, where babies are fed at three- or four-hour intervals, can give a very distorted picture. One has to remember that during the first two or three days of a

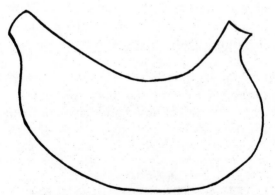

Actual size of an infant's stomach at birth (sometimes a picture is worth a thousand words!).

baby's life, she's often too sleepy to eat as often as she will in the future. Until she is at least four, five, or six weeks old, a baby who is breast-fed usually can't last for four hours between feedings.

Because a nursing mother can't see how much the baby is taking, her first thought as she feeds her for the tenth time that day is that she doesn't have enough milk. Almost everyone worries about this in the beginning, and we all need some reassurance. It cannot be stressed enough that two to two-and-a-half hours between some feedings is not uncommon in the early weeks, and that if the baby begins to go without eating for longer intervals at night, she may well have to make up for this by eating more often during the day (see Chapter 1, Breast-Feeding, for more information).

BREAST-FEEDING AND CRYING

In a study in Cambridge, England, Martin Richards and I found that mothers varied greatly in how they interpreted their babies' crying. In the first place, many were at a loss to explain it, particularly in the case of persistent crying in the evenings. In the second place, most breast-feeding mothers tended to assume that crying showed that the baby was hungry. Although a few mothers responded by feeding the baby regardless of how long it had been since he

was last fed, many breast-feeding mothers felt that if adequately fed he should be happy for three to four hours, and hence this more frequent crying must be a sign that their milk supply was inadequate. This "inadequacy" was the most common reason for giving up breast-feeding. But in fact the babies of the successful breast-feeders, who continued to feed for over six months, cried just as frequently in the early weeks as did the babies of those mothers who gave up: it seems that it is a general feature of the early stages of breast-feeding for babies to sleep for short periods and to take frequent feeds. We found that mothers who were willing to feed their newborn babies when they cried were more likely to be successful breast-feeders later.

—JUDY DUNN,
Distress and Comfort

SCHEDULE OR DEMAND

"You mean he's not on a schedule?" my mother who was staying with us kept saying. "He was on a schedule in the hospital, wasn't he? If you pick him up every time he cries and feed him, no wonder he has a stomachache, and no wonder he then needs to be picked up and held all the time—even when he's not hungry." But I can't not feed him if he's hungry, can I? If I try to

feed him and he eats, and no disaster occurs, I have to conclude that he was hungry, don't I? You can't make a baby eat who doesn't want to eat, can you? You can't overfeed a two-week-old infant who is nursing, can you?

Question: *Can you overfeed a baby?*

Answer: *No, every baby will stop sucking when he is full, and you won't be able to get another drop into him. If you attempt to force food into him beyond this point, he will only vomit.*

—VIRGINIA POMERANZ, M.D.,
The First Five Years

A: A baby's digestion is such that a full meal, taken calmly over a reasonable period—in twenty-five minutes, say, rather than in sips over an hour—will probably last him for between three and four hours. But that is once he is settled, once his digestion has begun to have a pattern. He has, after all, to learn to accept comfortable fullness and near emptiness, rather than the constant topping up of nutritional needs which went on in the womb. Furthermore, he has to accept our diurnal rhythm, to accept a long period unfed during the night. All this takes time. Because it takes time, the much disputed question about whether babies should be fed "on demand" or "on schedule" makes very little sense.

—PENELOPE LEACH,
Babyhood

IS THE BABY CRYING BECAUSE SHE NEEDS TO BE BURPED?

Often the baby will cry because she needs to be burped—even if you have already burped her a half-hour ago when you fed her. Newborns don't breath too regularly. Some collect a series of tiny bubbles of air, which take a long time to gather together into one large bubble that can be burped. If you suspect your baby is this way, sometimes holding her upright or placing her in a semiupright position in an infant seat after a feeding will help the bubble collect. A pacifier may also help to bring up the bubble (see discussion of pacifiers below and on page 43).

It never occurred to me that I wasn't burping Andrew enough—that twice a feeding wasn't enough for him, until the pediatrician suggested that I do it every three to five minutes, working on a burp for about a minute. After a few weeks, when his digestive system settled down, I didn't have to be so careful.

IS THE BABY CRYING BECAUSE SHE NEEDS MORE SUCKING?

Babies need a lot of sucking. It's good exercise and seems to relieve tension. Many interesting theories and research

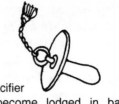

Dangerous Pacifier
Tassel can become lodged in baby's throat.
Flimsy metal ring could break off easily from plastic disc.
Plastic disc is not large enough and could get stuck in back of baby's throat.
Rubber nipple not well attached to plastic disk.

revolve around sucking in infancy. Margaret Ribble, author of *The Rights of Infants*, points out that "respiration, which is characteristically shallow, unstable, and inadequate in the first weeks after birth is definitely stimulated reflexively through sucking and through physical contact with the mother." She adds that the shallow and irregular breathing of the newborn deepens with sucking. And with this, the tendency to frequent paroxysmal crying diminishes. Sucking relaxes the muscle tension of the baby and quiets her random movements.

Jerome Bruner, another infant researcher, concurs with Dr. Ribble. He also notes that sucking relaxes the movement of the gut and reduces the number of eye movements the baby is making if given something patterned to look at.

Do not hesitate to use a pacifier between feedings. The baby's most intense

Safe Pacifier
All one piece of molded plastic, with large ring and disk.
Impossible for entire pacifier to fit into the baby's mouth and choke him.

desire to suck comes in the first four to six months. After this point, many lose interest. A good rule is to remove the pacifier once the baby is sleepy. In this way the infant will not become dependent on it when she is asleep—and you will not have to get up and replace it in her mouth quite so often. Be sure to use a safe pacifier.

IS THE BABY CRYING BECAUSE SHE NEEDS A DIAPER CHANGE?

A newborn baby always needs a diaper change if you take the idea of a "damp" diaper literally. The diaper is probably not what is disturbing the baby unless it is making the baby cold (see next page). In one experiment using agitated but well-fed babies, nurses picked up and changed the entire group. In half of the group, they simply removed and then replaced the wet diaper; in the other half they put on a new, dry one. *All* the babies settled down. Wetness made no difference at all. The babies apparently settled because of the warmth of the nurse's touch, the motion, and the change of position. By all means change the baby's diaper!

IS THE BABY CRYING BECAUSE SHE'S STARTLED?

Perhaps her Moro reflex is acting up.

The Moro reflex appears to be left over from man's more primitive times. A newborn may be startled by a loud noise or any sudden change of position—particularly if her head drops back. When the baby is startled, she throws out her arms and legs, cries, then draws her arms together as if to cling to her mother. It is thought that this response remains from the time when the infant had to grasp her mother for survival, protection, comfort, and mobility. Each time the baby cries, she may startle, which upsets her and makes her cry again. Thus the cycle can perpetuate itself.

If you pick the baby up and hold her securely, swaddle her, or simply place a firm hand on one of her extremities, this can help to break the startle-crying, startle-crying cycle.

IS THE BABY CRYING BECAUSE SHE'S TOO WARM OR TOO COLD?

Most of us run the risk of overdressing rather than underdressing the baby. This is just as well, because babies would rather be too warm than too cold.

Newborn infants have only rudimentary abilities to regulate their own temperatures in different environments. Moreover, they have very little insulating fat to keep them warm. Peter Wolff, an English researcher who has done perhaps the most extensive inquiries into why babies cry, found that those who were kept at 88 to 90 degrees cried less and slept more than those kept at 78 degrees. Wolff concluded that the colder temperatures probably weren't the cause of the crying, but that since babies sleep more deeply when warm, the colder babies may be more responsive to stimulation and therefore more likely to cry for other reasons.

Dr. Spock, a firm believer in fresh air and cool houses, suggests that parents keep indoor temperatures between 68 and 72 degrees. However, Penelope Leach, author of *Babyhood*, makes a very good point. She believes that cool temperatures may be fine when the newborn is wrapped up, but very inadequate if she is undressed for a diaper change or a bath. Parents who add more clothing to an already cold baby will not warm the baby up, but only insulate the cold. The infant must be warmed up first, then wrapped or dressed.

The hands and feet of a baby are not accurate gauges of how warm or cool she is, because they always feel cool.

The first time Katie slept for more than three hours in a row, I thought she was dead! We'd placed her basket on the kitchen table in the country, where we have a wood-burning stove. The wood stove was going all afternoon and we had friends over. It must have been a combination of our friends coming and feeling relaxed, and the warmth from the stove. This made sense to me. After all, she'd been inside me for nine months at 98 degrees.

IS THE BABY CRYING FOR SOME INEXPLICABLE REASON?

You have investigated every possible reason for crying. The baby is not hungry because she was fed forty-five minutes ago. She is not being poked by a diaper pin, doesn't have a wet diaper, isn't too cold or too warm, and isn't tired of being in the same position because you have switched her from back to stomach, from stomach to back, from prone to tilted. You've burped her, or tried to, several times, and she's still crying. You've even

FIG. 22

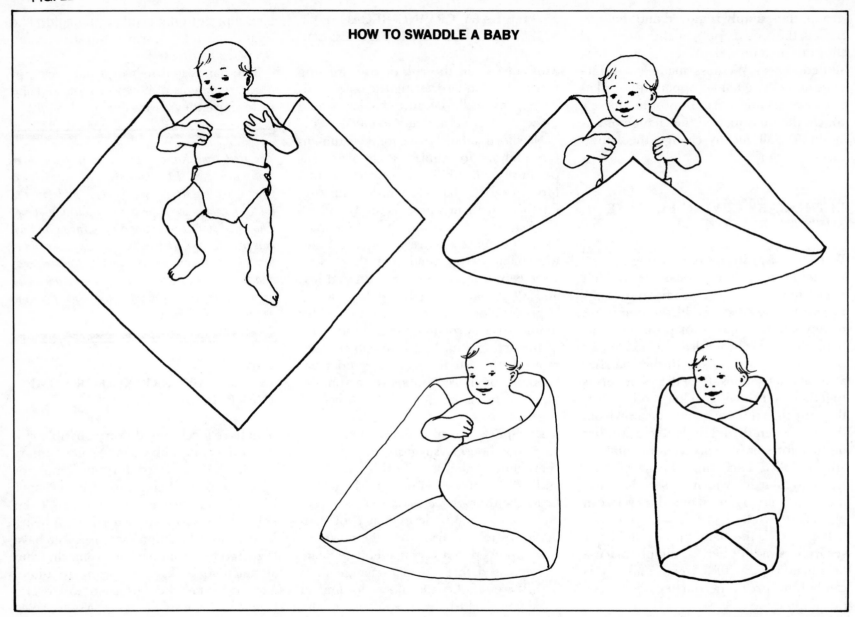

HOW TO SWADDLE A BABY

SWADDLING

You can't carry the baby all of the time when he fusses. Swaddling can be a very effective alternative because it provides the baby with the sensations of constant touch and warmth. A study done by infant researcher Yvonne Brackbill in 1971 showed that constant stimulation, through sound, light, swaddling, or temperature, increased the amount of time the infant spent sleeping, decreased the amount of time spent crying, slowed the heart and breath rate, and quieted random movements.

Brackbill also found that if two or more approaches were combined, such as swaddling with sound, the results were even better. When she compared the effects of different kinds of continuous stimulation, she found that swaddling was overwhelmingly the most effective. Shown here is one way to swaddle a baby so that the wrapping doesn't come undone.

taken her to look out every window in the house.

You're very tired, and beginning to feel inadequate. The sun is on its way down, or perhaps it has already disappeared over the horizon. The term *colic* flashes through your mind. But you can't quite believe that. After all, this doesn't happen every day—maybe every other

ROCKING

The age-old custom of rocking a fussy baby is certainly worth a try. Like swaddling, rocking is a source of consistent, mild stimulation. It may also recreate the gentle motion the baby felt inside the womb. Ashley Montagu, the author of *Touching, The Human Significance of Skin,* also suggests that the rocking motion helps to develop the efficient functioning of the baby's gastrointestinal tract by improving the muscle tone of the intestine. Perhaps this is true.

If you own a cradle but find that you are constantly walking the floor to quiet the baby, you may not be rocking the baby fast enough. It has been found that the most effective rate of rocking is sixty rocks per minute which is quite a fast pace to keep up. Sixty paces a minute, on the other hand, is a relatively slow walk for an adult. Also, if the baby rolls, instead of rocks, try placing two rolled blankets or towels on either side of her.

day, sometimes for twenty minutes and sometimes for two hours. The only alternative answer is "periodic, irritable crying," which is usually further explained as "unexplained."

On this and the following page are some of the age-old comforts (some of which are probably familiar) and some further reasons they work.

Question: *How did you soothe your baby?*

Answer: *Amanda was definitely a motion baby. The only way I could settle her was to hold and rock her, and sing to her, mostly songs that I had made up for her myself like "Quiet down, quiet down, quiet down, I'm so tired" to the tune of Brahms' "Lullaby." I had a rocking chair that squeaked and went along with the melody. The only problem was that I couldn't do anything else while I was rocking her, like read, because the chair had no arms. When we bought a hammock, life improved significantly because I could put her next to me or on me without having to hold her. Then I could read or crochet, or even sleep a little myself.*

A: *David rocked Matthew back and forth in the cradle. He was studying for his bar exam, and often read aloud in an appropriately monotonous voice. He'd sit at his desk and push the runner on the cradle up and down with one foot. His power of concentration amazed me. I think he bored the baby to sleep!*

A: *I wore Tosha in the Snugli baby carrier almost constantly. This was absolutely the only thing that worked. I cooked dinner this way, did housework this way, and sometimes even slept like this at night.*

A: *We walked and walked and walked and walked—back and forth. That's all.*

A: *We had a beautiful antique cradle that we bought for Benjamin at an auction. He rolled instead of rocked, and he hated it. So we often* took turns walking him. And sometimes we just let him cry because we couldn't figure out what the hell was the matter with him. One night I was so exhausted, discouraged, and dismayed by this eight-pound power figure who had transformed my life that I called my sister long distance. We went over every possible reason for his crying. She finally suggested that we get out of the house with him and go for a walk. This worked, for that night at least.

A: A ten-minute car ride usually did the trick.

A: We developed what we called the straight-jacket and wedge to cure Gregg of his twilight miseries. We swaddled him tightly and laid him on his side with his back against the side of his basket and his stuffed rabbit jammed against his stomach to hold him in place. But until we figured this out, he thrashed around so much that there was never any hope of calming him down. You have to swaddle the baby correctly though, or it just makes him angrier.

A: I'd take Nicky into the bathroom and turn the water on in the tub full blast to run a nice warm bath. Sometimes the sound of the water settled him, but if it didn't I'd take him into the tub with me and rest him on my knees. The water helped a lot. Of course we couldn't stay there forever, but at least this worked for a little while.

A: We relied on a pacifier, and it helped tremendously. The only problem was keeping it in his mouth. He also had one pacifier that he seemed to like better than the others, we think because the rubber was somewhat softer. When we realized this, we went out and bought ten of them.

CONCLUSIONS

The newborn baby has spent the greater part of his life in the womb, curled up in a small, warm place, bathed in amniotic fluid. He hears the rhythm of his mother's heart and feels the movements of her body. It is therefore not surprising that swaddling, walking, rocking, patting, or even taking the baby into the bathtub often work to calm an infant. These are very familiar, and thus reassuring, physical sensations. Who knows whether they actually relieve the discomfort or simply take the baby's mind or, more to the point, his body off it?

With each day other sensations such as your smell and your voice become more familiar to the baby. By a mere ten days of age, a baby is capable of turning toward his mother's nursing pad, indicating his ability at this age to discriminate between his own mother and another mother. By the second week of life, it has been found that the human voice is more effective at calming a crying baby than the sound of a rattle or a bell. It is also not surprising that researchers have found that by the fifth week, the mother's voice is the most effective means for eliciting sound from the baby.

We sometimes think of all these comforts as "techniques" for soothing a fussy baby. But an infant who isn't particularly irritable or "demanding" needs these comforts too. Touching, talking, holding, cuddling, and rocking are forms of communication and stimulation. They are what help an infant find his place in the world.

In the beginning of his life, the baby does not distinguish between his own physical sensations and those which are imposed upon him from the outside. It is through the repetition of physical contact with another person who satisfies the baby's very basic needs for food, warmth, and motion that the baby begins to differentiate himself from that source of relief or comfort. As he emerges as an individual, he begins to separate the "me" from the "you" and to realize that he does have an impact on his surrounding world.

Each time his cries are answered, he becomes more aware of the emotional subtleties or rewards inherent in the comforts parents provide. Eating not only means a full stomach, but close companionship, affection, conversation, and games. This emotional nourishment is as important as the physical because it is the basis for trust and love. Without this, how could a baby go on to learn about the world around him?

-7-
Colic

Question: *What is colic?*

Answer: *One guess is that both conditions [irritable crying and colic] are due to a periodic tension in the baby's immature nervous system.*

—BENJAMIN SPOCK, M.D.,
Baby and Child Care

A: Colic: a condition of severe abdominal discomfort common in infants under the age of three months or so; its causes vary, and may include swallowed air, excessive gas (a normal byproduct of digestion) in the intestine, allergy to the formula, or residual effects of maternal hormones.

—VIRGINIA POMERANZ, M.D.,
The Mother's Medical Encyclopedia

A: Colic: a paroxysm of acute abdominal pain localized in a hollow organ and caused by spasm, obstruction, or twisting . . .

—Webster's Dictionary

A: The infant susceptible to colic is an active, driving baby who is hypersensitive to the climate and stimuli around him. As his exasperating period of fussing creates tension in those around him, they overreact. They try too many ways to quiet him, feeling there must be a magic way or there must be something wrong that they should correct. Often there are three generations at work on each other. The tension around the infant builds up, he reacts to it with more of his own, his intestinal tract begins to reflect his increased tension—and what starts out as a two-hour period rapidly grows to four, eight, then twelve hours. His intestines are as hyperactive and hyperreactive as the rest of him to the increasing fatigue and breakdown in the family. This pattern becomes a vicious circle, and we call it "colic."

—T. BERRY BRAZELTON, M.D.,
Infants and Mothers

A: What is colic? It's pure misery for the baby. Piercing screams that go on for hours. They reach a crescendo, and I think surely it's over for tonight. She'll quiet for a few minutes as she gasps for air and her whole little body shudders. Then her face starts to screw up again and her fists clench. Her body gets beet red and she flails her arms and legs. If I feed her, she'll suck frantically for a moment, then push my breast away, enraged as if I've tried to trick her, and I guess I have because I know she's not hungry. Burping her when she's like this is almost impossible because she arches her back and screams even louder. The pacifier won't stay in her mouth, because it's always open with the howling. Sometimes she responds to walking and rocking. During the day, she's really terrific. I take her out and everyone tells me what a beautiful, adorable baby I have. She smiles at everyone. But I am a basket case.

Question: *What isn't colic?*

Answer: *A baby who cries in the evening, but in the same way and to the same extent as he does at other times of day, does not have the evening-colic syndrome. His evening crying is simply part of his normal crying pattern. A baby who cries in the evening and will take a feeding and be comforted by it has not got colic either. He is hungry. A baby who cries in the evening, brings up gas and then sleeps as usual has not got evening colic. He has gas. A baby who cries in the evening until he is picked up, and is then happy until he is put to bed again, has not got colic. He has probably decided to have the early evening as his wakeful period, and is simply not* *ready to be alone and asleep.*

—PENELOPE LEACH,
Babyhood

SOME SUGGESTIONS FOR COPING WITH COLIC

Though there is some disagreement about what colic is and about its cause and treatment, everyone agrees that it makes babies and their parents miserable. It usually strikes within a few weeks after birth, when the baby's crying pattern becomes so long, intense, and agonized that it can no longer be interpreted as the generally disorganized behavior of the newborn. It also seems to be an evening phenomenon (hence, "evening-colic syndrome") and is usually over by the time the baby is three months old.

If your baby is truly colicky and you haven't already consulted your pediatrician, by all means do so. It should not be diagnosed at home, just in case there is something more serious going on. Though many pediatricians are reluctant to prescribe medicines to soothe, a desperate parent can always ask. If the pediatrician is of the "all you can do is wait it out" school—and many seem to be—a combination of various soothing techniques may lessen the baby's discomfort. One of the very best descriptions of dealing with colic is in T. Berry Brazelton's book *Infants and Mothers,* but this can hardly be summarized in a quote because it is more of a process, almost a philosophy—rather than a treatment or cure per se.

One of the ironies about colicky babies is that they're usually charming when they're not having a spell. Despite their miseries, they seem generally to flourish. Unfortunately, parents aren't always as resilient. A series of bad nights which stretch out into weeks can bring parents close to the physical and emotional breaking point. When you begin to feel like this a good deal of the time, it's crucial to devise a strategy for your own survival.

STRATEGIES FOR PARENTS BY PARENTS

First on the list is for parents to remain allies with each other. It's nobody's fault, and you need each other to talk to rather than vent your feelings upon. Colic brings tremendous tension into a house.

My advice to a mother with a colicky baby is to sleep when he does or at least lie down and relax. To hell with housework. It takes all your energy, mental as well as physical, to help the poor thing through the night. It does end eventually. It just seems like forever.

Try to stay calm and get as much rest as possible. Get out of the house at least for a short time every day alone.

Get out of the house together for an evening. Don't feel guilty about inflicting a miserable baby on a good sitter, or a grandmother, or a friend who knows the full story. They don't suffer from the same battle fatigue you do.

Take turns. That's the only way. You and the baby go to one end of the house when it's your turn—and your husband to the other end.

In retrospect, I think that her colic was in direct proportion to my bad mood, and was triggered by tiredness at the end of the day. One of the best remedies was to hand her to my husband, fix myself a drink and take a bath and put my feet up. I had to learn not to feel guilty about handing her to him. Of course he'd been working hard all day, but so had I, and he was much better equipped at that point to walk with her. He also needed to get a chance to know her too.

SOME SUGGESTIONS FOR SOOTHING A COLICKY BABY

I learned to deal with Caroline's colic little by

little. I suppose that as she got older, her system also began to digest her food better. However, I do feel some of my remedies also helped.

1. *I warmed her formula instead of giving it to her right out of the refrigerator or even at room temperature.*
2. *I used Nuk nipples, which supposedly reduce the amount of air the baby swallows.*
3. *I stopped several times during a feeding to burp her. How many times depended on whether or not she was sucking smoothly or swallowing a lot of air. I adjusted the nipple ring so that it was loose enough that the milk flowed without her having to suck too hard.*
4. *I walked her in the Snugli baby carrier, which also sometimes helped.*
5. *So did letting her lie on a warm hot-water bottle.*
6. *I also rocked her across my knees.*
7. *If the gas didn't come up, I found that letting her lie on her side for a couple of minutes and then on her back before I held her over my shoulder also helped bring up the bubbles.*
8. *I also heard that fennel or dill water would help relieve gas, but never could find the correct "recipe."*

Dr. Alvin Eden, who writes for *American Baby* magazine, confirms this point. The recipe is, "Simply bring one pint of water to a boil, pour over one teaspoon of fennel tea, cool, strain, and give to baby." He also suggests using a pacifier, and helping the baby expel or pass gas "by gently inserting either an infant suppository or lubricated thermometer tip into the rectum." He adds, "A final word of advice: with the knowledge that colic is not a disease and therefore nothing to worry about, relax and enjoy your baby. A baby with colic is healthy. Once you accept this, you will be amazed how much the whole situation will be improved."

THE END OF COLIC . . .

No, I will never forget Jessica's colic. My favorite memory naturally is the last night of it. It was Fred's night on, and my night to sleep. But it was so noisy, I had to get up and see what was happening. I went into the living room. There was a bottle of Jack Daniel's on the coffee table, and a seedy-looking glass with a cigarette butt in it. The moonlight was streaming in the window, framing the cradle. Jessica was sound asleep. Fred was swaying back and forth in his Jockey shorts and black socks, rocking the cradle with one foot while he played his guitar. He was singing, "Your time is up. Your time is up. Your three months is over, or we're giving you away," in his best country-and-western style. That, believe it or not, three months to the day, or should I say night, was the end of one of the most horrendous periods in my life.

-8-
Sleep

All I want to know is how to get Andrew to fall asleep in less than the fifteen minutes it takes to settle him, and to stay asleep for more than half an hour during each of his naps. Then I'd also like to know how to get him to sleep past the uncivilized hour of five thirty A.M. You see, the child hardly ever sleeps, and I'm going crazy.

Babies always get the right amount of sleep— for them.

In any group of new parents the subject of sleep takes precedence over just about any other matter—sleeping through the night, sleeping on a schedule, getting the baby to sleep in the first place, night waking, waking up at a reasonably sane hour in the morning, and the hardest one—how long, if at all, to let the baby cry himself to sleep without damaging his psyche and your own.

We have great expectations about how long our babies should sleep, and even more about what we will do with the time when they are sleeping. If baby care weren't such a one-to-one, parent-with-baby-all-day-long, intense experience, we probably wouldn't be so concerned with the subject. But given the confines of the nuclear family and the role of the stay-at-home parent, the amount of time your child sleeps can, to a large extent, characterize how you experience his babyhood and how you feel about your own mental stability. Because, let's be honest, when the baby sleeps, you're off.

Everyone would like to have a child who loves to sleep, sleeps through the night practically from the time of arrival, takes long naps, goes to bed early and painlessly, never wakes up at night, and sleeps till eight in the morning. There are a few rare people who have babies who do almost all of these things. If they are honest, they will admit they are very lucky. If they are somewhat less than honest, they may suggest that you, too, might reap such benefits if only you "handled it" differently. However, han-dling is only part of it. The other part lies within the baby—his physiology, temperament, and metabolism. Some babies need a lot of sleep and are known as "good sleepers" while others—the "poor sleepers"—don't. Neither type is likely to remain the same forever, so do not allow yourself to feel either too terrible or too smug.

SLEEPING THROUGH THE NIGHT

Question: *When will the baby sleep through the night?*

Answer: *Supposedly at about eleven or twelve pounds, but do not count on it. Sleeping through the night, by the way, is a euphemism for five, six, or seven hours—in the beginning.*

For various reasons, few of us will ever forget feeding our babies at night. For some this can be a rather lovely and private experience, because the house is quiet, there are few distractions, and you can really be peaceful and focus on the baby. If you've never been a night person before, you may become familiar with your city's sounds and late-night activities, and even see the sun rise.

But this is a most positive view of the experience. The cumulative effect of sleep loss, coupled with other postpartum adjustments, can be lethal for parents—especially if the baby has night and day confused. It's vital that you make up some of your sleep the next day, keep life as simple as possible, and not expect too much of yourself during this time. And remember that you can only begin to cherish night feedings by knowing that *they will end.*

Elizabeth was fourteen weeks old before she slept through the night. She was premature, which may have had something to do with it, but she was also a baby who had day and night all mixed up. She slept after each of her daytime feedings and was wide awake at night. Because I was so incredibly anxious at first about her physical well-being, I played along with this— kept her company and all, watched late movies on the late show, etc., until I had to hire a baby nurse because I was so exhausted and frantic that I could hardly function. One thing I didn't know was that I could have put her to sleep on her back, the position she preferred. I was so afraid that she would choke.

Question: *What is the best sleeping position for a newborn baby?*

Answer: *Pediatricians think that it is much more important to satisfy the baby's natural urge to repeat a comfortable pattern in sleep than to worry about some of the pros and cons that are presented for each sleep position.*

SOME SUGGESTIONS

1. It's really helpful to get it across to the baby that *it is nighttime.* Use a low-wattage bulb to light the baby's room, or your room. You don't have to be cold, but the more businesslike the feeding is, the less interested the baby will be in having your company.

2. Get organized in advance. If you are bottle-feeding, prepare everything you will need. You might consider the luxury of commercially prepared formula in disposable bottles, which needn't be refrigerated unless the bottle is unsealed. A bottle prepared in advance need not be heated. You can take the chill off it by running it under warm water.

3. If you are breast-feeding, your husband can, if he's willing, get the baby for you and bring him into bed, burp him, change him, and return him to bed.

4. Night feedings are also an excellent time to introduce a relief bottle if you are breast-feeding. Your husband can take over. The usual advice is to wait three or four weeks until your milk is established, and it is sound advice. However, there are plenty of people who breast-feed successfully even if they do miss the two A.M. feeding every couple of nights from the very beginning. Your milk supply is influenced by the baby's sucking, as well as your state of fatigue.

5. If you have difficulty getting back to sleep, don't lie there feeling frustrated. Either do some relaxation exercises (see page 114), or read a book, or turn on the late show.

6. It's crucial that you make up your sleep loss during the day. See Chapter 11, Postpartum, for making life simpler.

7. No pediatrician or current child-care book I can find suggests taking the baby into bed with you. The La Leche League, however, is all for it, and lots of people do it without smothering or rolling on top of the baby. It seems logical that this will no more "spoil" an infant than will

holding it or rocking it. In fact . . .

8. *Whatever it takes to get your baby to sleep, do it without being afraid of "spoiling."*

BEDTIME—FOR THOSE WHO HAVE REACHED THE AGE OF SPOILING

As Richard Flaste of the *New York Times* so aptly put it, "This is dedicated to the same boat—you know, the one we're all in."

The baby is tired after a long day, and you are even more tired. You long for adult companionship and conversation, some time alone with your husband, a chance to put your feet up, to read a magazine, to have a pleasant, uninterrupted late dinner, or just to stare aimlessly into the television while you "cool out."

You've put the baby to bed, and maybe even before you've had a chance to get out of the room and begin to feel pleased that you've pulled it off, you hear a whimper. Your heart rate speeds up slightly as you tiptoe away. By the time you've reached the next room, there is no doubt in your mind. The baby is not asleep. He is crying. Your jaw is tense. But you are still standing firm.

You glance casually at the nearest clock. The crying has grown louder, but

you turn on the water in the kitchen so that you can't hear it so well. You rattle the pots and pans in the sink and look at the clock. Three minutes have passed. You turn off the water. The crying has become more persistent.

You consult your mate: "What time is it?" A full five minutes has gone by. You sit, take a deep breath, and control the tears of rage that are beginning to cloud your vision. You grope for the silverware. "I can't take it," you growl. "You set the table!" Scenes from your former life flash through your mind of impromptu dinners at the Chinese restaurant around the corner. The loud, persistent cries are now punctuated by gasps. There are seconds of silence when you know the baby is shuddering between gasps. You tell yourself: we must stand firm. Before you became a parent you had visited couples with no backbones whose "spoiled" babies dominated and ruined the evenings. You vowed, "This will never happen to us."

Your mate has set the table and slyly located your dog-eared copy of Dr. Spock. He quotes, "After three months you can begin to grow suspicious." "Be quiet!" you yell—and apologize for flying off the handle. He needn't read further. You already know it by heart. You know real-life, true horror stories to back it up. The baby is now shrieking, gasping, shuddering. You turn to the clock. A full

seven minutes has gone by. The baby is coughing between shrieks. The rice is ready.

You begin to waver. The noise is giving you a headache and your heart is pounding. He is, after all, only a baby and you're worried. You feel yourself being drawn into that horrible slough of despondency. You are ambivalent: Your dinner is finally ready; you long for peace. The baby is coughing and spluttering; he will choke to death. You rattle the pots and pans in the sink. You turn to your mate for support, but he is wavering, too. He asks, "Do you think something is wrong?" You glare at the clock. A full nine minutes has gone by. You've never let him cry this long. He is, after all, only a baby. Dr. Spock is an ogre. What does he know about babies? He's probably retired now and living off the royalties of his book.

Should you or shouldn't you?

THE BEDTIME DILEMMA CLEARLY STATED

My main problem with Geneve is sleeping at night. And I've yet to find a satisfactory solution or attitude. I'm unwilling to spend two hours getting her to sleep and I'm equally unwilling to let her cry and cry. She can work herself into all kinds of anxious, fearful, hysterical, emotional states. Most of the time I nurse her to sleep (she's seven months old), which I'm told is a bad habit to get into. But she often wakes up as I move her to the crib, and then I stay in the room with her. When she gets sleepy and starts to cry, I rub her to sleep. Sometimes the rubbing doesn't do any good and after a while I leave and she cries herself to sleep, but sometimes I can't stand the crying or she starts to get hysterical and I go back in. Sometimes she's more than amenable and goes to sleep, sometimes my going back starts the whole cycle all over again, and sometimes going back isn't enough, doesn't seem to comfort her, so I pick her up and either that works and she calms down and goes to sleep (frequently only to wake as I put her back in the crib . . . oh God, oh God) or it doesn't and I burst into tears of frustration and we both have a good cry. This doesn't happen all the time, or even most of the time, just often enough to make me feel that I really don't know what the hell is going on!

SOME SUGGESTIONS, PHILOSOPHICAL AS WELL AS PRACTICAL

1. A bedtime ritual, lasting fifteen or twenty minutes, can really help a baby prepare for sleep. A bath, a song, or a book physically immobi-lize a baby, but more to the point, they are one-to-one projects that give the baby your full attention. But it's not just the ritual that is impor-tant. If you're anxious or in a hurry, the baby will sense this and will be-come more anxious. Sometimes, no matter how you feel, you must force yourself to be calm and take the extra five minutes that you may not feel you have left in you. Then leave with the conviction that the baby can put himself to sleep.

2. Encourage the use of a transitional object—a blanket, cloth diaper, doll, scarf, stuffed animal—whatever the baby is interested in. A bottle is a somewhat less desirable transitional object but, if it works, use it (see Teething and Teeth, page 219). Hav-ing a "relationship" with such an ob-ject is really a great stride forward in the baby's development, because it means that she can find comfort without you, and this is the begin-ning of independence. A baby will begin to form an attachment to an object at nine or ten months, but many do so as early as five months.

3. It makes for much more sanity and less resentment in a household if the father becomes as skilled as the mother in all aspects of the baby's care, including putting the baby to bed.

4. Don't put the baby to bed *before* a baby-sitter comes (see discussion of separation anxiety, pages 143–145).

NIGHT WAKING

Question: *Why do babies wake up at night?*

Answer: *Sometimes it starts from a bad cold or ear infection that wakes her with real discom-fort. This makes parents quick to run to her again on subsequent nights when they hear a whimper, even though the cold is subsiding. Sometimes the wakefulness seems to start during a painful stage of teething.*

—BENJAMIN SPOCK, M.D.,
Baby and Child Care

A: According to recent studies of sleep, sleep cy-cles in infants are regular and are characteristic of them. An active, noisy baby . . . may be active and noisy in his sleep. Three to four-hour cycles usually make up the night's sleep. Each cycle can be broken down into various types of sleep. In the middle of each cycle is approximately sixty minutes of deep sleep. The hour on each side of this deep sleep may be a lighter, dreaming state in which movement and activity (or dreaming) comes and goes. Then, at regular intervals through the night, an infant comes to a semi-conscious, semi-alert state. In this period, he may suck his fingers, cry out, rock or bang his head, move around the bed, practice his newly learned tricks, fuss, or talk to himself . . . and then settle into his conditioned sleeping position to get himself to sleep again. When his parents are nearby and respond to these cries and the activity, they quickly become a necessary part of his pattern of getting himself back to sleep. It seems an important role for us as parents to "condition" them to use their own resources for sleep as early as we can. This is an important part of acculturation.

—T. Berry Brazelton, M.D.,
Infants and Mothers.

A: *Laura has not had a full night's sleep since Katie was born. Katie is now eighteen months old so you can imagine the tension, exhaustion, and frustration (including sexual!) in our house. Laura is now afraid to complain because everyone has pointed out that Katie's waking is now a conditioned response. She wakes, cries, and knows that Laura will rush in to quiet her. At first there was usually an understandable reason to go in. Katie had a cold, we had tried out a new baby-sitter, she was getting a tooth, Laura had had a bad day at work and transferred her anxiety onto Katie, or she was being weaned from the breast to the bottle and needed extra comforting, or she was frustrated because she couldn't walk, or she was overstimulated. Now there aren't any reasons left, and I've concluded that on some level Laura really needs to be needed in this way.*

EARLY-MORNING WAKING

The sun is just appearing over the horizon as you are roused from a deep, comfortable sleep. The baby is up. You can hear the toys being thrown out of the crib one by one and know that as soon as they are all on the floor, your time is up. This is when you consider making blackout curtains or having them made to order if you don't sew. This is when you wish you'd started having children earlier, for by now they would be seven, able to make their own breakfast, and maybe bring you a glass of orange juice in bed. You certainly deserve it. Until this phase passes—and it does seem to be cyclical, perhaps having something to do with the seasons or the baby's mastery of a new skill—the only fair and reasonable solution is turn-taking: one morning off, one morning on.

A PLACE TO SLEEP

CRIBS

A crib must be absolutely safe, because you aren't there (and don't want to be there) all the time to see what your baby is doing in it. Thanks to the Consumer Product Safety Commission's standards issued in 1973, full-sized baby cribs must meet mandatory safety standards, which are quite stringent (see box). You do not have to worry about safety when you buy a new crib, in other words; your choice will be dictated by appearance and convenience.

Options. Cribs come in two basic types—single- or double-drop side. The latter costs more, and is useful only if you don't place the crib against the wall. A single-drop-sided crib is slightly more stable and less expensive than a double-drop-sided one. Cribs also come with solid-paneled headboards or slats all around. The slatted versions provide the baby with more visibility, but they are more expensive. You will also find that you can pay considerably more for a crib that is covered with decorations—balls that twirl on the headboards, fancy decals, or canopies and ruffles.

MATTRESSES

A good mattress is well worth the money you spend on it—especially if you are using a second-hand crib that comes with an inferior mattress. Many children use their cribs for the first three years, and if they do not need a great deal of firmness and support because they don't weigh much during infancy, they will by the time they are two and a half—and using the crib as a trampoline.

Options. There are three options—inner spring, foam, and hair-filled. Inner springs are recommended because they hold up best under use. A foam mattress will lose its firmness before a hair-filled one will. But the hair-filled type may cause allergies. In any case, a mattress will have a longer life if you turn it periodically.

CRIB BUMPERS

Crib bumpers are important for the baby's comfort and safety. They soften the corners where babies like to snuggle, and keep arms and legs from dangling between the slats.

Options. Crib bumpers come plain (usually white or pastels), with patterns, or in clear, inflatable versions. Choose patterned over plain. Your baby will enjoy staring at Raggedy Ann and may give you a few minutes' extra sleep. The clear, inflatable bumpers are more expensive, easier to store, and give the baby a view, though distorted, of the world outside.

Safe Usage. Crib bumpers, by law, must tie into place or snap in at least six places. Check periodically to make sure that the bumper is secure and that the elastic hasn't broken. The baby can chew on this and possibly choke. Bumpers become a hazard once the baby can stand—they provide a stepping-stone out of the crib.

BEDDING

Sheets. Three fitted sheets are the minimum you will need—one on the bed, one in the laundry, and one on the shelf, about to go on the bed. Patterned sheets cost more than plain. You can make plain sheets very interesting by tie-dying or trying out some of the ideas suggested in the clothing section.

Protecting the Mattress. A mattress protector, a plastic casing that zips around the mattress, may seem like a redundancy with a new, vinyl-covered mattress. It's an option. A mattress pad that covers the entire mattress is also an option. While the baby is still small and immobile, a piecemeal approach makes more sense. Use small pads under the baby. If they get wet you don't have to change the entire bed.

RESOURCES

Crying, Colic, Sleeping

Arnstein, Helene S., *The Roots of Love,* Bantam Books, New York, 1977.

Brazelton, T. Berry, *Infants and Mothers,* Dell Publishing, New York, 1969.

Dunn, Judy, *Distress and Comfort,* Harvard University Press, Cambridge, Mass., 1977.

Leach, Penelope, *Babyhood,* Knopf, New York, 1976.

Montagu, Ashley, *Touching, The Human Significance of Skin,* Columbia University Press, New York, 1971.

Winnicott, D.W., *The Child, the Family, and the Outside World,* Penguin, New York, 1964.

-9-
Bathing

Some parents actually enjoy bathing their newborns. For others the bath can be a nerve-wracking ordeal. For these people, twenty Red Cross baby-care courses or hospital demonstrations can't dispel the fear that their floppy, slippery, tiny baby will slide through their fingers and onto the floor. You can always resort to rubber dishwashing gloves or cotton gloves for better traction. Or the baby's father, who probably has bigger hands than the mother, can undertake this job.

But more to the point, if you or the baby don't feel confident about baths at first, or if you don't have the time, don't worry about it. Take solace in the fact that some child-care experts feel baths are unnecessary for the first six months as long as the diaper area is washed daily. On the other hand, if your newborn seems to like the water, it can be a wonderful soothing technique on a hot August afternoon.

Once the baby is sitting, you may discover that there is nothing better for holding her attention than water, the most available and the cheapest of all toys. All you need in addition are some measuring cups and spoons and a washcloth. A bath, as ordinary as it seems, is truly a learning experience. Think about the varieties of sensations the baby gets from the water alone. There are the tactile sensations—the temperature difference between the water and the air, the semiweightlessness and the general sensuality of water. Water also provides some of the most dramatic evidence of cause and effect, that is, the baby's own power to influence her environment. She can splash, make waves, blow bubbles, and pour. And if you have any doubts about her abilities to drink from a cup, give her one in the bathtub and see how she practices.

SUPPLIES

The bath will go more smoothly if you get everything organized and near you before you undress the baby. It's easier if all this is kept in one basket, box, or pan.

- [ ] mild soap
- [ ] tearless baby shampoo
- [ ] washcloth
- [ ] cotton balls (optional)
- [ ] large towel or apron for you, made out of toweling
- [ ] skid-proof surface to line tub or sink (a towel or rubber mat)
- [ ] clothing and diapers

HOW TO GIVE A SPONGE BATH UNTIL THE NAVEL HEALS

Choose a warm, draft-free location and a waist-high surface (a kitchen or bathroom counter or tabletop). Place the baby on a towel, and have a bowl of water nearby if you aren't near the sink. Some newborns panic when they are completely naked, and if this is the case, keep the baby's diaper on when you wash his top and an undershirt on when you wash his bottom. Following are some specifics.

1. Face: Do not use soap on the baby's face. Wash with clear water. (He'll probably hate it.)

2. Eyelids: Use water and a washcloth or cotton balls. Wipe from the nose outward, using a different part of the washcloth or a new cotton ball for each wipe.

3. Ears: Ears clean themselves naturally. Don't put anything smaller than your elbow into your baby's ears. *No Q-Tips inside the ear!* Wipe the outer ear with a washcloth folded over your finger, and clean behind the ears as well.

4. Nose: You can soften, then remove, dried mucus from the baby's nose by using the corner of a damp washcloth.

5. Head or hair: Once a week is plenty. Use tearless baby shampoo or plain, mild soap. Do not be afraid of scrubbing the fontanel—it is covered by a tough membrane. For hair washing, the sink is useful. Soap the baby's head, then rotate the baby so that his head only is over the sink and rinse him beauty-parlor style.

6. Navel: Don't wash with water until it is healed. Dab with rubbing alcohol several times a day. When the navel is healed, it should be washed at each bath. You'd be surprised what accumulates there.

7. Genitals (girls): There is usually a whitish, cheesy material which accumulates in the folds of the labia in girls. This is perfectly natural and will go away on its own. Some pediatricians, however, think it should be cleaned. Don't scrub. Use the corner of a washcloth or a piece of cotton. Take a few swipes at each bath, using a different part of the washcloth or a new cotton ball for each swipe.

Genitals (boys): Wash the penis as you would any other part of the baby. If the baby is not circumcised, it may be painful to retract the foreskin and wash underneath until he is about six months old. Dr. Spock, however, doesn't feel this procedure is necessary. He suggests leaving the foreskin alone.

8. Fingernails: Keep the baby's nails short so she won't scratch herself or you. Cut them when she's drowsy or asleep. Tiny babies have thin, almost transparent nails. If you put a little powder or cornstarch under each nail, you will be able to see what you are cutting.

HOW TO GIVE A BATH ONCE THE BABY'S NAVEL IS HEALED

I found the kitchen or bathroom sink the most convenient place to give a tiny baby a bath. Special baby bathtubs, when full, are very heavy to lift and empty. They also aren't useful for very long and have to be stored someplace. Fill the sink with a couple of inches of water and test the temperature with your elbow or wrist. Your fingers are not an accurate gauge. Place a towel, a piece of foam, or a rubber mat in the bottom of the sink to provide some traction. Then lower the baby in by slipping your hand under the baby's back, supporting his head with your wrist or arm, with the fingers of your hand crossing to the baby's armpit on the side away from your body (see illustration). This way you have the other hand free to soap and rinse the baby, one part at a time. A totally soapy baby is impossible to hold onto.

I gave Jessica a bath by placing her in her infant seat in the kitchen sink. This way I didn't have to worry about holding on to her. The seat was plastic, and it didn't matter if it got wet. Instead of the cushion, I used a towel to soften it.

I took Nicky into the bathtub with me. I had to compromise on the temperature, but in the middle of August this was no great sacrifice. Your legs are the perfect resting place for the baby.

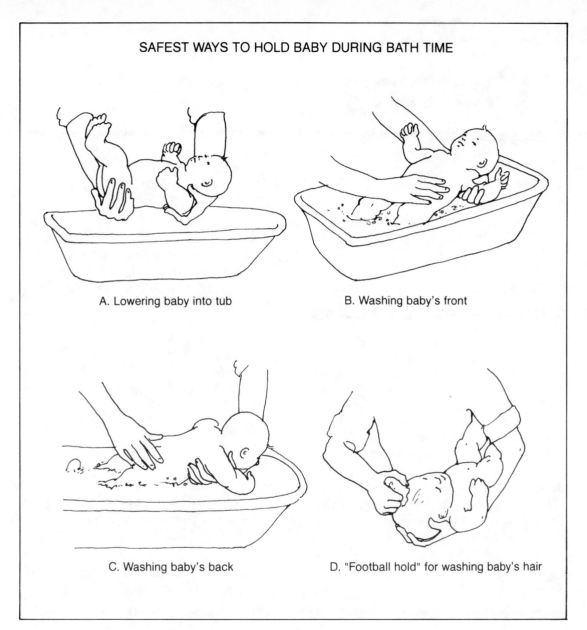

SAFEST WAYS TO HOLD BABY DURING BATH TIME

A. Lowering baby into tub

B. Washing baby's front

C. Washing baby's back

D. "Football hold" for washing baby's hair

Just leave a thick towel on the floor by the tub to put the baby on before you get out.

I liked the Tubby. I never had any fears bathing Karina in it. At ten months she still enjoys playing in it on a hot day. Because it's inflatable, it's easy to store or take to the beach.

SAFETY IN THE BATHTUB

Be sure to turn off the hot-water tap first after filling the bathtub, so that any drips that might come out are cold water. Also see baby-proofing suggestions (pages 193–202) for lowering the hot-water temperature throughout your house while you have young children. Hot tap water can cause bad burns. *And never leave the baby alone in the tub,* even when she can sit up on her own!

-10-
Clothing

BUYER BEWARE

It is hard *not* to get carried away when picking out baby clothes. Because miniature shirts, dresses, and nightgowns are so very appealing, it's easy to overstock. Late in pregnancy, especially, it's natural to become obsessed with being thoroughly prepared. But it really isn't necessary to buy *everything* at once. The baby's wardrobe should be based on your budget, the gifts he receives, the time you have to spend caring for the clothes, and—most important of all—your access to a washing machine. What you start out with also depends on the season of the baby's birth.

If keeping costs down is a priority, you will find that clothing sales are usually held in January, March, April, and July. Visits to thrift shops, the Salvation Army, tag sales, or garage sales can also be very rewarding, and friends with older children are often more than happy to provide hand-me-downs. Second-hand clothing is soft and comfortable, and is usually past the point of shrinking and fading. For ideas on brightening up recycled clothes, see page 103.

FACTS AND OPINIONS

The average baby will double his weight in five months, triple it in a year, and grow about eight inches in the first year.

I didn't have any friends or relatives with babies, so I put myself in the hands of a department store sales clerk. I spent close to $100 on clothes—at least three of everything in yellow, white, and shades of bilious aqua. After Betsy was born, it took me about a week to figure out what was easy to get on and off her and what looked good. I put the rest away, so I wasn't reminded of my folly. I'd recommend buying a few really useful things like stretch suits and front-opening T-shirts, and at most, one each of the other things.

SUGGESTIONS FOR WHEN YOU BUY

1. Start with the six-month, mediums, or up-to-eighteen-pounds size—three ways of saying the same thing. From then on follow this chart:

Weight	Size
19–22 lbs.	12-mo.
23–26 lbs.	18-mo.
27–29 lbs.	24-mo.

2. Make sure clothing provides access to the diaper area.

3. Make sure that a garment opens down the front, so you don't have to pull clothing over the baby's head. Babies hate this.

4. Look for snaps and metal zippers. Plastic zippers stick when they get .wet; tiny buttons are difficult to handle.

5. Try to buy clothes that have similar washing instructions.

6. Esthetic appeal and comfort are also

important. Are the seams well constructed and soft? Bright colors are hard to find for newborns, but are certainly more interesting for the baby to look at. They also look cleaner far longer than pastels.

THE LAYETTE

BASICS

2–4 knit undershirts. An undershirt and a diaper are all a summer baby needs for comfort and freedom of movement. In winter a shirt will provide extra warmth under a stretch suit or a gown. Choose snap or tie-front opening shirts, because babies hate to have clothing pulled over their heads. See tie-dyeing on page 104, to make a plain white shirt more interesting, if you have time.

2–4 stretch suits. My collaborators agree that the stretch suit is the best buy in baby clothing. A one-piece terry cloth suit with front snaps from neck to crotch to toes combines the assets of booties, tights, and shirt. It can be worn day or night and stretches enough to fit all babies. You can even cut the feet out to make it last longer. Stretch suits are available in both summer and winter weights.

1–2 nightgowns. These long-sleeved, front-opening gowns are useful for cold weather babies and usually cost less than stretch suits. They are either sewn shut on the bottom or have a drawstring to "bag" the baby. (Buy only the latter for accessibility to the diaper area). Though gowns are awkward when the baby begins to crawl, they can be made into adorable dresses for girl toddlers.

1–3 receiving blankets. A one-yard square of soft, lightweight fabric, these are useful for swaddling (see page 77), as towels, or as portable changing surfaces. They are extremely easy to make if you sew. Good materials are cotton or synthetic challis, which come in beautiful bright colors that are more interesting than pastels.

1 sweater. A sweater is useful especially during transitional seasons. Look for front-opening, tightly knit sweaters so that the baby's fingers don't get caught in the weave.

1 hat. A hat is a must. In summer, the entire baby, including the head, should be kept out of the direct sun. Unfortunately, almost all baby hats have strings that tie under the baby's chin. Babies hate this. A good winter baby hat is a knitted "helmet"—basically a bag with a small opening for the baby's face, like skiers wear—

no strings to tie and then have untied by the baby. If you want to make a simple baby hat, see the box on pages 94–95.

LUXURIES

Kimonos. These mysterious garments look like long bathrobes, and unless someone tells you that they're supposed to be versatile, you might never guess. They can be worn with the opening either down the front or down the back. The theory behind this is if the baby is lying on his back, the kimono is worn with the opening down the back and is spread out and away from the diaper area, so that it doesn't get wet. When he's on his stomach, the kimono is worn with the opening down the front. Long before the baby outgrows this garment, however, he will become an active wriggler and kicker. A kimono bunches up and gets in the way because it's so long.

Sacque Sets. These two-piece suits have a short front-opening top and matching waterproof-liner pants. They are common gift items and are usually quite dressy. But they are quite useless in cold weather unless you put tights on underneath, which makes changing the baby a more complicated process than most of us wish to get involved with on anything other than special occasions.

How to Make a Baby Hat in Less than an Hour

Anyone with beginning sewing skills and an hour can make this simple hat designed by Joan MacNamara. The directions that follow are for a six-month-old size. If you wish to make the hat reversible, use two different colors of fabric and sew buttons on the inside as well as the outside of the hat.

Materials Needed:
fabric: ⅓ yard of 36″ or 45″ fabric
lace edging: 14″
buttons: 2 or 4 small buttons, under ½″ in diameter
elastic cord: two short pieces for button loops
tissue paper or newspaper: to make a paper pattern if you don't want to mark cutting lines directly on the fabric
ribbon: 24″

1. Fold fabric as shown below. Lay out the pattern and cut out two identical pieces, piece #1 for the outside of the hat and piece #2 for the lining of the hat.

2. On right side of piece #1, pin elastic as shown to form loops in corners B and C. Sew loops in place.

3. With right sides together, pin pieces #1 and #2 together, leaving the longest edges (A and A¹) open. Stitch along remaining edges, allowing a ½″ seam allowance. Trim seams. Turn right side out. Press flat.

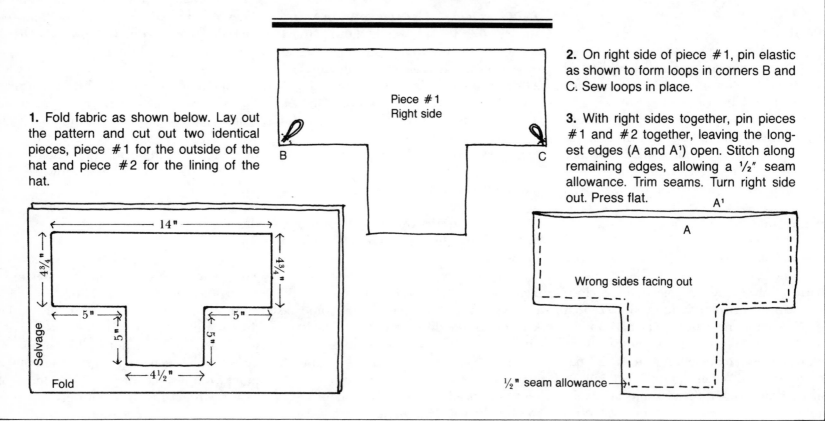

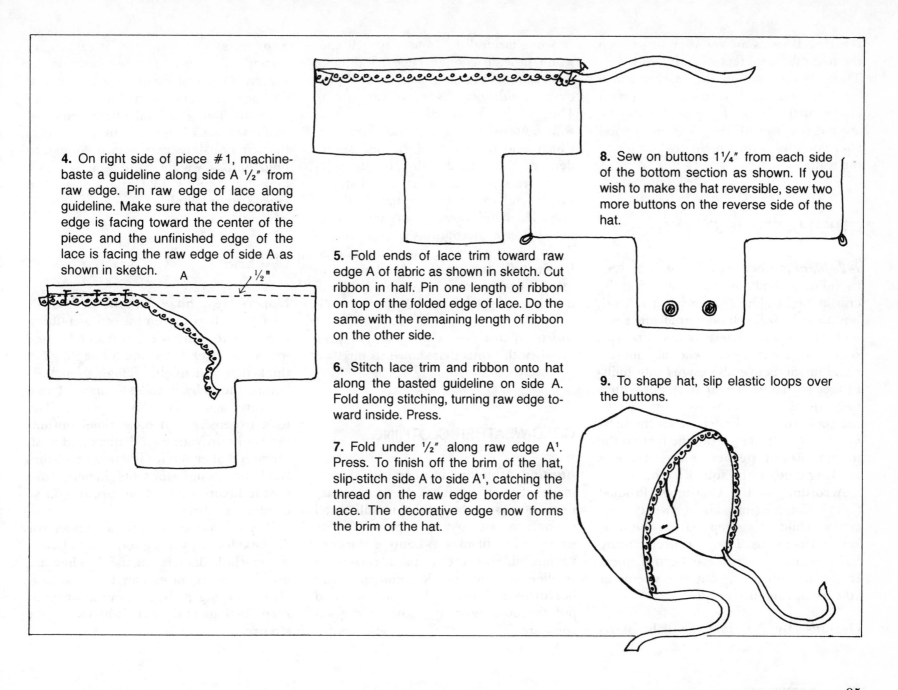

4. On right side of piece #1, machine-baste a guideline along side A ½″ from raw edge. Pin raw edge of lace along guideline. Make sure that the decorative edge is facing toward the center of the piece and the unfinished edge of the lace is facing the raw edge of side A as shown in sketch.

5. Fold ends of lace trim toward raw edge A of fabric as shown in sketch. Cut ribbon in half. Pin one length of ribbon on top of the folded edge of lace. Do the same with the remaining length of ribbon on the other side.

6. Stitch lace trim and ribbon onto hat along the basted guideline on side A. Fold along stitching, turning raw edge toward inside. Press.

7. Fold under ½″ along raw edge A¹. Press. To finish off the brim of the hat, slip-stitch side A to side A¹, catching the thread on the raw edge border of the lace. The decorative edge now forms the brim of the hat.

8. Sew on buttons 1¼″ from each side of the bottom section as shown. If you wish to make the hat reversible, sew two more buttons on the reverse side of the hat.

9. To shape hat, slip elastic loops over the buttons.

Booties. Booties are an attempt to keep the naturally cool feet of an infant warm. There is one set on the market which won't fall off, made of corduroy with an elastic in the back of the heel and a tie around the front. Knee socks are a good alternative or supplement to booties in the winter.

OTHER USEFUL CLOTHING

1–2 blanket-sleepers. These are very useful once the baby starts traversing the crib at night. The blankets will fall off, but the baby will still be warm if she's in a blanket-sleeper. These come in two styles: bags for babies who do not yet stand up, and coverall designs with built-in feet for later. If you start out with a bag, invest in a "grow sleeper," which has tucks that can be let out as the baby grows. To help skid-proof the feet on the more grown-up sleepers, place a piece of masking tape on the sole of each foot.

According to the Consumer Product Safety Commission, about twenty percent of children's sleepwear on the market still contains Tris, a cancer-causing flame retardant which has been banned. If you are unsure about the sleepwear you are buying, be sure to ask.

Overalls. By the time the baby starts crawling around the house, stretch suits won't provide enough knee padding or warmth on cold floors. Two to 4 pairs of overalls with *snap crotches* are very useful. They come in two designs, a coverall with buttons or snaps at the shoulders, which tend to stay on the round shoulders of the typical baby, or the old-fashioned style with bib front and straps, which tend to fall off the baby's shoulders. The latter, however, are more practical because the buttons can be moved down the straps as the baby grows taller. If you twist the straps several times to make them shorter, these overalls will not slide off the baby's shoulders.

Shirts. With large neck openings—preferably with prints that show less dirt!

COLD-WEATHER CLOTHING

Bunting. A bunting is a bag with sleeves made of snowsuit fabric. It is a luxury item, because a baby who is still small enough to put up with bagging can be wrapped in a blanket. A bunting is inconvenient if you use a pack carrier, a stroller, or a car seat. Recommendation: borrow one if you really want one and put the bunting money toward a good snowsuit.

Snowsuits. A snowsuit that is easy to get on and off is crucial for your sanity in the winter. Optional snap-on mittens and feet are also very useful for babies who have the ability to pull off mittens and don't yet wear shoes. Look for fabrics that are not slippery; it's hard enough to hold onto a wiggly baby as it is. Also, look for zippers that the salesperson swears are infallible.

DIAPERS

Diapers are a huge part of your baby's wardrobe. If you aren't a pro at putting them on to start with, you *will* be one within a week. It's mind-boggling to think that you might change thousands before the baby is toilet trained. There are three approaches to diapering. The least expensive and most time-consuming is to own your own diapers and wash them. A diaper service is a middle-of-the-road approach. Disposable diapers make up the luxury route. You can, of course combine all three.

If you decide to use a service or disposables, it's still a good idea to have a dozen cloth diapers on hand. They are useful in emergencies, can double as towels or burping pads, and can be used to keep portions of the baby's bed and your lap dry.

THREE WAYS TO FOLD A SQUARE, FLAT DIAPER

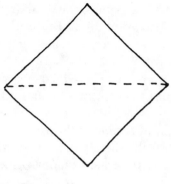

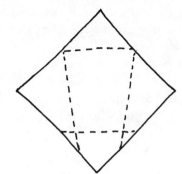

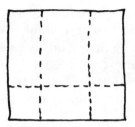

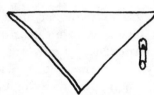

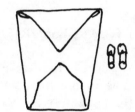

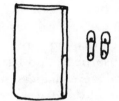

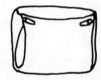

1. Triangular Fold. Fold the diaper into a triangle and fasten the three corners with a single pin.

2. Kite Fold. Fold in two sides to give diaper a long, pointed shape. Fold over top and bottom flaps; secure with two pins. This method provides a thick center panel.

3. Triple Fold. Fold over one-third of the diaper. Then fold the rectangle in thirds as you would a letter. Fasten the diaper with two pins. The extra thickness should go at the back for girls and in front for boys.

CLOTH DIAPERS

If you plan to use your own diapers, you will need between four and six dozen and a small, rust-proof diaper pail with a tight-fitting lid.

Cloth diapers come in a variety of fabrics and styles. My recommendation is the prefolded, gauze kind, because they provide the most softness for the baby and are the easiest to care for. But read the following to come to your own decision.

Choices in Fabric. Cloth diapers are made of cotton gauze, bird's-eye, or flannelette. Gauze diapers are generally softer, more absorbent, and lighter than the others. Bird's-eye diapers are somewhat more durable and less expensive, and flannelette, though less absorbent, is warmer.

Choices in Style. Flat diapers are the least expensive and most bothersome type of cloth diapers. They come in squares, rectangles, or stretch rectangles which can be folded in various ways to fit the baby as he grows. If you are faced with a large, square diaper and a very small baby, page 97 shows three ways to fold the diaper to make it fit.

Prefolded diapers are designed to have up to six layers of thickness where it counts—down the middle. Some additional folding might be necessary to make the diaper small enough for a newborn.

Fitted or contour diapers are hourglass-shaped with snaps. They come either in one size which is supposed to fit from birth to two years, or in several sizes which must be replaced as the baby grows. They are quite expensive, and I've never met anyone who uses them.

DIAPERING ACCESSORIES

Pins. The secret behind a durable, safe diaper pin is in the head. A good old-fashioned metal safety pin with a strong head will do the job. So will a pin with a plastic head, as long as it is reinforced with metal. The pins that most often hurt babies are those with plastic ducks and rabbits on the heads. These can chip apart and scratch the baby. To keep pins sliding easily, poke them into a bar of soap left in its paper wrapper (so that the soap flakes don't scatter).

Clips. It takes a certain practiced hand to use a diaper clip, but once you master it you will never poke the baby or yourself by accident. If you do use them, keep them in a safe place, away from the baby.

They are small and very swallowable.

Powders and lotions. Neither powder nor lotion is necessary, or nature would have provided them. But both are awfully nice to use. Don't shake the can of powder directly onto the baby or he might inhale a cloud of it, which is unhealthy for his lungs. Put it in your hand first. Cornstarch is an inexpensive natural substitute, and Ammens Powder, not marketed specifically for babies, is miraculous at clearing up a mild diaper rash.

Diaper liners. A diaper liner can be useful for saving wear and tear on cloth diapers, particularly when you are traveling. After you fold the diaper, place the liner inside, then pin the diaper together. Look for the type made with green and blue dots and waves. These are the softest.

Waterproof pants. Waterproof pants prevent leakage onto a baby's clothing, your lap, your visitors, and your furniture, but they keep the baby wetter because moisture which might otherwise evaporate or be absorbed into the baby's outer clothing is trapped, increasing the likelihood of diaper rash. The best kinds of pants are made of soft nylon, which doesn't get stiff with repeated washing and drying. If you use plastic pants, they will come out softer if you dry them in the dryer (but use a *very* low heat) rather than hanging them on a line.

A PLUG FOR DIAPER SERVICES

If you want to save time, a diaper service can give you several free hours a week that you might otherwise spend washing, folding, and carrying heavy diaper pails. Diaper services use special soaps, bacteriostats, and rinsing agents that insure against bacterial buildup or soap residue from washing to washing. Diaper services also usually provide newborn-sized diapers, a boon to any new mother who has never diapered a baby before. Shop around for the cheapest and best service in your area.

DISPOSABLE DIAPERS: BANKRUPTCY NOW, ECOLOGY LATER

It is true that millions of trees go into the making of disposable diapers and that the plastic backings on them do not biodegrade. They also cost about four times as much as owning and caring for your own cloth diapers. But many parents feel that the convenience is worth the financial and ecological cost. We rationalize that there are many positive things we can do for the environment once our children are toilet trained, and we will arrive at that point somewhat poorer in pocket but richer in spirit. Even if you don't use them regularly, these diapers are invaluable for travel and other special occasions. The following list offers some suggestions for getting the best use from disposable diapers:

1. If you use only disposables, buy them by the case through your local drug or discount store to save time as well as money.

2. If you remove a dry diaper by mistake, a piece of masking tape can repair the damage.

3. Perhaps this is obvious, but the sizes on the boxes often have little to do with the size and shape of your baby. Don't graduate to the next larger—and more expensive—size until you have to.

4. Change the baby often. These diapers hold more moisture than you think, but they do not contain bacteriostats, and cause rashes in some babies.

5. Disposable diapers can be altered for a better fit: Pull the leg area out, then tuck it in around the baby's legs to avoid leaks. You can also add absorbency by double-diapering: Lay one on top of the other and put a hole in the seat of the top one. Then diaper the baby. To keep the diaper from acting as a wick and dampening the baby's shirt, the plastic lining can be folded or turned down to shorten the length of the diaper. Don't do this if your baby can't tolerate the plastic next to his skin.

6. Proper disposal: Regardless of what the directions say, don't flush these diapers, especially if you have a septic tank. When you put them in the trash, fold them so that the plastic layer is outside and seal them in plastic bags. A study done by the Environmental Protection Agency showed a significant number of intestinal and polio viruses in the stools of babies recently immunized with live polio vaccine. This can be a real hazard for sanitation workers.

LAUNDRY

DIAPERS

For the early weeks when your baby's skin is very sensitive, here is a conservative approach to cloth diaper care. Later you can experiment with detergents, bleach, and fabric softeners.

1. Soiled diapers should be dunked up and down in the toilet as you flush to remove the bulk of the bowel movement. (It is not necessary to rinse diapers which are merely wet.)

2. Soaking: place diaper in a small, covered diaper pail containing borax and water (one teaspoon borax to one gallon water) to soak until you are ready to wash.

3. Wash diapers on the hottest cycle, using a mild soap, not detergent.

4. Rinse at least twice to remove all soap residue. Add ¼ cup of vinegar to the final rinse. If the water in your community is hard, rinse at least three times.

MISCELLANEOUS—THE LAUNDRY IN GENERAL

1. A little baking soda and water will remove the spots and odor of the baby's spit-up.

2. Once your baby starts eating solid foods, the laundry will take on a new aspect. Fresh stains—eggs, fruit and berry juice, and liquid vitamins—can be removed before they set with cold water. If they are allowed to set for a period of time, soak in cold water for a half-hour or work undiluted liquid detergent onto the spot.

3. For mystery stain removal, see page 103.

CHANGING TABLES

THE IDEAL CHANGING TABLE IS . . .

1. Homemade, from an old dresser that is waist high and repainted with lead-free paint. This way you will have convenient storage and will not strain your back leaning over.

2. The top is covered with a soft, waterproof or water-absorbent surface—a towel, carriage pad, or piece of foam. A strap (which is optional) can be made from an old belt nailed or stapled to the top of the dresser.

3. Overhead, at adult eye level, one or two open shelves are useful for storing diapers, powder, and oil. From the bottom of the shelf, you can hang baubles and bangles to interest the baby.

4. A towel rack is also convenient for hanging towels and clothes, and as a support and distraction for the baby when she insists on standing.

5. A paper-towel or toilet-paper dispenser will save on cotton and premoistened towels, and so will a bowl of water.

6. If there is still room, a mirror adds great distraction value.

7. You can also collect all the baby's laundry in one place if you hang a laundry bag from two hooks at one end of the changing table.

Question: How do you know how much clothing to put on the baby?

Answer: *A good rule of thumb is to dress the baby the way you would dress yourself. Remember in hot weather that a baby's skin burns easily, and that his head needs protection from direct sun if he's going to be exposed to it for more than a few minutes. An overdressed baby may get prickly heat. A baby who is not dressed warmly enough will cry, and his skin may look mottled. A baby's hands and feet will never be as warm as the rest of his body, no matter how hard you try. A pediatrician will assure you that this is nothing to worry about.*

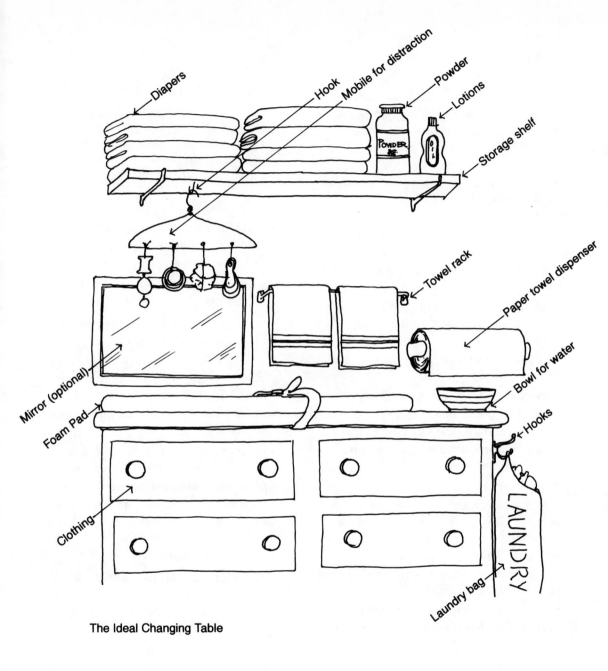

Diapers

Hook

Mobile for distraction

Powder

Lotions

Storage shelf

Towel rack

Paper towel dispenser

Bowl for water

Hooks

Mirror (optional)

Foam Pad

Clothing

LAUNDRY

Laundry bag

POWDER

The Ideal Changing Table

SHOES

Question: *Why are stiff, high, hard-soled, difficult-to-put-on shoes made for babies?*

Answer: *There is no good reason. Ankle support is not necessary or nature would have provided it.*

Good Advice

Babies don't need shoes until they walk outside, and then sneakers are excellent for several reasons. They provide good traction, they are flexible, and they are cheap. If you buy your baby cheap shoes, you are much more likely to replace them at the right time—which for Xantre was as often as every two or three months. It's heartbreaking to spend $16 on shoes for a six-month-old who can't walk anyway, and then have to put them away after two months.

After a baby is standing and walking there's real value in leaving the child barefoot most of the time when conditions are suitable. The arches are relatively flat at first. The baby gradually builds up the arches and strengthens the ankles by using them vigorously in standing and walking. . . . When you always provide the baby with a flat floor to walk on and always enclose the feet in shoes (with their smooth insides), especially if the soles are stiff, you encourage the child to relax the foot muscles and to walk flat-footed.

—Benjamin Spock, M.D.,
Baby and Child Care

HOW TO FIND SHOES THAT FIT

1. Always take the baby with you to the shoe store so she can try on the shoes. She's much more likely to be relaxed if you, rather than a stranger, fiddle with her feet.

2. Socks are important for the fit of a shoe. If you are buying shoes for winter, bring along a pair of heavy socks for the fitting.

3. After putting on both shoes, let the baby walk around the store so that you can see if her walk is normal.

4. Make sure that there is a half-inch of space beyond the longest toe. If you can't feel this space, the shoe is too hard.

5. Request extra, longer laces which will make it easier for you to tie the necessary double bow.

SUGGESTIONS FOR MAKING THE OLD AND STAINED LOOK NEW

1. Patches on worn knees and elbows renew the life in pants, sweaters, and jackets. A very simple way to make a patch is to cut out two pieces of fabric that are the same size and shape. Sew them together, leaving a small opening, so that you can turn the patch inside out. (If you want, you can stuff a knee patch with polyester quilting for extra softness. This patch is easy to sew on because the edges are already finished.

2. New buttons, trim, embroidery, or appliqué (either your own handiwork or premade iron-on appliqués) can transform a dreary pair of overalls into something special.

3. You can also make an old pair of overalls into a toy. Using Velcro strips, you can stick on colorful shapes made out of different fabrics, which the baby can pull off and play with.

4. Stains can either be removed (see number 6) or covered by dyeing (see directions for simple tie-dyeing), embroidery, or appliqué. You can also crayon over them with indelible Pentel crayons, which are colorfast.

5. Because of many, many launderings, Follow the directions on the package.

secondhand sleepwear may no longer contain the original fire-retarding agents. Here is a "home brew" fire retardant that works.

9 oz. borax
4 oz. boric-acid solution (available at your drugstore)
1 gallon warm water

Combine all three ingredients. Soak the clean sleepwear in the solution until it thoroughly penetrates the fabric. Dry as usual.

6. Mystery Stain Removal for People with Patience

a. Try washing the clothing as you would anything else.

b. If this doesn't work use an enzyme presoak. If this fails use a mild treatment of chlorine or sodium perborate bleach or hydrogen peroxide.

c. If this doesn't work use the oxalic acid treatment: Spread stained material over a bowl of boiling water. Apply a few drops of oxalic acid solution (one teaspoon of crystals to one cup of water) to the stain. Rinse quickly and very thoroughly by dipping into hot water.

d. If none of the above works, use a strong chlorine or sodium perborate bleach or consider dyeing the clothing.

When Anna was three months old, I began to feel like I was going stir-crazy. I felt confined to the house because of the cold weather, tired from her night waking, and very lonely. I still hadn't adjusted to a nonworking life and missed the routine and friends from my old job.

A La Leche leader put me in touch with a neighborhood woman, Judi Weber, who had a baby, Justin, near Anna's age. Judy, an ex-stock broker, had recently opened a recycled clothing store for infants and toddlers. She'd rented a small storefront and initially stocked it with clothing from thrift shops and the Salvation Army. She also took in some new, handmade items from local women—tie-dyed shirts, crocheted hats, bags, and sweaters. Used toys and larger pieces of baby equipment like cribs, high chairs, playpens, car seats, and rocking chairs were also sold on consignment.

Once the store had been open for a few months, Judi started a credit system where parents could trade their children's outgrown clothes for credit (play money) to be used toward 50 percent of a new purchase. With this incentive, there was always plenty of inventory and turnover. Nothing cost more than $4 or $5 and many items went for less than $1.

I was delighted when Judi offered me a job two afternoons a week. I was able to bring Anna with me, which was good for both of us. In the back room she and Justin took naps in a playpen and Port-a-Crib (also available to customers when not in use). The floors were carpeted and baby-proofed for crawlers, and we never had to worry about the secondhand toys remaining perfect. Anna and Justin became close friends over the months and were seldom bored with each other or the customers.

Budget Baby had a lot to offer parents as well. Because we encouraged browsing and talking, the store soon became a meeting place. We had a comfortable old porch swing where mothers could nurse and rock their babies, sit and talk, or eat their lunches out of paper bags. A bulletin board had information on baby-sitting, day care, play groups, pediatricians and clinics, exercise and Lamaze classes, and current newspaper clippings. Eventually Judi stocked some books on baby care and nutrition and gave a psychologist friend use of the store to run a group for new mothers one evening a week.

My salary wasn't that large, but I really enjoyed using my imagination to renew some of the old clothes which came in. When I'd worked full-time all those years before Anna was born, I hadn't had the time to knit, crochet, embroider, and sew and felt great using these skills again.

But more important than this, the store helped me make new friends with women in the community. The play group which Anna has belonged to for over a year is made up of Budget Babies, and the cooperative nursery school she'll go to the following year grew out of parents I met through the store as well. As for myself, the work at the store convinced me that I enjoyed business and might even have a flair for it. I've recently finished an evening course in running your own small business, and am thinking about opening a health food store and restaurant geared mainly for children. I think every neighborhood would benefit from a place like Budget Baby. Does your community have one?

—BETTE LACINA

SECOND HAND IS BEAUTIFUL

TIE-DYEING

Materials

1. Garments to be dyed (2 or 3 undershirts, a crib sheet)
2. Dye
3. Large pot or other equipment as recommended in dye instructions
4. String, rubber bands
5. Scissors
6. Newspapers to cover work surface

Dye

The most commonly known dyes are the packages available in grocery stores and five-and-tens. These powders are mixtures of both cotton-fiber and synthetic-fiber dyes suitable for any garment. They are inexpensive and easy to use but have two drawbacks: (1) you can rarely get a strong, vivid color, and (2) the garment will fade slightly each time it is washed. This means the garment must be washed separately, preferably by hand, and that it will become paler with use.

The most effective dyes are commercial colorfast dyes used with all-cotton fabric. These are usually sold in bulk quantity to wholesalers; some distributors will sell them in small quantities. The procedure for using these dyes is slightly more involved, but the finished garment will be a beautiful machine-washable color. *(Note: These dyes require lye. Use with extreme caution.)*

Garments

If using a "grocery-store" dye the fabric content of the garment will not matter. If you are using commercial dyes, select all-cotton items. Your baby will probably have many: cotton knit T-shirts, crib sheets, washcloths and towels, etc. A great combination is to dye an undershirt and a pair of cotton training pants the same color. This will give your baby a cool, color-coordinated outfit. Plain white sheets can be dyed to match the other colors in the nursery, eliminating a monotonous "baby-white" look. Look at the clothing and linens you use for your baby for possibilities.

Tying

A length of string or a rubber band wrapped tightly around a section of fabric will prevent the dye from soaking into the fibers, so wherever you tie, the folds of the fabric will remain white. With this rule of thumb in mind, tie sections of the fabric either randomly or following a planned design.

Using either string or rubber bands, gather up and tie sections of the fabric. You can make several of these ties across the surface. Try tying a section, then fastening a second tie an inch or so below the first. This can be done repeatedly. The effect

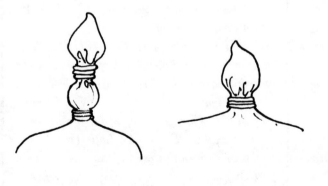

when dyed and untied will be a series of concentric circles.

To make stripes, gather across the entire width of the garment and secure with string. This is a great method to use along the bottom edge of a T-shirt, around the sleeves, or repeated several times on a sheet.

Any combination of tying can be used on a garment. Play with it, see what effects you get, experiment. As you become more experienced, you will be able to anticipate the results and you may want to design specific patterns.

When the garment is tied, prepare dye bath according to directions on the package. Soak the piece in clear water; dye according to directions.

Using scissors, snip the strings and rubber bands and unfold the garment. Hang to dry.

Several dye baths can be used on a garment. A shirt can be dipped into a clear yellow first, then tied and dipped into a red. The ties will keep the folds the original yellow, and the red dye will most likely blend with the yellow to create a shade of orange.

Or try this three-step method: Tie the white fabric; dye it a light color; without untying the first strings wrap additional sections of fabric. Dye again. This will give you some white circles, some light-colored circles, and a main color a blend of the two dyes.

When you are dyeing fabric in more than one color, read the directions to see if the fabric should be allowed to dry before dipping a second time. A light color works best for the first dye bath, followed by a darker color. Remember that the finished shade will be a blend of the two colors. For example:

red + yellow = orange

red + blue = purple

blue + yellow = green

NOTE: To order small quantities of excellent dyes not available in the consumer marketplace, contact:

Aljo Mfg. Co.
116 Prince Street
New York, N.Y. 10012

Resources

Clothing

Buying Clothing for Small Children (Cornell Miscellaneous Bulletin #100) Cornell University Ithaca, N.Y. 14850

Little Clothes for Little Prices; Fix It, Change It, Cover It; and *The Basic Materials,* an excellent manual in three parts. For further information, write to:

Curtain Productions, Inc. 1300 Salanoni Avenue Huntingtcn, Ind. 46750

Mothercare Stores, Inc. 529 Fifth Avenue New York, N.Y. 10017

(Write for a free catalogue featuring brightly colored, well-made, relatively inexpensive clothes for babies.)

Sew For Babies by Kerstin Martensson— available at many fabric stores or write to:

Kwik Sew Pattern Co. 300 Sixth Avenue N. Minneapolis, Minn. 55401

Memo to Parents Re: Your Child's Foot Health American Podiatry Association 20 Chevy Chase Circle, N.W. Washington, D.C. 20015

Part IV
LIVING WITH MOTHERHOOD

-11-
Postpartum

THE PHYSICAL ASPECTS OF POSTPARTUM

After the birth of your baby, your body undergoes as many changes as it did during pregnancy, except that the changes occur more rapidly and far less attention is paid to them. Most of us experience postpartum, the six-week to three-month period during which our bodies return to their prepregnant state, without fully understanding the dramatic physical and emotional changes we are experiencing.

Postpartum is actually a time of far greater physical and emotional stress than pregnancy. Besides having to cope with fatigue, the stresses of the birth, the constant physical and psychic demands of newborn care, you are experiencing the greatest maturational event in your life. You are suddenly no longer a daughter, but a mother, with expectations, responsibilities, feelings, and needs which differ from anything else you have ever experienced.

To help cope with the stresses of the postpartum period, it is very important to understand what is happening to your body and to take steps to insure and maintain good health. It is also crucial not to forget the very real connection between your physical and your emotional well-being.

Question: What changes will my body undergo during postpartum?

Answer: Hormonal Activity. During pregnancy the placenta produces very high levels of estrogen and progesterone. After the delivery of the placenta, the levels of these hormones drop dramatically and immediately. It is thought that this rapid change in the hormone levels may account for sweating, heart palpitations, and hot and cold flashes similar to those experienced by some women during menopause. It is commonly thought that these abrupt drops in estrogen and progesterone may account for the mood swings characteristic of

postpartum blues. However, there is no medical evidence that this is the case. It's more likely that stress is the culprit.

The Uterus. After birth the uterus begins its dramatic transformation from a two-pound organ back down to a two-ounce organ; it takes about six weeks. The reduction of the uterus to its prepregnant size—involution—occurs in several ways. The muscles contract to clamp down on the open blood vessels where the placenta had been attached to the uterine wall. These contractions prevent excessive loss of blood or hemorrhaging. Sometimes, particularly in nursing women and multiparas (women who have had more than one child) these contractions can be felt as afterpains. In multiparas the uterus must work somewhat harder to regain its former shape and size. Nursing also helps the uterus contract because when the baby sucks, oxytocin is released by the pituitary gland. This releases the milk but also serves as a stimulant for the uterine muscles to contract. Besides these contractions, involution is occurring via the actual reduction of the size of the uterine muscle cells. Protein within the cells is metabolized by the body and sloughed off through the urine. **Suggestion:** Beginning as soon as you wish after delivery, lie on your stomach with a pillow under your hips and relax this way for about half an hour at least twice a day. This will help drain and tone the uterus, relax your abdomen, and relieve some of the back strain you may be feeling.

The Lochia. This is a discharge, continuing from three to four weeks after birth, that starts out as bright red. After three or four days it will begin to change color, growing paler pink, then yellowish or white. A foul odor to the discharge may mean infection, in which case you should contact your doctor.

Menstruation. The non-nursing mother will probably have a period six to eight weeks after the birth. The nursing mother, because she maintains high levels of the hormone prolactin, may not have a period for up to a year. Prolactin tends to suppress the action of the ovaries, but this is not a reliable form of birth control!

Urine and Bowel Function. You will have to urinate frequently after delivery

---

EPISIOTOMIES / CARE OF STITCHES

Most women have an episiotomy with their first vaginal delivery—a small cut between vaginal and anal openings to enlarge the birth ring and prevent it from tearing. While some women experience the healing as a mild discomfort and inconvenience, others describe their stitches—especially if they are accompanied by hemorrhoids—as the least pleasant aspect of childbirth. They wonder if they will ever be able to walk and sit comfortably, not to mention make love again. The stitches will feel better every day, and by two or three weeks you might find yourself forgetting to sit down delicately. In the meantime you can minimize the discomfort in several ways, including exercise.

1. It's important to rinse the perineum with plain water after urinating or having a bowel movement to avoid infection. Most hospitals provide new mothers with a simple plastic squirt bottle. Continue to use it once you are home.

2. Heat is also an excellent treatment, because it helps relax the muscles and stimulate circulation. A simple reading lamp will work, but a sitz bath may be more relaxing: Fill the tub with no more than two or three inches of warm water. Elevate your legs over the bathtub for twenty to thirty minutes—*two or three times* a day. Or take hot showers.

3. If you have hemorrhoids as well, skip the heat lamp, but the other suggestions for stitches will help. So will cold witch hazel compresses. Also, be sure to drink lots of fluids and eat plenty of fresh fruit and bran, so that you will not get constipated.

4. The Kegel exercise. Exercising the perineal area is probably the furthest thing from your mind, but you can begin by doing the Kegel exercise.

During pregnancy the perineal area or pelvic floor can be stretched and weakened by the growing weight of the uterus. During birth the muscles are further weakened by the tremendous pressure of the baby's head as it pushes through the birth canal, and then, to add insult to injury, they are severed by the episiotomy.

---

as your body relieves itself of excess fluids—including the 30 percent increase in your pregnancy blood supply. Drink two to three quarts of fluid per day, nursing or not, to purge your body of wastes and toxins. Some women are also bothered by constipation. Fluids, fresh fruits, raw

vegetables, and a little bran added to your cereal will help.

The Cervix. It will be about four weeks before the cervix closes. Until it does, the uterus is vulnerable to infection. This is why intercourse and the use of tampons,

Unless this area is strengthened and repaired by exercise, the muscles will begin to sag like an old hammock. This can be the root of other more serious gynecological problems, such as prolapse of the uterus, in which the uterus falls into a stretched vagina.

If you are not already familiar with the Kegel exercise, postpartum is an excellent time to start. To locate the muscles, spread your legs apart while you are urinating, and try to stop and start the flow. Your ability to do so is an indication of your muscle tone, which after a vaginal birth may be minimal. Tense and relax these muscles a few times to the count of five on the first day, and build up gradually to as many times as you like.

This exercise, as mentioned before, will help with painful stitches, hemorrhoids, bowel movements, and the general toning of the entire perineum and vagina, which can make for better lovemaking. The beauty of this very important exercise is that it can be done almost anytime or anyplace.

How the Kegel Exercise Works
The perineal area or pelvic floor is a thin sheet of muscle which supports the pelvic organs: the uterus, the bladder, and the bowels. It is penetrated by three openings: the urethra, the vagina, and the anus. The urethra and the vagina are surrounded by one large sphincter which interlocks with the anal sphincter like a figure eight. Contracting the major sphincter will cause the other to contract as well, and thus exercises the entire area. This is the basis of the Kegel exercise.

douches, and vaginal sprays are forbidden until after the postpartum checkup.

The Pelvic Floor or Perineal Area. The network of muscles surrounding the vagina, anus, and urethra will be tender, swollen, and stretched after birth. The episiotomy will also add considerably to discomfort. Exercises, sitz baths and time will help (see box above for suggestions and exercises). A nursing mother should also know that her vagina may feel dry once she resumes lovemaking. This is due to the fact that during lactation the ovaries produce little or no estrogen, which, besides activating the ovaries, serves to lubricate the vagina. An estrogen cream, prescribed by your doctor, will help with this problem. K-Y jelly, available without a prescription, will also help.

Abdominal Muscles and Your Lower Back. During pregnancy the abdominal muscles stretch to twice their prepregnant size to accommodate the growing fetus. It is vital to get these back in shape, not only for vanity's sake, but also because it is these muscles which support your lower back. During the first month postpartum the abdominals are undergoing their natural involution, and strenuous exercises such as sit-ups are useless and should be avoided. The following exercise, which can be done as soon as you feel up to it after the birth, will gently tone abdominal muscles and relieve back tension.

1. Lie on your back with knees bent and feet flat on the bed or floor.

2. Take a deep breath and relax.

3. Press the small of your back against the floor and contract the muscles in your buttocks. Your back should be perfectly flat.

4. Hold this position for the count of five. Then relax and start over. Repeat no more than four or five times

a day during early postpartum.

For safe exercises to be begun later, see suggestions on page 115.

The Breasts. Whether you nurse or not, your breasts may become engorged two to four days after delivery. This hard, rather painful swelling is caused by a combination of the increased circulation of blood to the breasts, the swelling of the tissues, and the pressure of the milk. If you are nursing, it can be relieved by frequent feedings, warm showers or ice packs, and a good, firm bra. If you aren't nursing, the latter three suggestions will make you feel more comfortable. Women also wonder if nursing will change the shape or size of their breasts. Any changes that do occur are due to pregnancy, not nursing.

Hair. Some women lose a lot of their hair four to six months after the baby is born. This can be alarming, but it is quite normal and should stop within a month. The hair that grows when you are pregnant simply has a shorter life than your usual hair.

Skin Changes. Your skin can be affected by hormonal changes during pregnancy. Some women develop a darker pigmentation on the face, or a brown line from the navel to the pubic bone, or darkened areoli. These should disappear within a

---

FIGHTING TENSION, FATIGUE, AND OVERWEIGHT

Being tense, tired, and overweight are three of the most common complaints during the early months of motherhood. Maintaining your energy level and being able to relax are very important in terms of your ability to function physically, and getting back to your former weight is important in terms of your self-image. Though it is safe to lose up to a pound a week during postpartum and/or lactation, many of us find that getting back to our prepregnant weight is a much slower process. Following are some suggestions for fighting fatigue and tension and losing weight summarized from *Mother Care* by Lyn DelliQuadri and Kati Breckenridge.

Losing Weight

1. Apportion your daily food intake so you get more calories from protein than from fats and carbohydrates.

2. Eat more food in the early part of the day, when you need it most and have the energy to prepare it. Make the lighter afternoon and evening meals especially high in protein.

3. Try several small meals throughout the day as an alternative to three big meals.

4. Prepare one big salad a day and add all the seasonal raw vegetables you can find.

5. Eat foods high in protein, iron, calcium, and vitamin-B complex. Take the vitamin supplements you took during pregnancy.

6. Avoid eating processed foods. Their chemicals and high salt, sugar, and starch content do you no good. Read labels carefully.

7. Try to relax when you eat.

8. Eat slowly and chew your food completely.

9. Drink at least two quarts of water, juices, and low-fat milk throughout the day.

10. Restrict your coffee and alcohol intake. Both are drains on your energy.

11. Don't skip meals, use diet pills, or attempt fad diets or fasting. In each case your body is required to work much harder with much less nourishment. During postpartum, when your system is already depleted and working hard to recover, you can cause yourself damage by dieting in these ways.

month or two. During pregnancy red stretch marks may show up on your breasts and abdomen. After several months these will fade to white and shrink, but they will never totally disappear. Rubbing your skin with lanolin, vitamin E oil, or vegetable oils may help smooth and soften them. Beyond this, nothing, save a good suntan, helps.

Varicose Veins. If you've suffered from these during pregnancy, they will usually decrease in prominence or totally disappear after the birth. The toe-pointing exercise on page 116 will help, and so will elevating your legs a couple of times a day.

Weight Loss. According to Gideon Panter and Shirley Linde's *Now That You've Had Your Baby,* you can expect the following weight loss after the baby is born:

7 pounds	The "average" baby	
1½ pounds	Placenta	In the delivery room
1½ pounds	Amniotic fluid	
2 pounds	Other fluids and blood	One week postpartum
3 pounds	Surplus fluids	
2 pounds	As the uterus shrinks	Six weeks postpartum
17 pounds total		

FIGHTING TENSION, FATIGUE, AND OVERWEIGHT

Fighting Fatigue and Maintaining a High Energy Level.

Certain vitamins and minerals also play a key role in providing energy and fighting fatigue. These are vitamin-B complex, iron, and calcium.

Vitamin-B Complex. This contains about twenty B vitamins. Besides combating fatigue, B-complex aids in digestion and promotes healthy skin, eyes, and blood. Good sources are liver, wheat, brewer's yeast, and dark, leafy green vegetables.

Iron. This is essential to enable the red blood cells to absorb oxygen and carry it throughout the body. If you are iron deficient, you will feel weak, look pale, and your vital functions will be slowed down. Constipation can also result from iron deficiency. Foods high in iron are meats, poultry, organ meats such as liver and kidney, shellfish, eggs, dried beans, dark green vegetables, whole grains, wheat germ, cereals, and dried fruits (particularly apricots).

Calcium. This mineral repairs and builds bones and teeth, and works in combination with vitamins C and K to help them coagulate blood and build cells. Calcium is also thought to combat fatigue by increasing the oxygen content of the muscles. If your body is low in calcium, you may become irritable. Foods high in calcium are milk (skim milk and buttermilk have less saturated fat and slightly more calcium), cottage cheese, yogurt, salmon, and dark green vegetables.

CESAREAN POSTPARTUM

The cesarean mother is experiencing all of the "normal" postpartum feelings and adjustments as well as those resulting from major surgery. For several days after the birth, you may feel the effects of the anesthetic—discomfort in one or

FIGHTING TENSION, FATIGUE, AND OVERWEIGHT

Easing Tension

Being able to relax and truly rest during postpartum is just as important as exercise. The following is an exercise recommended in *Mother Care,* by Lyn DelliQuadri and Kati Breckenridge. It takes about fifteen minutes and is amazingly restorative at any time, be it postpartum or not.

1. Take the phone off the hook and close the curtains. Lie quietly on your back on a bed with a pillow tucked under your lower back. Be still a moment with your eyes open, then gradually let them close.

2. Lift your head slowly as though to touch your chin to your chest. Feel your neck muscles tense, then let your head sink back onto the bed.

3. Lift your right arm, keeping the elbow straight. Feel the tension in the muscles and then relax completely so that your arm drops back onto the bed. Repeat with your left arm.

4. Push your shoulders forward so that they try to meet across your chest, then let go. Feel them sink back onto the bed.

5. Tighten the muscles of your stomach. Feel the tension, then let go. Feel the muscles loosen as you breathe.

6. Lift your right leg, keeping the knee straight. Feel the tension in the muscles, then let go so that the leg drops back onto the bed. Repeat with the left leg.

7. Tighten the muscles in your face—squint your eyes, clench your jaw, frown. Feel the tension and then let go. Feel your face muscles smooth out and release.

8. Continue to lie relaxed, focusing your attention on your muscles loosening and your body sinking into the bed. Notice that your breathing is slow, relaxed, and regular. (Your body temperature will also decrease slightly.)

9. Open your eyes slowly and lie still for a moment. Then stretch, rise, and move slowly into your normal activities.

both shoulders due to the gas and blood that collect under the diaphragm, considerable abdominal discomfort from the incision, horrendous gas pains, and constipation.

You can better cope with the gas pains if you get up as soon as possible and walk around in an upright fashion. The following breathing exercises, recommended by Bonnie Donovan in *The Cesarean Birth Experience,* will help you to cope with an attack of gas.

1. Join your hands on a small pillow placed over the incision.

2. Breathe in deeply and then exhale.

3. Take another deep breath and hold it for a count of five (or ten, if you can). Then exhale.

4. Take a final deep breath in and let it flow out.

One consolation for the cesarean mother is that the recovery is rapid. Each day you feel so much better and more able than you did the day before. Within a week you will be jumping out of your skin to get out of the hospital.

Beyond the physical discomforts that a cesarean brings, there are some psychological ones. Even though cesarean procedures are generally becoming more flexible in some hospitals, many of us are not "awake" in the delivery room, do not have our husbands with us, and are not allowed to hold our babies until several hours after the delivery. We know about the importance of the early bonding of mother to infant, yet many C-section patients may not feel as capable of taking care of the baby as the other women on the maternity floor do. We may also worry about getting a good start with breast-feeding and, particularly if we were asleep during the delivery, may feel left out of one of the most important events in our lives, and feel guilty for feeling this way.

While the vast majority of the other mothers on the maternity floor will be sprinting around—in your eyes, at least—and talking about their labors and deliveries, you may be walking slowly, or be tied to an IV, and not have much to say. There is a need to talk about childbirth and to feel that it is personal and unique. This is how we begin to come to terms with it. Talk to your doctor and your husband about the delivery, and talk to other women on your floor who have also had cesareans. There is also a group called Cesarean Sections, Education and Concern (CSEC), which has been formed to give support to mothers who have had sections. (See Resources for how to contact them.)

One other problem can be ambivalence about taking care of yourself and the baby at the same time, once you do get home. Help really is essential so that you don't wear yourself out and can

spend your energy both recovering and caring for the baby. There is certainly no need to lie prone in bed all day, but you can simplify the logistics of caring for your baby by camping out in one room of the house for the first week. You can feed, change, comfort, and put the baby to sleep on your bed. Have the telephone by your side, as well as plenty of nutritious snacks and fluids, so that you don't have to make unnecessary trips to other parts of the house. And let a helper do everything else that needs to be done around your house.

ADDITIONAL EXERCISES RECOMMENDED FOR POSTPARTUM—A PEP TALK

Following are some additional exercises that are safe to do before your postpartum checkup. Again, many of these should be familiar if you participated in childbirth-preparation classes. Most of us find it rather difficult to get motivated to

do these, weight loss being a much more tangible goal. But your muscles will never be quite the same unless you do some exercises. *Back problems caused by weakened abdominal muscles during pregnancy only increase after delivery* and grow progressively worse as you bend and lift a baby who grows heavier and heavier. Exercise is also excellent for getting you out of a funk and making you feel like you are doing something good for yourself.

After the six-week postpartum period, it is usually fine to resume your pre-pregnancy exercises, but check with your doctor if you have any doubts. At this point you might find it worthwhile to join or form a group in your community. Still later check to see if your local Y provides child care for infants over six months. Some do for a small fee so that you can dance, swim, or do deep knee-bends in the peaceful company of adults.

1. *Chin raising.* This will help relax your upper back and your neck and prepare you for doing sit-ups later. Lie flat on your back with your arms relaxed at your sides. Lift your head up and bring your chin as close to your chest as you can. Do ten or so.

2. *Hand clapping.* This will help strengthen the muscles underneath your breasts and improve the circulation in your chest and breasts.

    a. Lie on your back with your legs stretched out in a relaxed position.

    b. Place your arms straight out at right angles to your body like a T.

    c. Raise your arms over your head and clap your hands together. Then return to the original position. Do five or six times.

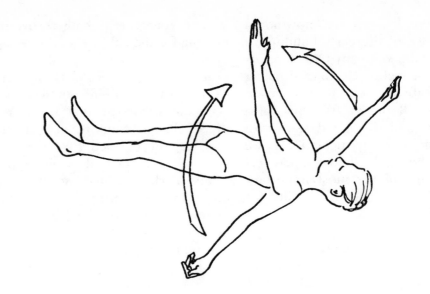

3. *Toe pointing.* This will help improve the circulation in your legs and is especially good if you have varicose veins. It can be done either lying down or sitting.

    a. Lying down: Make yourself comfortable with your legs stretched out and together. Point your toes and hold to the count of five, then relax. Repeat five or six times.

    b. Sitting: Sit on the edge of your bed, using your arms for support. Point your toes forward as far as possible, then bend your ankles toward you, then relax.

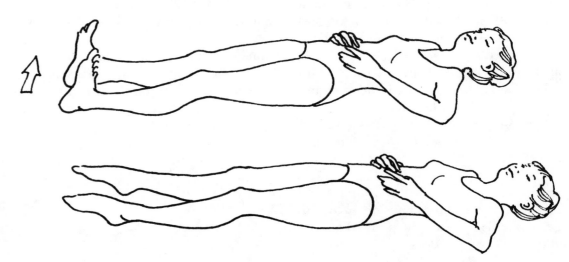

4. *Hip rolling.* To make a dent in your waistline: Lie flat on your back and draw both legs up. Keep your shoulders flat on the bed, with your arms relaxed and out from your sides. Twist both legs together to the right, then bring them back up and twist both legs to the left. Do five or six times.

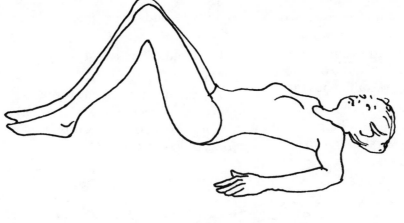

5. *Stretching and reaching.* To make a dent in your waistline:

a. Stand up and raise your hands over your head and look at the ceiling. Stretch up as far as you can on your toes.

b. Relax your left arm slightly as you stretch your right arm up as far as you can. Raise your left hip and heel slightly. Then relax.

c. Repeat—stretching your left arm and lifting your right hip and heel slightly. Do five or six times.

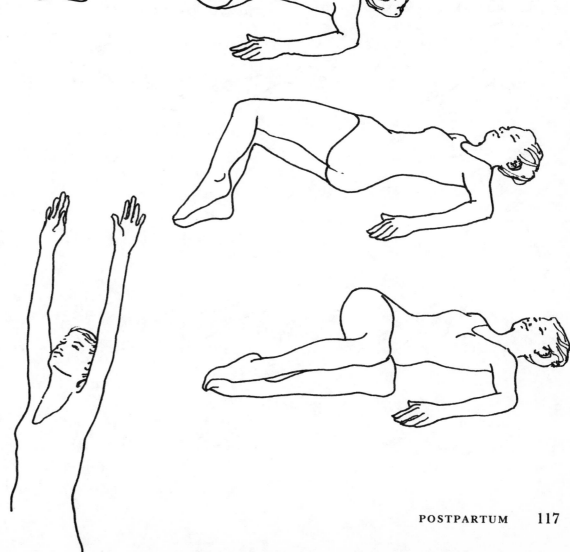

6. After the first month your abdominal muscles will have shrunk back to within ten percent of their original length. It's now time to begin gentle abdominal exercises. Here is one which Dr. Panter recommends in *Now That You've Had Your Baby . . . :*

Abdominal strengthening. To help flatten stomach and strengthen back muscles:

a. Lie flat on the floor. Raise right arm and left leg toward each other.

b. Hold to the count of two, then lower.

c. Then raise left arm and right leg toward each other. Keep arms and legs very straight and point your toes. Do six to each side.

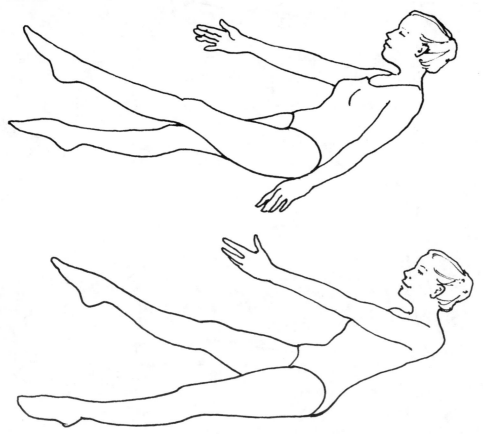

A FINAL WORD ABOUT YOUR BACK

She only weighed nine pounds at the time. I was kneeling and leaning over, and twisted to pick her up off the floor when something happened to my back. I'd suffered from backaches during pregnancy, and assumed that this was normal. I didn't do any postpartum exercises because, realistically, who has the time or the energy? I hardly had time to take a bath, no less exercise. To make a long story short, I was flat on my back for eight days, on medication and in horrible pain. I had to find someone to take care of both of us. I felt so vulnerable and angry, and aware that I just couldn't afford to be helpless now!

Suggestions.

1. Never bend from the waist without bending at the knees. Avoid any position in which your back is arched.

2. Carry the baby high and close to your chest rather than on your hip (easy to say and hard to do)!

3. Never twist your body to lift an object or the baby up or down; face the baby or object squarely.

4. In general, when you are seated, it is restful to the back to have the knees higher than the hips and firm support for the lower back. If you are

standing for a long time, cooking, for instance, you can give your back a partial rest by placing one foot on a low stool. You'll also find a rocking chair very restful, because the back-and-forth motion changes the groups of muscles being used.

POSTPARTUM BLUES

Most, but certainly not all, women experience some kind of mild depression after the birth. It has been thought that this may have some connection with the tremendous drops in estrogen and progesterone that follow delivery, and the triggering of the milk let-down reflex by yet another set of hormones. However, recent studies have shown that adoptive mothers and some fathers experience "postpartum blues." Hormonal changes, therefore, are probably only one of many contributors to the emotional volatility a new mother can feel. The anticipation as well as the fatigue of childbirth, the continued interruption of sleep—particularly **REM** or dream sleep, necessary for anyone's psychological well-being—the isolation, as well as the growing awareness of the realities of parenthood: all create stress.

Traditionally these "blues"—manifested as sadness, anger, a general frenziedness, and even paranoia, a distinct feeling that no one cares—begin to be felt about two to four days after delivery. But many women do not experience them until a week or two later. For some these feelings pass in a day or two, but for many of us, they come and go in waves that gradually diminish over the course of the next few weeks.

In any case, it's important to realize that these feelings are quite normal, and they will pass as you become more familiar with your baby and her needs, as well as your own new needs, and as your body restores itself. The worst is usually over when the baby begins to show signs of sleeping through the night.

In the meantime, talk about your feelings—your sadness or your anger—and cry all you want to. A great deal of tension has been stored up as you awaited the birth—anxiety about the baby's well-being, about the pain of childbirth, about your ability to take care of a helpless infant, and more. Talking can only help.

If you continue to feel depressed and find that you are unable to function in terms of taking care of your baby or yourself at any time, be it during postpartum or later, get professional help. Some of the signals of a deeper depression can be changes in your appetite or sleep patterns (either constant insomnia or constant sleeping), a serious inability to concentrate, and lack of interest in the world around you.

WHERE TO GO FOR HELP

There are several places where you can go for help: your obstetrician, your childbirth-preparation instructor, the social services department of the hospital where you delivered, or your family doctor. You can also get in touch with a local health clinic or any of the family-service organizations such as the Jewish Family Service or the United Way. If you have a local chapter of the National Organization for Women (NOW) in your community, they will be able to refer you for appropriate counseling.

SOME EARLY POSTPARTUM FEELINGS

In the hospital I was so high after the birth that I couldn't sleep the first night. I was so relieved to have delivered a healthy baby. I had to hold him and look at him and talked incessantly about his birth to anyone who would listen. Two days later when I was at home and got on the scale, then looked in our full-length mirror, I was really depressed. I looked seven months pregnant—I had only lost fifteen of the twenty-seven pounds I had gained, my stitches were killing me, my back hurt, and I was still in my grungy nightgown at 2:30 in the afternoon. I looked at the baby who had finally fallen asleep on our unmade bed. He already had dirty fingernails and white pimples on his cheeks! He was a mess. I was a mess. I started to cry.

My postpartum depression started on the third day in the hospital. I was feeling very down for a number of reasons. I had a postoperative fever after the cesarean and wasn't allowed to have Caitlin with me. My breasts were aching and the hospital only had two breast pumps available for the entire floor. I was sure they were out to undermine nursing for both of us. No one visited me that day, and my doctor dropped by to tell me she was going to the country for the weekend. I felt totally neglected. The final straw was the arrival of my special bland dinner for cesarean patients—white bread, white butter, white fish, white milk, white potatoes, and white custard. When I lifted the metal dome lid off, the dinner was covered with white ice crystals. They had forgotten to put it under the microwave oven. I was very paranoid at that point, and took all this to mean that no one cared for or appreciated me. I fell apart. I did regain some of my humor, though, within a day or two.

I cried a good deal on and off for the first few weeks. It wasn't always sadness, though. I cried because it felt good to let go of all the feelings I was having. Every time I thought of my own mother, I cried. I think I wanted her to be with me even though Bill was at home with me and being very helpful.

I felt very mortal, very fragile, yet also somehow part of the continuum of it all. On the one hand, I wanted to survive because I was strong and had to take care of this tiny, helpless baby, but I also knew she would go on living after David and I were dead. This didn't depress me so much as it moved me and unsettled me.

I was filled with what they call free-floating anxiety. You know—something awful is going to happen.

There were days when I just didn't think I could continue to cope. I was bone tired. Every day seemed like an eternity. It's all a blur now.

I felt bad about my irritability at Fred. He was being so incredibly wonderful and helpful—cooking, cleaning, taking over so I could sleep. He went to Bloomingdale's to get me a nursing bra, and I yelled at him when it didn't fit—things like that.

I had a recurring bad dream. I kept leaving Elizabeth on the subway. I'd realize this as I stood clutching her diaper bag, watching the train disappear down the tunnel. I'd get control of myself by saying, "It doesn't matter. That train will come back on the other side of the platform on its way uptown." I'd cross over and wait for it to return, but when the train did come, I couldn't remember if it was the right train. The passengers were all in a hurry and pushed me aside when I stopped to ask where my baby was. One woman said, "How could you be so careless as to have forgotten your baby on the New York City subway? Don't you know it goes all the way to Canarsie? You're not fit for motherhood!"

Order and cleanliness were all I craved besides sleep. The dirty dishes and the sea of laundry that had accumulated when I was in the hospital really got me down.

I didn't feel depressed during postpartum. I felt numb. When a friend came by to see Jenny for the first time, she asked, "Isn't your love for her so incredible that you'd sacrifice your life for her or even kill for her?" I dwelled on this for days. I wasn't so sure that I would have at that point. I wondered why I didn't love my baby as much as Eleanor suggested I should. Maybe I was abnormal. Several months later, I began to understand what she was talking about.

I had no postpartum blues until the baby was six months old, so I can't say that I was typical. At six months I was still fat, still too tired for sex, still uncurrent, and beginning to wonder whether or not I would ever feel like anything but a mother. Cabin fever was part of the diagnosis.

GETTING THE REST YOU NEED

To help mothers cope with the postpartum pe-

riod, we think fathers have a human and moral obligation to make sure the house is clean and that adequate food is provided for at least a week's meals, when they bring their wives home from the hospital. If he's very lucky, the pregnant woman awaiting her firstborn will be so bored and restless in the last weeks before delivery that she'll have scoured the house herself and frozen some meals. But that doesn't usually happen. Either the woman is too uncomfortable to be able to do much heavy housework, or the mother-in-law who has arrived to help out has served all the goodies ahead of time. Or the wife has never been much of a housekeeper or cook and doesn't realize that she'll feel even less like it after the baby comes.

So the house may be a shambles when labor begins. It doesn't matter. It also doesn't matter whether the husband has ever wielded a broom before. He can and must learn. The most intense postpartum depressions we heard of were triggered by the sight of a sinkful of dirty dishes, or the vacuum in the middle of the living room, or a bedroom strewn with toys. This is one time when the stakes are enormous, and no husband with genuine concern for his wife will subject her to this kind of stress. He can fight about liberating women later, but during her hospital stay he simply must man the mop, or suffer the consequences.

—VIRGINIA BARBER and
MERRILL MAGUIRE SKAGGS,
The Motherperson

SOME SUGGESTIONS

1. *Sleep whenever you can*—when the baby sleeps, or when your husband or helper (if you have one) is available to care for the baby. Take the phone off the hook. Some phones will stop beeping if you dial one or two numbers and stick a pencil in to lock the dial in place. If you are breast-feeding, your husband can bring the baby to you, change him, burp him, and stay up with him if he needs comforting—at least on some nights. *You have to function well in your job, too, the next day.* Relax several times a day.

2. Enlist the help of your husband for housework as well as care of the baby. Baby care is a learned thing, not instinctive. Newborn infants in need of comforts will accept them from anyone, and the only reason that mothers usually become more skilled at this is because they get so much practice. Never do housework when the baby sleeps!

3. Do not at this point ponder being too organized or efficient. Other mothers with babies whom you may know probably have older babies or older children and have had lots of practice at organizing their lives in order to maintain their psychic survival. There is plenty of time for this in the future.

4. Drink plenty of fluids (two to three quarts a day) whether you are nursing or not. These are needed to restore the fluid balance in your body and to help flush it of wastes and toxins accumulated during pregnancy. Also continue to take prenatal vitamins containing iron. Anemia adds to fatigue.

5. Try to spread your visitors out over the first couple of weeks. Company is especially nice and necessary once husbands or household help leave.

6. Rely on all the conveniences you might ordinarily consider to be luxuries—disposable diapers, nutritious take-out foods, having the groceries delivered, etc.

7. Try to get out with the baby as soon as you feel up to it. Even a short walk to the grocery store or around the block can be restorative. One of the most difficult parts of caring for a newborn—or any baby—is the lack of eventfulness. Getting out, even though it takes some planning, really punctuates the day.

8. The one thing about babies is that they grow and change daily, weekly, and monthly. Interrupted sleep, fussy periods, and full-blown colic all do end.

9. Be in touch with your own doctor and the pediatrician if you have any questions whatsoever.

RESOURCES

Postpartum in General

Boston Women's Health Collective, The, *Our Bodies/Ourselves,* Simon & Schuster, New York, 1976.

DelliQuadri, Lyn and Breckenridge, Kati, Ph.D., *Mother Care,* J.P. Tarcher, Inc., Los Angeles, 1978,

Noble, Elizabeth, *Essential Exercises for the Childbearing Year,* Houghton Mifflin, Boston, 1976.

Panter, Gideon G. and Linde, Shirley Motter, *Now That You've Had Your Baby,* David McKay, Inc., New York, 1976.

Cesarean Recovery

Ask at your hospital about a local chapter or write to:
Cesarean Sections, Education and Concern (CSEC)
Nancy Cohen
140 Vale Road
Needham, Massachusetts 02192

Donovan, Bonnie, *The Cesarean Birth Experience,* Beacon Press, Boston, 1977.

-12-
The Transition Into Motherhood

People will tell you before you have your baby that your life will change. They're right. But the trouble is we seldom have a realistic notion of how great the changes can be. Perhaps this is because the changes are so far-reaching and complex that they are hard to communicate. Then, too, most people assume that the changes are unique to themselves. ("If something as universally accepted and approved of as motherhood is this hard for me, then it's got to be *my* fault.")

We have largely abandoned the myth that marriage consists of living happily ever after, but the myth still persists to some degree that mothering is, or should be, a self-fulfilling and joyous duty. But the truth is that we go through a huge transition and maturational change when we have our first baby. The supports we have formerly relied on and taken for granted can all change radically or even disappear: a marriage that functioned smoothly; perhaps a job that provided satisfaction, self-esteem, and monetary returns; a circle of friends who share in-terests and offer support; mobility, the freedom to come and go without think-ing; and time—so much time—to our-selves.

As women, we have far more choices today about our own lives and destinies. We push ourselves—and are pulled—in many directions. But after the baby is born in almost all cases a couple reverts to more traditional roles. The woman, particularly if she stays at home, usually assumes the greater part of the baby's care. What does this mean?

It means a lot of physical work—feed-ing, changing, bathing, protecting the baby from danger, and soothing the baby when she needs comfort, regardless of how you may feel. It means making a million small decisions that involve the heart as well as reason—not just "Do I put this undershirt on the baby?" but "Can I possibly leave her in the care of a person who neither knows her well nor loves her as much as I do?" It also means conquering many logistical problems, in-cluding getting to the grocery and back in less than thirty minutes before the baby falls apart. It means routine, details, and very little free time.

The pressures and duties can appear as heavy limitations on our new freedoms. We sometimes respond with tremendous efforts to make good use of our little bits of free time. If you stay at home, there may be a million projects—things you wanted to do once you weren't working. But it can be difficult to feel a sense of accomplishment when what you start is seldom completed as quickly as you wish it were. And then what, if anything, does a "project" have to do with the rest of the world? Being a mother can mean wondering if you are still an interesting person, and whether you work or not, you may question your ability to be a "good mother."

Your relationship with some people may also change. You may be drawn closer to your mother or further apart— or both at the same time. And you may find that some old friends, particularly those who are single and those who are childless, may not understand how you are feeling. They may not be able to offer you the support they once did because, you suspect, they do not fully understand the changes you are going through. You may hardly understand them yourself.

If you do not return to a job, you may find yourself resenting those who still work—for example, your husband. When he walks out the door for what you may begin to perceive as an eight-hour break, God forbid that he fails to return exactly when he says he will, because it can be lonely to be at home with a baby all day. You may have many rational discussions but just as many irrational ones (arguments) about sharing child care. And you may feel that you are in the ridiculous position of asking for favors if you suggest he take care of *his* baby for an entire afternoon. There is less time for a husband and wife to spend together and less privacy. Spontaneity no longer exists. You may not feel like making love because you are tired or simply not interested. This can add to the tension.

You may discover that the other side of mother love and mother instinct is anger and feelings of inadequacy and ineptitude. And you may feel guilty, ungrateful, or immature for complaining about your lot because mothers have, after all, always done these things. But why was it such a well-kept secret? Well, it wasn't a secret. It was just that mothers of previous generations did not have the range of alternatives against which to measure the duties of motherhood that we have.

Yet the fact remains that the rewards are many. It's just that they are not nearly as tangible as the sacrifices, and are harder to articulate. The apparent limitations on freedom, for example, are anything but limiting. They are part of a profound growth process that can expand your horizons more than anything else ever has.

I've yet to meet anyone who doesn't feel she has grown, expanded, and matured through becoming a parent. In terms of what you may have come to expect of your life, parenting is a high-risk undertaking. But any venture that promises great rewards must be risky. Though few of us slide easily into motherhood, *we would never not be that baby's mother.*

Question: *What were the difficult adjustments you had to make when you became a parent?*

Answer: *Having a baby is such a huge decision. It's a privilege for a woman to have this choice nowadays. But in some ways it makes it even harder. You postpone pregnancy—because you don't think you're ready yet, because you're still trying to find out who you are. Another year goes by and another. You think about it a lot. You finally decide to go ahead, and make this rational choice to have a baby. During pregnancy you're a star. Life goes on as usual. You're well-fed, well-rested, well-exercised, and well-read. When you enter the delivery room, maybe you're even in control and on top of it. Then it's over. Suddenly you have no more choices, and you're out of control. There isn't even time to think about your identity. There's hardly time to brush your teeth! Do you understand, at all, what I'm talking about?*

A: *The most difficult adjustment for me was becoming relatively inactive after working for nine years. I missed the stimulation I received from other adults while teaching. But basically I was in such a state of euphoria after his birth, that I only started feeling these things after the first six months when life had become more routine. I also still find getting up at 5:30 very frustrating. Who can ever accept that?*

A: *I never realized how incredibly difficult it would be to leave Ann with a sitter—as tired as I felt and as crazy as I was to get out. I haven't yet found one whom I feel 100 percent confident about.*

A: *Doug and I hardly make love anymore. I'm out by 10:30. It's causing a lot of tension between us.*

A: *Sometimes I feel a day is lost. Paul will come home from work and ask me what I've done today. Well, I haven't done anything except the usual. Sometimes I feel like nothing is happening. There are so few events in my life. It takes such discipline to create them!*

A: Lack of mobility was the biggest shock. A short trip eight minutes away to the grocery store requires real planning. I suppose this is temporary, and someday I'll have all the time I need. But when?

A: The most difficult adjustment was having so little time to be alone or with my husband. This is easing off considerably now that Joel is older. I made my baby my priority, but I almost lost myself in the process. I'm not convinced that this is the way it should be. I had assumed a child would integrate easily into our lives, but it didn't work out that way.

A: The biggest adjustment for me was not being told that I was doing a good job all of the time.

A: Strangely enough, I have found the constant interference of strangers the most difficult adjustment. (Is she too cold? Where are her mittens? Should she be out today? etc.) People feel they have the right to criticize, comment, compare (Isn't she walking yet?) when it comes to babies, whereas they wouldn't dream of doing this in any other situation.

A: The time adjustment is hardest for me. I know that I'm grabbing for time for myself so much that this sometimes destroys my pleasure in being with the baby. I wish I could let go, let her in more instead of being so afraid that she will engulf me.

A: My self-esteem plummeted. I felt less competent all the way around. I used to run a department with twenty people in it. Now I don't know how I did it. I did have an interesting discussion with another woman, though. She felt that baby care was a right-hemisphere kind of experience (feelings, emotions, intuition), in battle with the other hemisphere (the exercise of logic, reason, etc.). When you have a baby, you're also tuned in on a different level. Your hearing changes, your sense of touch changes, you sense things about a baby, a cry can affect your whole body—definitely left-hemisphere stuff. Your brain just simply isn't functioning in quite the same way as before. And maybe this is what has shaken my confidence. The part of me that had gotten tremendous satisfaction from being able to think problems through to completion is totally boggled.

A: I am not what I would describe as bored staying home with Timothy, but I am afraid that I am becoming a boring person.

A: When Eliza and I spend the whole day alone together without seeing or talking to another adult I get a little crazy. If we're alone for a couple of days because the weather is bad or she is sick, as she has been so often this winter with ear infections, and John is away on a business trip, I really get crazy.

A: We are broke! That's been really hard. Without my job, we have nothing extra.

A: The most difficult adjustment for me was to learn to accept imperfection—or rather my own limitations; that is, to realize that I can't do it all myself as well as I would like to do it, and to accept this about other people as well.

A: As far as I am concerned, one of the biggest problems I had adjusting to motherhood was the isolation and the loneliness of it all. I simply didn't know anyone in my community with a young child or a baby. My other friends worked, and when I did see them I felt this pressure to live up to their vision of my former self. I felt they didn't know what I was going through. If they tried to commiserate, I was on the defensive because how could they possibly know? I didn't want them to think it was that bad. If they didn't want to hear about Nell, I was on the defensive because she really was the center of my life. It wasn't their fault. You really need a peer group when you're a mother. Only somebody who is in the same boat can offer quite the same kind of support, sympathy—and respect for what you're doing.

A: We had to adjust to what I called custody battles . . . we were in the midst of one of our many arguments that started with the birth of the baby. This argument was based on another argument where Peter had gotten so mad that he had stomped out of the house. Our current argument had to do with my anger that he had the freedom to walk out, whereas though I might have wanted to, I never would or could run out and leave the baby with anyone as angry as he was. Anyway, we were arguing away. He said, "I want a divorce!" I said, "So do I!" He then said: "I want custody of Amanda." I was stunned. I said, "You do? Are you serious? You've got to be kidding!" Something clicked with both of us: I could see it suddenly occurred *to him what a tremendous amount of work it would involve, and that, just as suddenly, he appreciated what I had to do. We ended up laughing at the absurdity of it all.*

A: I don't feel nearly as glamorous or sexy anymore. I found even by the time I was six months pregnant that I'd stopped using flirting as a way to relate to the men at work. Flirting was not a big part of my life, but it's hard on the ego to feel like such an old bag, an old shoe without possibilities anymore. Now, practically the only man I ever talk to is my husband.

A: It's clear to me that along with the birth of your first child comes the implied dismissal of the child in you. Who's going to take care of you? The biggest adjustment for me was actually believing that I was a parent. Isn't that what it's really about for all of us?

Question: *What are some of the rewards of having a baby?*

Answer: *I could not possibly have imagined the flow of love that keeps you going.*

A: My baby has taught me more patience. I am more patient with myself and everyone else.

A: Sara has given me a sense of fulfillment, a broadening. I am more assertive, more confident, feel more of an adult now that I have someone to protect, someone who depends on me.

A: There is no doubt that the birth of my son has cramped my freedom. But he has brought out that aspect of my character that is more sharing and patient and understanding.

A: I think having Eliot has sort of shaped me a bit, made me more aware of responsibilities. Having someone depending on me for everything is a very sobering experience.

A: I feel that the baby has provided me with a sense of direction in that my day is pretty well planned out for me. If nothing else, it's taxed my sense of organization and my own creativity to think up interesting things for us both to do. I do see how important it is, though, to keep up my own interests.

A: Having Elizabeth really was the beginning of our marriage, even though she came four years after the ceremony. Until her birth Carl and I had functioned more or less autonomously, in our different jobs and interests. We spent many evenings apart because he was involved in politics and I in the theater. We'd had lots of fun together, but we'd never worked together—had so much joy together—the way one does with a baby.

A: I am a more physical person now that I have a baby—quicker to love and hug everyone. I'm also much more easygoing now. I enjoy singing and dancing now—since I did so much of it with the baby.

A: I think I can understand much more about human survival just watching Dana as he struggled to master each new physical feat. He practiced—was frustrated—and would repeat something over and over again, until he could do it. One can't help but be impressed and inspired by that kind of determination, that

energy and curiosity.

A: I am much more tender. I am easily and deeply moved by stories about any form of child neglect or abuse—though I'm clearer now on where that anger comes from.

A: After many, many struggles Mike and I have finally worked out a division of tasks around the house that mushroomed when Lucy was born. You wouldn't believe the laundry that a baby generates, the crumbs, and all those toys, with little pieces.

A: I learned to let go a little, which includes letting go of the baby a little each day as she becomes more and more of a person.

A: I always knew it was worth it, but the day Andrew and I had our first private joke confirmed it. I had just mopped up an unbelievably messy bowel movement—the fourth of the day. I don't usually let him go diaperless in cold weather, but I was sitting there in a state of despair on his bedroom floor, and he crawled away, pulled himself up to stand at the end of his dresser—and then he peed. As I was thinking—oh, Andrew, how can you do this to me—he let out a scream of delight. He was so thrilled by the spectacle of his huge stream of pee going across the room and the sound it made when it hit the floor. He looked at me. He was waiting for a reaction. I started laughing. Then he started laughing, then he got down and crawled over to me, pulled himself up on my shoulder, and gave me a huge hug. I will always remember this as being the first time when I knew that he knew that I was okay. He was really communicating. This is the direct feedback that we all need, and when it finally does happen, what in the world is comparable? It's enough to make me cry.

A: Having Natalie has made me more political, more in touch with my community. You do not have to be a card-carrying feminist to have your blood boil at the lack of child-care resources in a city of eight million people. I've become a joiner after having been a loner for most of my life.

A: We have many new friends. We've actually met two couples with babies whom we like to spend time with.

A: We're pretty broke, but life is much simpler. We no longer entertain on the grand scale that we once did—or feel that we have to seek entertainment—be cultured—do so many things to improve our minds. We're entertained enough as it is by Matthew. He's very funny.

A: Everyone talks to you when you have a baby. Suddenly you are available to strangers. You meet people. In an odd way you're respected and trusted when you're pushing a baby carriage.

A: At first I made frantic, fruitless efforts to organize the unorganizable. But now I am organized. You have to be.

A: Having her really helped me learn the value of my own time and my own work. I don't waste my time now. I either do something, or simply try to enjoy myself the way she does—wholeheartedly.

A: Becoming a mother has given me more respect for all the other mothers I know—my own included. I see how very difficult and humanizing the job is, and I cannot help but feel that we are all basically pretty good people who are trying very hard.

A: Rewards? It's obvious. The birth of your own baby is nothing short of a miracle. Loving and nurturing a child is an extraordinary experience!

RESOURCES

The Transition Into Motherhood

Barber, Virginia and Skaggs, Merrill M., *The Motherperson,* Bobbs Merrill, New York, 1977.

Bernard, Jessie, *The Future of Motherhood,* Dial, 1974.

Bittman, Sam and Zalk, Sue Rosenberg, *Expectant Fathers,* Hawthorn, New York, 1979.

Chess, Stella et al., *A Psychological Approach to Parenthood without Guilt,* Penguin, New York, 1977.

Lazarre, Jane, *The Mother Knot,* McGraw-Hill, New York, 1976.

Le Shan, Eda, *How to Survive Parenthood,* Warner, New York, 1973.

McBride, Angela Barron, *The Growth and Development of Mothers,* Harper & Row, New York, 1973.

Rich, Adrienne, *Of Woman Born,* W. W. Norton, New York, 1976.

-13- Getting Control of Your Time and Your Life

After Julianna was born, for the first time in my life, I found myself secretly poring over articles in women's magazines with titles like "Ten Ways to Save Hours Every Day, and Still be Fresh, Thin, Healthy, Beautiful, Interesting, a Fun Supermom and Sexy to Boot." I had become part of a huge audience for self-help literature—the harried housewife, the harassed mother—but I had to get control of my time and my life somehow. I didn't know where to begin.

People may tell you that a baby is time-consuming and that your life will change drastically. Still the amount of time a baby requires comes as a shock to all of us. You are not incompetent, crazy, or lazy if you find yourself still in your nightgown at ten in the morning, even though you've been up since six. If you feel somewhat out of touch with current events, and have not read a newspaper in weeks or a book in months, you're not unusual either.

If you are relaxed and easygoing and have been able to rid your life of many of its "shoulds," so much the better. You are one step ahead of most of us and *should* skip this section. If your baby is under six months old, you may also skip this section. It's too soon to worry about being organized.

A SELF-HELP EXERCISE

A terrifically useful exercise is to keep track of how you spend a day. In a notebook mark off the hours in fifteen-minute intervals. Carry this notebook around with you, and make notes about what you have been doing, *including your feelings* (pleased, harassed, tired, happy, angry, delighted, proud, guilty, grateful, lucky, etc.). Later, when you have time, fill in the notes in more detail and expand your feelings. Put an *A* next to any entry that has caused you anxiety—even if it is something as intangible as the weather. Put the whole thing away for a few days, then come back to it.

A number of things will become clear. The most strikingly obvious will be the extent to which your time is fragmented. You will also be amazed at the tremendous number of decisions you make in a day, and the amount of physical work you are doing. *You should feel good about this!* A pattern will emerge around the *A*s. Some of them, as in my case, will have to do with concrete, practical matters—a snowsuit which is difficult to get on and off the baby, or cats that need to be fed, or a hundred and fifty trips up and down the steps. But just as many of the *A*s will have to do with attitudes. I discovered, for example, that I spent considerable time worrying over trivial matters, and that I was overly critical of myself as a housewife and mother. I was pretty resentful that I had no time to pursue my work or other interests—even though I was still quite unclear about those interests in the first place. I did not want a job as much as a balance to mothering. And I was not allowing myself enough time to derive any satisfaction from the small amount of editorial work I was doing in an effort to create this balance.

Then what do you do? Attack those things that are bothering you, *but not all at once.* Group the practical *A*s into one list, and the attitudinal *A*s into another list. Establish priorities. The two groups are interrelated, but do not fall into the trap of dealing only with the practical *A*s. The attitudinal *A*s are even more important and take the most time and effort to scale down and/or eliminate. They are deeply ingrained in all of us.

A DAY WITH AN EIGHT-MONTH-OLD

Following is a minute-by-minute account of a day with an eight-month-old. I kept track of several days in search of the "typical" one, which I never found. This was the grimmest day, and I must confess that I chose it on purpose. Anyone reading this has got to feel more efficient and organized than I. The details exist because I carried around a tape recorder thinking that I would write an article on saving time when you have a baby. Instead, I decided to write a book. But books and articles aside, the exercise was extremely useful for me: I was able to make some changes that improved the quality of my day-to-day existence.

6:35 A.M.: Hear Caitlin crying, but am determined to leave her in crib until at least 7:00 because she woke up twice last night. I reason she must be tired. Hope she'll become interested in toys I dumped into crib at 2 A.M.

6:40 A.M.: Can't stand crying, so get up to look in her room. It's my morning on while Charlie sleeps. Toys on floor. Caitlin tangled in blanket and trying to stand up. Has hiccups. Bring cup of water because I'm trying to get her to use cup. She chokes and splutters with first sip. Give up. Change her, noticing all those iron drops she has to take are making her constipated. Carry her to phone to call pediatrician, but look at clock realizing he doesn't take calls until 7:00.

6:50 A.M.: Take her downstairs and put her in playpen with some toys. I warm up a bottle because house is freezing. Worry about dumping her into playpen, but floors still cold, not to mention dirty.

6:55 A.M.: Hand her bottle which she can hold herself. Worry if I should do this. Maybe she needs to be held? Wonder if I should ask pediatrician about this. But don't have time to hold her because have to make pureed apples and pears to go with cereal from scratch. We're out of bananas. Put kettle on for coffee.

7:00 A.M.: Call pediatrician to tell him iron drops are making her constipated. He recommends more water, fruit, and some Maalox if it gets really bad. Decide not to ask about holding her own bottle, feeling he might think it a foolish question—knowing he would suggest the cup, which is a pain in the neck.

7:10 A.M.: Finish straining fruit. Then feed her breakfast on my lap. High chair tray still dirty from last night. Bad housewife! Take it off and soak in sink. She keeps sliding down in the high chair anyway.

7:25 A.M.: Carry her upstairs to dress her. Look for sweater, but realize it is still in dryer two flights down. Decide to dress her in two undershirts plus polo shirt. She wiggles, rolls over, and almost falls off changing table. Blow on her stomach. She laughs. Put on her white booties, which are black on the bottom. Feel bad again about dirty kitchen floor.

7:30 A.M.: Pick her up, go back downstairs, and put her on kitchen floor so I can finish making coffee. She pulls herself up to stand by counter, edges over to stool and pulls it down on herself with a crash. Her head goes "crack" on the floor. She screams. Pick her up to comfort her.

7:35 A.M.: Realize I've let coffee boil over on stove. Put her down on floor. Dump coffee out and start over. Baby has put a penny she found on floor into her mouth. "No!" I scream, prying open her mouth to retrieve penny. "No mouth!" Put her down. She whines to be held.

7:40 A.M.: Carry her back upstairs to tell Charlie to get up. Think about getting dressed myself, but realize new batch of coffee is probably boiling on the stove. Leave baby on bedroom floor for father, who is just waking up, to watch. Run down and turn off coffee.

7:45 A.M.: Return and discover baby has been put back in bed and is sucking her thumb. Explain that she shouldn't be in crib now because it isn't time for nap, and I don't want her to fall asleep now. I need nap time later to work. Explain she is bored, not tired. He's irritated. Says it's hard to shave as baby crawls around, stands up, and falls down all the time. The crib is safer. I say, "That's not news to me."

7:50 A.M.: Get dressed myself while Caitlin plays on floor with my shoes. "No mouth!" I scream. Ask Charlie if he'd mind watching her while he does his exercises so I can finish making breakfast and get laundry out of dryer. He says fine.

8:05 A.M.: Discover washer is not working and panic. Call Charlie down, feeling very unliberated. "Where is baby?" I ask. "In living room," he says.

"Did you put loveseat in front of stairs?" I ask. "No," he says. I run out just as she is about to go upstairs. Grab her. Push loveseat across stairway. Put her back and return. Washer is not broken. The hose was bent, and that is why water wouldn't fill up. Charlie is irritated, though, because broken antique desk is in the way. Further claims that furnace is drying out the wood. We argue. Desk wouldn't be here if he would fix it as promised. Argument curtailed because we hear a crash from living room. Rush out. Phone on the floor, baby trying to dial. Grab her. Replace phone. Search through toy basket for her plastic phone. Give it to her. No interest.

8:15 A.M.: Leave baby with Charlie and go upstairs to finish making our breakfast. Charlie calls me down to see Caitlin doing exercises on mat with him. We both laugh. He's doing pushups and she is too, sort of. Hear on radio that it will snow by noon and realize I've put baby's snowsuit in washer. Panic! No possibility of going out for next two hours.

8:20 A.M.: Sit down alone with cup of coffee, pencil, and paper to make a to-do list so I won't panic about what I will do all day.

8:25 A.M.: Cats meowing to get fed, so get up and feed them. Start to clean up kitchen and scrub high-chair tray.

8:40 A.M.: Charlie brings Caitlin upstairs, reporting she had great fun standing and looking in bathroom mirror as he took shower. Pats it, babbles at it. I hold her and she feels damp all over from steam, but decide to let it go as house is warming up now. She jumps up and down in my lap, then sneezes. Feel like a bad mother.

8:50 A.M.: Put her in Jolly Jumper in kitchen doorway. She twirls around and makes pass at cat's tail as he goes by. Look for iron drops, which I'd forgotten to give her at breakfast. Water plants. One is dead.

8:55 A.M.: Warm up coffee and sit down with Charlie to eat. We both talk to baby as she bounces happily in doorway. Wonder if all this bouncing is good for her legs.

9:05 A.M.: Charlie leaves, late as usual. I swear I hear Caitlin say "Bye-bye." Continue to work on to-do list, which reads: pay bills (find them first), shop for dinner, go to cleaner's, go to library to get new card and find out hours, pick up cat medicine at drugstore, ask tenant for rent, mail it to bank, find mail deposit slips (find stamps first), work on manuscript of friend's book. Desperately need my broken desk fixed, so I can put all this stuff in one place.

9:10 A.M.: Baby has hiccups and is

fussy. Take her out of Jumper. Give her iron drops, which she spits out on white shirt. She cries and rubs eyes. But don't want to put her to sleep yet—until she has iron drops, or I'll forget again. Dryer buzzing.

9:15 A.M.: Carry her down to dryer and get stuff out. Bring it to living room to sort. Move loveseat to block stairs. Get her cup of water for hiccups. She chokes and splutters. Throws cup at loveseat. Carry her back upstairs to get bottle of juice, which stops hiccups. Go back down to continue sorting laundry.

9:25 A.M.: Baby starts to cry, so pick her up to take her to bed, but phone rings. Answer it. It's friend asking me how I'm doing with proofreading. Say I haven't gotten to it yet, but definitely will. Just haven't had time. Baby crying, can't talk now.

9:30 A.M.: Take her up to her room. Change her and put her down for her nap. Put toys in crib for her to play with. Run down to get iron drops. But baby out like a light by time I get back.

9:45 A.M.: Sit down to start proofreading. Phone rings. It's Charlie. Report that baby said "Bye-bye"—maybe. We agree. She's a genius. Charlie reminds me to pay mortgage. Tell him it's on my list.

9:50 A.M.: Sit down to start proofreading again. Can't spell any better than the author. Not cut out for this kind of work. Feel depressed. Vow that Caitlin will learn to spell. No progressive education for her!

9:55 A.M.: Get up to search for dictionary. Remember it's in baby's room, which used to be study and still has all our books in it.

10:00 A.M.: Go back to proofreading.

10:45 A.M.: Snow has started falling heavily. Go up to see if baby is awake. She is. Bring her downstairs. With great difficulty, put her in snowsuit, which has zippers running down the insides of both legs. Put on a pair of socks, two pairs of booties, but wonder if that is enough. Put her in playpen, and run upstairs to get pair of Charlie's socks. She cries as I leave. Come back, and put the big black socks on. She looks absurd. Am all ready to go. Then decide to call drugstore just to make sure cat medicine is ready; put baby on floor. She makes a beeline for cat. Drugstore line is busy.

11:10 A.M.: Finally out the door.

12:00 noon: Get home, but without cat medicine because vet hadn't called in prescription yet. Library won't give card unless I show proof of address, which I didn't have with me. Typical New York attitude! Feel like a failure.

12:10 P.M.: Put Caitlin in high chair. Give her chicken and sweet potatoes. All over her face. She rubs potatoes into her hair and keeps sliding down in high chair. Take her out. Hold her in my lap.

12:20 P.M.: Put her on floor so I can unpack groceries. She knocks over the cat food, which I forgot to elevate, and samples it. "No!" I scream.

12:30 P.M.: Carry her downstairs to help sort laundry on the living room couch. Move loveseat to block stairs. She pulls pile of towels down on herself and laughs. So much for folded towels. She crawls around, heading for the rubber tree. Pick her up and place her in front of toy basket, which interests her for a while, until I finish folding laundry and put it in basket out of the way.

12:50 P.M.: Look at book and a women's magazine with Caitlin. Notice she likes pictures of babies in Pampers ad. Laughs at them. Also keeps looking out the window at snow. Points at it. We stand at window and talk. The snow is already about three inches deep. I wonder how I'm going to get back out to drugstore to get the cat's medicine.

1:05 P.M.: Take her upstairs and change her. Put her in crib and start out the door. She's standing up, crying and banging on the crib. Go back, lay her down. Wind up musical mobile, cover her up and start out door. She's standing up and crying and banging on the crib again. Go back, lay her down, pat her on her back and rock the crib back and forth. Wind up mobile and start out the door. She starts to cry again. Go back, wind up mobile, give her a kiss. Go toward door, this time close it behind me. Go downstairs. Turn on water in kitchen so I can't hear. Wash her lunch dishes, and eat the remaining tablespoon of potatoes and chicken, and drink a cup of coffee.

1:20 P.M.: Sit down to do proofreading.

2:15 P.M.: Hear her crying. Am determined to leave her there, once again reasoning that she should play with the toys I dumped in.

2:20 P.M.: Can't stand crying. Go upstairs and get her out of bed. Put her on bedroom floor and make phone call to new acquaintance with baby. Ask her if she knows how to keep baby from sliding out of the high chair. She suggests a piece of foam for traction. Tell her about proofreading. She says, "Oh, can't take full-time motherhood?" I grow defensive and explain that I only do it while she naps and at night. Baby has crawled under the bed and bumps head. Cries. Put down phone to reach under and get her. Hold her on my lap and continue conversation. Acquaintance wants to know how

I plan to get any work done during naps and at night. She's too tired to do anything. Plans to return to work part-time when baby is in nursery school. Explain that I plan to find some child care, so I have more time to work. She points out that this will require all the money I make and adds that eight months is a terrible time to introduce baby-sitters, due to separation anxiety and stranger anxiety. Grow more defensive. Explain that I plan to find wonderful person and introduce her gradually. "Good luck," she says. Baby starts to cry, and use this as excuse to hang up. Cross acquaintance off list of possible new friends.

2:30 P.M.: Take Caitlin downstairs and put her in Jolly Jumper while I look for bills and checkbook. Talk to her while I write checks. Call vet about missing cat-medicine prescription. Says he called it in in the morning.

2:55 P.M.: Call drugstore to make sure. They have it now.

3:00 P.M.: Go through whole snowsuit routine again. Find stamps for bills. Look out window. Snow now six inches deep. Decide I can't use stroller and will have to carry her. Pick her up to go out, but realize she's had bowel movement all over overalls and snowsuit because disposable diaper tape has come undone. Plan to write angry letter to Pampers

company with a carbon to Consumers' Union. They've ruined my day.

3:05 P.M.: Carry baby upstairs. Take all her clothes off and wash her off in bathroom sink. Re-dress her in three layers of clothing because snowsuit is wrecked.

3:25 P.M.: Finally go out the door carrying her wrapped in a blanket, under my cape.

4:00 P.M.: Return with cat medicine. Had to wait for prescription to be filled. Decide to take my business elsewhere—to a druggist who tells the truth and has chairs to sit on. Undress baby and put her on kitchen floor while I catch the sick cat (we have two of them). Try to get medicine down his throat, but he throws up. Decide to wait until Charlie gets home so he can help hold him. Baby edging toward the radiator. Grab her. Say, "Hot."

4:15 P.M.: Give her half a bottle, which she drinks while I feed cats. Sit down to think about dinner. Phone rings. It's Charlie telling me he's bringing Herb home because the snow has gotten too bad for Herb to make forty-mile drive up Palisades Parkway, which has probably been closed anyway. "Can't Herb stay in a hotel?" Too late for that because Charlie already invited him. "What about the dirty floors—and the messy house?"

"Herb doesn't care," Charlie says. "I do," I say. Charlie says he will cook. I say okay. He then asks about the sidewalk. Has it been shoveled, apologizing immediately for asking such a stupid question, but tenant has a right not to kill himself. It's in the lease. At least sprinkle with rock salt.

4:30 P.M.: Take baby to utility room to look for rock salt. Wrap her in blanket and stuff her under my cape. Go out and throw the salt on the sidewalk. Let baby throw some too. She loves this.

5:00 P.M.: Put her on kitchen floor. Feed cats, but she won't let them eat. Keeps grabbing tails, even though cats are up on counter. Put cats and their dinner out in entryway. Slam door. Yell at cats. Baby cries. Pick her up to comfort her.

5:15 P.M.: Warm up her dinner. Give her pots and pans to play with while I search for spaghetti for our dinner.

5:30 P.M.: Feed her her dinner in my lap. She keeps grabbing spoon and won't eat spinach. Give her piece of banana which she can hold. Eats some. Throws the rest on the floor.

5:50 P.M.: Take her upstairs and undress her for bath. Turn on shower to warm up bathroom. Undress her for bath, which she loves. She sits and splashes, drinks water out of measuring spoons, and I wonder if bath water is harmful to drink. To tired to argue. Tries to stand up holding onto soap dish. "No," I keep saying as I sit her down, "you'll slip." Each time I sit her down, she tries again—laughing. Finally distract her by turning on the water. She's interested in measuring spoons, so I clean the toilet while she plays. Face fact that her hair needs washing. A terrible scene follows.

6:10 P.M.: Take her out of tub into her room to put on her pajamas, which I forgot to bring into the bathroom. She shivers. While dressing her, phone rings. Carry to our room. It's Sears Roebuck about the dryer warranty. I ask how they have the nerve to call at such an hour. The baby is naked and crawling across our bed to the edge. I slam phone down. Feel better having yelled at someone.

6:15 P.M.: Finish dressing her in pajamas. Phone rings. It's Charlie saying he's halfway home but subways are running slow. Thinks he and Herb will walk the rest of the way home. "No, please," I say, "that will take hours. Stick with subway," I advise. He says, "Don't put Caitlin to bed, though, so Herb can meet her. Just relax," he advises.

6:20 P.M.: Take his advice. Turn on television and watch the news with Caitlin on the bed. Play peek-a-boo with pillows. Give her old *TV Guide*, which she tears up while I start to put laundry away. Why am I doing this? I stop putting laundry away and get back on the bed with the baby. We play hide-the-toy-under-the-pillow. We play airplane. I hold her hands while she jumps up and down. She's laughing. I jump up and down with her.

6:55 P.M.: Hear door downstairs opening. "Daddy's home!" Visible delight on Caitlin's part. Carry her down and hand her to Charlie. Remember that I have to find snow shovel. Go down to utility room to find it.

7:05 P.M.: Come up with shovel. Charlie and Caitlin are looking out the window at the snow. Suggest that I shovel snow while Charlie puts baby to bed and Herb makes me a drink. They agree. I go outside, happy to be alone in the dark and the snow. "Don't forget her iron drops, they are by her crib."

7:30 P.M.: Come in, noting that the light in her room is off. She must be asleep. My "real" work is over—for today, at least.

As you can see, there were many *A*s in this day. I made some changes *over a period of months*. Here's what they were.

1. I decided to give the cats to my par-

ents-in-law, who live in the country. The cats weren't getting the attention they used to get from us. They were one more thing for me to think about. (I also lent my in-laws the rubber tree, which flourished for two years under my mother-in-law's green thumb.)

2. I borrowed a snowsuit from a friend with an older baby. This snowsuit was easier to get on and off. Zippers on outside of legs, and it had feet attached to it. I didn't see the point of buying shoes until she could walk. I kept the other snowsuit in case of "accidents."

3. I found a new drugstore that delivers. I also found out that my grocery store delivers. Had never thought to ask before.

4. I decided to spend an evening every two weeks making enough baby food to last that long, and freeze it. I also bought some commercial baby food to have on hand when I didn't feel like being organized.

5. We totally baby-proofed the house and installed safety gates, which we had resisted doing because we knew we would be moving into our tenant's apartment, which was much safer, in two months.

6. I realized that I hadn't eaten anything but breakfast all day and had had several cups of coffee. Still haven't conquered this problem, but went out and bought a bottle of wheat germ and immediately felt healthier just looking at it.

7. I decided to make some plans for the rest of the winter so that neither the baby nor I felt so isolated. This meant overcoming shyness and calling some of the mothers I hardly knew in my community and inviting them over. By the following fall, I'd found four compatible friends, whom I started a play group with.

8. The housework, particularly the undone laundry and the dirty floors, were making me feel like a "bad housewife." I vowed that when we moved we would have the washer and dryer as close to the bedroom as possible, and that Charlie and I would do the laundry in the evenings. Charlie agreed to wash the floors, but only when he felt like it and as long as I didn't nag him. The floors are still often dirty, but I keep telling myself that I'm a nice person even if I'm not the greatest housekeeper.

9. We decided we had to get our morning act together. We tried getting organized the night before, but this didn't work. So we abandoned our system of one person getting up while the other one stayed in bed, except on weekends. We decided it was more important for him to get out of the house on time and come home on time, when I was desperate, than take care of baby in the morning and leave late. We're still working on our morning act. It's far from perfect, but we *try* not to fight then, at least.

10. I took the phone off the hook when the baby napped, so that I could work. I was still frustrated, and eventually allowed that if I was going to write anything, I needed longer blocks of time during the day. I was too tired at night. I needed some child care. After much searching and trial and error, I found two good people, who have worked for us since. I treat them like gold. But did not, and have not yet, overcome guilt about choosing to work, be it for the six hours a week when I started, or the thirty-five when I finished. My problem, but certainly a common one.

11. I also decided that I needed some time to have fun alone and with Charlie. On weekends he takes care of the baby one afternoon, while I do the mornings. During these times we do what we want to do

even if it is totally frivolous. We try to go out together at least twice a month.

12. Since I was destined to live in a multiple-story house, I cut down on some of the stair-climbing by leaving diapers and extra clothes on each floor.

13. Rather than nag Charlie about fixing my desk, I paid to have it repaired by a professional. At least the bills are all in one place, even if they don't get paid on time.

14. I finally read our copy of *How to Get Control of Your Time and Your Life* (by Alan Lakein, Peter H. Wyden, New York, 1973), a book almost as useful to a new mother as Dr. Spock's. I actually did the exercises in it, which have to do with establishing priorities. I realized that the first place to start was with my to-do list. I tended to put the most important to-do's last—like my work. I stuffed the exercises into the book and looked back at them a year later, and was surprised at how many more things I was doing and how much better I felt about myself.

-14-Parent Information and Support Groups

I wish, in addition to preparing for natural childbirth together, that Bill and I could have prepared for the difficulties of adjusting your life to a new baby. I don't mean how to give them baths, hold them, mix up formula, or sterilize bottles, either, but how to understand them and deal with some of the very real logistical and psychological problems that new parents face.

I found that I could get an abortion, contraception, or rape and sex counseling, but nothing in the direction of postpartum support. Doesn't anybody care about what happens after the baby is born? When I called various mental health and women's centers, I was invariably told that they didn't deal with that *area. If I asked if they could refer me elsewhere, they admitted that they wouldn't know where to refer me. One center asked that if I found a place, would I please let them know.*

Life with a baby can be much more pleasant if you have people to talk to who are experiencing the same things you are and have many of the same questions and concerns that aren't always the pediatrician's bailiwick.

Following is a description of a parent information and support group for mothers and their babies by Phyllis Silverman, a group leader trained in early childhood development. Included are some suggestions about where to find a group for yourself or how to start one on your own, as well as a progress report on how we're all doing.

When I began to lead new-parent groups, I wanted to share the information on child development and infancy I have access to as a professional. I felt the newest research and theories on infancy would be of interest to parents in understanding babies, their growth and development, as well as their highly individual differences and personalities, and what this means in terms of parenting.

For instance, parents have found it helpful to know that all children under the age of three go through many alternating cycles of dependence and independence. Understanding the deep attachment of the six-month-old and how this relates to the often rather sudden clinging at that age can help a parent to deal with the very practical necessity of finding appropriate and consistent caretakers. Or the "refueling" behavior of the newly mobile eight-month-old may make more sense if a parent knows how important this "touching base" or holding on is for the baby to recharge before going off on another independent jaunt. This kind of behavior can be mistakenly interpreted, and parents may wonder whether all their love, concern, and attention suddenly added up to spoiling the baby?

Parents may also wonder and worry about an eight- or nine-month-old who appears to be going on a hunger strike. So strong are some babies' drives for autonomy that they may stop eating until Mom surrenders the spoon and introduces finger foods. They may also wonder why the baby won't sleep very much anymore. I don't pretend to be an expert on sleep (frankly, I don't think anyone is), but I can think of many reasons a baby might fight sleep. A new walker, for instance, is often so exhilarated with this new world suddenly available that he literally fights leaving it for quiet restfulness. The baby is not spiting or fighting parents, but rather voting in favor of something else. Sharing this kind of information and talking about it in a group can give perspective as well as some solutions for the day-in day-out care of a baby.

An informal group that meets in a comfortable, safe space is also a place for parents simply to observe how other parents and their babies act together. If the babies have mastered crawling, I've found it helpful to have someone else on hand, skilled with babies, to care for them in an adjoining room. The door is left open, so the babies can crawl back and forth as they wish. Parents enjoy hearing what their babies have been up to from someone else, and we are all continuously amazed to see how well the babies relate to the others—how they "talk," touch, and play, and imitate each other—refuting the theory that socialization does not occur until children are at least two or three years old. The babies I have worked with for the most part come to recognize each other through this weekly contact and genuinely seem to enjoy each other.

As I gather experience running groups, I've found that having information per se on child development and providing the infants with pleasant, stimulating social experiences are only two of the benefits for parents and babies. The groups have many other functions. The often-isolated new mother, who lives away from her family or doesn't relate well to them, can meet other new mothers. A woman with her first child, often out of the nine-to-five job market for the first time and without an accessible or necessarily sympathetic community of friends or much experience structuring her time, can meet new people. In every group some participants have developed friendships.

The groups are also a forum for sharing basic how-to information on many of the daily aspects of baby care—preparing your own baby food, where to buy equipment, or find baby-sitters, and so on. But just as important, a group can give feedback which corrects distorted perceptions or information ("all babies sleep through the night by the time they are three months old," "weaning from the breast to bottle is a simple matter of doing it"). Talking together confirms that the way a new mother can feel—inadequate, anxious, frustrated, tired, or angry—is not unusual.

One of my groups, for instance, spent many weeks discussing the lack of support for mothering and how it has affected their own self-esteem. While a mother alone at home is likely to blame herself for not being better organized, more energetic, and "content," and feel guilty for having negative fantasies or thoughts about her baby, mothers together discover that this is normal.

It is much healthier for parents to express their feelings honestly and to work toward solutions openly than to feel angry toward their young children and guilty for feeling this way, which is so often the case. The approach of questioning and looking at problems and finding solutions which a group offers is very helpful for parents to use on their own when the group ends.

New-parent groups are beginning all the time. Many are advertised in community newspapers. Some are offered through local Ys, school boards, and child-development departments of colleges. I offered mine through Elizabeth Bing, a pioneer in the prepared-childbirth movement. She has access to many new parents through her prepared-childbirth classes. She felt, as I and many others do, that parents need support through pregnancy and birth as well as during the actuality of living with a baby.

If there doesn't seem to be anything going on in your area, you might take the initiative and approach the chairman of the child-development department in a local college or ask about resource people at a local counseling agency or the hospital where you gave birth. If you are looking for other new parents to be in your group, your prepared-childbirth instructor or your pediatrician can be helpful. If you ask your pediatrician, be sure to stress that you are looking for parents with normal questions, fears, and problems. Some pediatricians feel that such groups are only for parents with extreme problems, and that is certainly not the case. Remember also that not all pediatricians are amenable to such groups, preferring to do all the problem solving themselves.

The emphasis in any group will, of course, depend on the leader as well as the participants. If you are in a position to choose a leader, I think a firm grounding in child development is necessary if the group is going to have an "educational" focus. It is important, though, that any leader, regardless of his or her focus, be an objective person who is accepting of many lifestyles.

You may, on the other hand, wish to have a parent-led group, which can still offer a great deal of support and an opportunity to share feelings and practical information. Though this group will provide less of a developmental structure from which parents can make decisions, one way to extend your experience and knowledge is by reading together and/or inviting guest speakers from various fields—child psychology, nutrition, day care, and so on—to the group. Here, again, it is important to hear people with various points of view who are flexible enough to tell both sides of the story, particularly if you are dealing with relatively controversial subjects such as going back to work, group care for infants, or when to wean from the breast.

One final word: Our groups ranged in size from five to eight. Fathers were welcome but rarely came because we met in the late morning, during business hours. While I feel that women have a great deal to share with each other, fathers need support, too. If the group agrees to it, one evening meeting every four or five weeks may be substituted for a day meeting so that fathers can attend.

We really are a society in which the roles of parents are undergoing the stress of change—a society that has given lip service to the importance of the mother and the family, but has not provided the structural supports that will strengthen them. As a leader of parent workshops, I have had many doubts about the way I wanted to try to lead them, but I've never doubted for a moment their importance to the parents who have participated.

—PHYLLIS SILVERMAN

Dear Phyllis,

We wanted you to know how much we missed you at our lunch. We had a wonderful time. Five of us were able to get there, which we considered quite a feat — five baby-sitters, five lunches, five naps, and we don't know how many dollars to pay for it. But it was certainly worth it because we knew that we couldn't have managed to all meet sans babies at one time and in one place. And, of course, we hardly knew each other then.

There we were in our "real" clothes, having cocktails before lunch in a restaurant — the sort with candles on the tables and numerous dark corners where one suspects lovers might meet. The nicest part, though, was that after talking, eating, and drinking for two hours, we realized that we hadn't mentioned our babies (or my child) yet because there was so much else to talk about. We are all so interesting.

April is teaching dance therapy six hours a week as an assistant, and has been asked to take over the course next semester. Marilyn is taking a course one night a week in filmmaking, and Barbara, who joined the group after it moved to my house, somehow convinced Chase Manhattan Bank to give her back her old job on a half-time basis for exactly half-pay with benefits. Hooray for Barbara! (And the bank.) Her husband is taking care of Elizabeth in the afternoons, and she reports that he promptly found himself some relief child care.

Margie is planning a trip with her husband to some not-yet-determined warm climate. The big question is whether to take the baby or leave her with her grandmother, who will do it, but doesn't

seem thrilled by the prospect of taking care of an almost-walking eleven-month-old for a week. The baby apparently cries whenever her grandmother picks her up.

Cheryl, who couldn't come, was traveling in Israel with her husband and Anna. And Florence, who also couldn't come, is fine. I ran into her a few weeks ago at the Museum of Natural History — under the whale. Paul, who is now walking, was climbing the steps with his father — up and down, up and down — so we had a few moments to chat. She's doing some secretarial work at home for a lawyer, and is contemplating returning to school. She reports that Paul has a better social life than she does now that she and some friends have organized a play group.

Marilyn did want me to tell you that Andrew has turned out to be "a totally delightful child, even though he still doesn't sleep much." He and the two other "downtown" babies are in a play group. April added that "Samantha is walking and talking. She's not a baby anymore. Oh God! It was so hard! It seems to have taken so long to get to where we are. Yet it was over so quickly. I'm a little sad!" Between trips back and forth to nursery school, I, as usual, am slaving away on this book, convinced as always that people are much better than books. But what do you do until you find them? But the purpose of this letter is mainly to thank you from all of us — for listening and watching, for helping us to interpret, and understand, but mainly to talk — about our babies and ourselves.

Best wishes,

Frances

cc: Elizabeth Bing

Part V

CHILD CARE

-15-
Separation

YOU DESERVE A BREAK: A PEP TALK

One of the hardest things about being a parent is allowing yourself to get away from your child and accepting the idea that it's all right to take some time off. Deep within, you secretly wonder whether the baby will survive in the care of someone else who neither knows him as well nor loves him quite as much as you do.

In some ways making the break is easiest if you *must* leave the baby regularly, for example, if you work. It can be harder for a full-time, "non-working" mother to find a balance between time with the baby and time away. Some women don't feel they can justify the expense of child care unless they have something "pressing" to do. Such mothers may find it easier to take advantage of free child-care solutions, such as enlisting their husbands, trading off with another mother, participating in a baby-sitting coopera-

tive, or seeking the help of a close friend or relative.

In any case, you need and deserve a break, purely for your own enjoyment—even if you do nothing but sit in a coffee shop alone and read magazines. You truly deserve time to yourself, because baby care and all the back-up work that goes into it is a physically and emotionally demanding job. Once you're actually able to do it—that is, find someone to take care of the baby, and return to find the baby *still alive*—you will find it easier to do so each succeeding time. It does take practice, but eventually you'll wonder how you ever functioned without some time off, and you will be amazed at how delightful your baby is.

WHAT YOUR SERVICES AS A MOTHER ARE WORTH

If you are a typical "non-jobholding" U.S.

housewife, you fill at least 12 well-defined occupations valued in the open market at a minimum of $300 a week for an actual pay in dollars of $000.

If you are among the tens of millions of American women classified as "married, not in the labor force," you put in 100 or more hours per week working at these occupations—and frequently many, many more—again, for the dollar pay of $000.

You have no set hours and it's normal for you to start early and stop late. You have no specified schedule for rest. You have no assurance of any vacation worth the name at any time for any duration. You get little, if any, recognition for your job performance as such. It's taken for granted that you'll be good . . . .

Imagine what our GNP would swell to if we counted in just the $300 a week being earned by tens of millions of women!

—SYLVIA PORTER,
Sylvia Porter's Money Book

Dear Ellen,

Enclosed is a check. Though I realize you are a mature woman and a mother yourself now, and you can do whatever you like with this money (truly, there are no strings attached), I hope you will use it to get some baby-sitting help with Mark, so that you can get out a little bit. When I talked with you on the phone, you sounded so frazzled, depressed, and I daresay lonely. This certainly isn't good for you, or the baby. I only wish your father and I didn't live a thousand miles away, so that we could help you and Carl out. We do miss our first and only grandchild, and would love to see more of him than his photographs, as adorable as they are, can ever reveal.

With almost thirty-one years of perspective on your babyhood, it strikes me as having been less stressful for me than what you convey about life with Mark. There probably isn't a mother in the world who isn't tired some of the time, but some of your other complaints strike me as not being entirely your fault. When you were a baby shortly after the war, everyone else I knew was having babies, lots of them and very close together. We were somewhat younger than you and your friends are, and were not "dropping out" of the job market or "taking a break" from it, because many of us really hadn't entered it in the first place.

This street was also never empty then during the day the way it is now, and I was never lacking for company. I simply opened the front door. I was also fortunate to have a (compatible) sister-in-law right down the street, with children near your age. You have none of those things — no relatives nearby, no friendly neighbors whom you know (yet, at least), and no old, close friends who have become parents yet.

Back then, we also didn't have all the experts telling us what to do, nor did we know about women's liberation, and perhaps we <u>were</u> exploited. (In some way maybe we were lucky. Don't bristle!) This is not to say, however, that most of us didn't rely on our educations, our heads, and our organizational skills and derive great satisfaction from our volunteer work for numerous useful and I feel important organizations, and that many of us didn't pursue graduate degrees

which later served us well when we finally did go back to work. Many of the grandmothers I know are holding down jobs, myself included.

I doubt that you remember traveling with me to Jefferson City to lobby for funds for day care, then a relatively new, and as always, controversial area. You were two and threw a horrible temper tantrum on the steps of the capitol building. And this isn't also to say that some women weren't frustrated as housewives and mothers, very lonely and bored with the monotony of taking care of small children. They just didn't talk about it, which was too bad. Some of them did turn into alcoholics and have nervous breakdowns (I won't name names). I can think of several of my friends and their young children who would have been much happier if they spent fewer hours cooped up in the house together.

I am not suggesting that you get a volunteer or a paid job unless you want one, but I am suggesting that you get out and maintain your interests and have some fun. None of us had a great deal of money when our children were small, but we all had some household help because it was easy to find and very cheap. We didn't agonize the way you seem to about leaving the baby for an afternoon. We were not guilt-ridden when we did our volunteer work.

So do take some time off. You are involved in one of the hardest jobs you'll ever have, even if it doesn't pay a nickel. I respect what you are doing, and so does anyone else who has raised children. And if you are so angry about the lack of support for the venerable institution of motherhood, do something about it. You've got a voice, a telephone, a typewriter. If you want day care, I doubt that anyone is going to hand it to you. You have to get involved.

Well, I'll get off my podium now! My love to all — especially the baby!

Love,

Mom

P.S.: We have all sorts of things in St. Louis for new mothers. Enclosed is a clipping about a postpartum hotline. They even have a course in new-parent education at Forest Park Community College. Why don't you check and see if there is anything going on in your area?

SEPARATION—MOTHERS

How comfortable you feel about leaving the baby in someone else's care depends most of all on the person you leave her with. You must trust the caretaker, because it simply isn't worth leaving if you don't. And you must be able to communicate with the person about the baby's needs, your needs, and those of the caretaker. Naturally, communication is easier with a grandmother or a close friend, but most of us don't live near our families and can enlist the help of friends only up to a point. Eventually we must rely on strangers.

Genuine trust and clear communication do not occur instantly, but over a period of time. This is why it is natural to have some ambivalent feelings about separating from your baby at first. It takes practice on everybody's part, and the best practice is through a series of small separations that allow everyone a chance to get to know everyone else. If this approach sounds overprotective, believe me—it's an investment of your time and thought that can save you considerable agony in the future.

GOOD ADVICE

From the vantage point of preschool-age motherhood, the most important point I would make,
the biggest mistake I made, the most distressing problem I have and have had, has to do with sociability and separation.

If I were to do it over again, I would do my darnedest to get someone else to take care of the child for at least a couple of hours a week, from as early as possible. Ideally, perhaps, this is another mother whom you can trade off with, and as the babies grow, they will become playmates (babies do not stay babies very long!). Three important results should be achieved: (1) Baby or child gets used to having you come and go, knows that when you leave, you will also return. (2) Baby learns that someone other than you can also take care of her acceptably. (It is important that you really trust whomever it is you leave the child with. This person should care for the child and should have a philosophy similar to yours on how children should be brought up.) (3) It helps preserve or restore your sanity. The person, or perhaps better, different persons, who care for the child should also be other than the father, that is, in addition to the father's help.

I did almost none of the above. At eleven months, I took Ricky to visit his grandparents. I went out one evening and they had to hold him the whole time. If they put him down once, he just made a beeline for the front door out of which I had disappeared. When Ricky was two, I went to work for a little while. Every time I left him at the baby-sitter's, he screamed his head off until I was out of sight (at least). At four he was still very shy about going to new places with or without me (turning on his heel
and running at the door of a classmate's birthday party), and usually refused to go to anyone else's house to play unless I stayed with him, and even then he was diffident. At five he still doesn't like to go to other kids' houses to play, or get into any unfamiliar situations. How much of this is related to his having been cared for only by me for the first year, I'll never know.

SEPARATION—BABIES

There is much to be said for getting some practice at separating in the early months of the baby's life. At that time she is still amenable to meeting new people and is not in the midst of a separation-anxiety crisis, which is a perfectly natural cross-cultural phenomenon. Distress at your departure is a behavior pattern that tends to emerge when the baby is between six and eight months old, rises to a peak in the middle of the second year, and begins to decline gradually, and *may* end by the time the child is three. Experts disagree as to when and how (and indeed if) you should separate from a baby who experiences separation anxiety. I feel you're being unnecessarily hard on yourself if you don't have some free time away from the baby.

There is no simple explanation for separation anxiety. It seems to be related to the baby's newfound mobility, which fills him with both a sense of power (Whoopie, I can crawl away from you, Mom!) as well as a sense of fear (Will you be there when I come back because I really love you and need you to hold onto, so that I can "recharge" and crawl off again?).

Separation anxiety is also related to the baby's growing ability to remember, or to hold an abstract concept in his head. By six months he is beginning to be able to remember something when it is out of sight. He will look for an object hidden under a blanket, and will become mildly upset if he can't find it. He is not quite able to deal with the discrepancy between his memory of the object and its absence. Previously, however, he'd lose interest in finding the object because everything "out of sight" was literally "out of mind"—including his mother.

But now the baby can connect the concrete reality of his mother putting on her coat to his past experience of his mother then leaving. Anticipation of separation causes him anxiety. What he cannot yet remember is that she will come back. Understandably enough, he becomes upset. Fortunately, he is apt to forget in a short time that his mother has left. Babies don't dwell on things for very long—particularly if the caretaker is familiar and sensitive, understands what is happening, and distracts the baby.

Separations have to be handled with some care and tact, whether you are using a familiar caretaker or not. Sneaking out of the house while the baby is asleep is deadly! Waking to find a stranger is terrifying. Moreover, this can set up a dreadful pattern for the future. Going to bed can be a difficult separation for the baby under the best of circumstances. If past experience has given the baby reason to believe that parents may vanish and be replaced by strangers when she is asleep, the problem is exacerbated from her point of view: Going to sleep becomes, in her mind, dangerous! This is because the baby comes to associate her going to sleep with her parents' leaving.

But certainly some prior experience at separating and some prior knowledge of a caretaker who is already known and trusted by both parent and baby can make the anxiety connected with separation easier to handle. And though we as parents feel bad leaving a crying baby, it's important to remember that the baby is working on the problem of separation himself. One of the ways in which the baby does this is through playing peek-a-boo.

TWO APPROACHES TO SEPARATION ANXIETY

This prewalking period is no time for any un-necessary separation from you or from familiar surroundings, no matter how short. Dr. John Bowlby, a scientist who has done perhaps the finest research to date on the nature of parent and child attachment says, "The protest, despair and detachment that typically occur when a child over six months is separated from his mother are due to loss of maternal care at this highly dependent, highly vulnerable stage of development. The child's hunger for his mother's presence is as great as his hunger for food, and her absence generates a powerful sense of loss and anger."

He adds that the trauma of early loss or separation from the mother can carry over to produce similar responses in older individuals. Such disturbed adults tend to make excessive demands upon others and, if these are not met, to react with anxiety and anger.

—THE PRINCETON CENTER FOR INFANCY AND EARLY CHILDHOOD, The First Twelve Months of Life

I had read John Bowlby and did not want to raise a psychopath! I hadn't used any sitter until Paul was nine months old, a time when he was very attached to me, very clingy and cried every time I left the room. I was therefore very conscious of introducing a sitter gradually, so that she and Paul felt comfortable about all aspects of his care. The first week, I simply had her come by to play with him when he was awake and in a good mood. She acted like a friend who'd come to visit both of us. The second week she came at lunchtime, so that she could have some experience at feeding him. I hovered in the background and did the laundry. The third week, she came while it was time to put him down for a nap. I hovered in the background again. When he woke up, Linda went in to get him. Now this might all sound very protective, but by the fourth week, he didn't even cry, which I expected him to do, when I went out the door.

PEEK-A-BOO

. . .Peek-a-boo and all the variations of this game will occupy the baby interminably. He will play the game by pulling a diaper or his bib over his face, then pull it off with cries of delight. He will play hiding games with any cooperative adult, watching them disappear with a solemn expression on his face, greeting their return with joyful screams. He can keep up such games much longer than you can.

What is the pleasure in these games? If the disappearance and return of loved persons is such a problem to him, why should the baby turn all this into a boisterous game? The game serves several purposes. First, by repeating disappearance and return under conditions that he can control (the missing person can always be discovered again with brief waiting) he is helping himself to overcome his anxiety in connection with this problem. Second, the game allows him to turn a situation that would, in reality, be painful, into a pleasurable experience.

—SELMA FRAIBERG,
The Magic Years

-16-
Who Will Take Care of the Baby?

"Oh, just go out and get a baby-sitter!" It sounds so simple, but it's not. Finding and judging good child care, be it for three hours a week or for fifty, isn't easy. In fact it's one of the hardest jobs in parenthood. Good people are hard to find. Child care is not a particularly well-paying field, nor is it nearly as respected as it ought to be. Given these realities, many baby-sitters don't stick with the job for too long. Herein lies one of a parent's biggest problems: insuring the continuity of care that babies need and thrive upon. Parents, of course, need this too.

Putting the issue of continuity aside for a moment, there are a few points many of us have found useful when looking for child care. The most important thing to remember is perhaps the simplest: You cannot possibly duplicate yourself. You are the baby's parent, and there is no one like you who will have the same kind of relationship with your baby. You are not really looking for the much-touted "mother substitute" as much as you are looking for mother complement(s)—a few consistent people, in addition to you and your husband, whom the baby comes to know and trust. Different people have different qualities and experiences to offer a baby, which is very positive. This is what our lives are all about—the richness and variety of experience and relationships.

What we're all looking for are warm and trustworthy people whom we can talk to, who have a positive view of the world, who enjoy babies and find them interesting. There are many questions you can ask a potential baby-sitter or family-day-care mother or day-care administrator, but do not dismiss your gut feelings when it comes to making a final decision. It is also a good idea to interview several people. You'll become more practiced as you go along. This way you can build a list of reliable people you may need to count upon in the future.

Following are some general suggestions from parents on evaluating caretakers. Following that are more details on the options for different child-care arrangements. (If you work outside the home and need child care on a regular basis, see "Child-Care Choices and Options for Working Parents" on page 157.)

EVALUATING CARETAKERS

Question: How did you find and evaluate child care for your baby? Can you make any useful suggestions for parents?

Answer: It is hard in an interviewing situation to know how well a person will take care of the baby. The baby should be there, though. I found one good ploy was to leave the room for a few minutes to get a pencil or something. If there's no action between the sitter and the baby, this is a very good clue. Does she talk to the baby, and let him come to her? I had one marvelous Englishwoman who couldn't get a work permit, whose husband was a foreign student. She walked right in, greeted me and the baby. She was at ease. Somehow she included the baby in the conversation. She looked at him as she talked to me. She asked me almost as many questions as I asked her. She even asked the baby questions! I felt very good about her. She was warm and demonstrative. When she left, she picked up the baby and gave him a hug. She was a mature woman who felt good about herself, and, I sensed, the world. Come to think of it, this is the heart of it. She was positive. I've never found anyone quite as terrific as Marlene. When she left (a chronic problem with most child-care arrangements), I was really sad. She had become a friend of the entire family.

A: How well a person accepts criticism or direction is crucial. One woman made me feel like a perfect idiot for writing everything down. Doubtless she'd had more experience with babies than I had, but I could see she was the type who was going to do it her way. I learned through experience that, right off the bat, you should ask a sitter how you are going to handle differences of opinion because it's inevitable that this is going to come up. They start out as little issues which you think aren't worth mentioning. It's a beautiful day outside. The sun is shining. You return home to find the baby has been in all day. You let it pass because you can't always get it together to get out yourself either. Some other small thing happens. You come home and the baby's in the playpen. You don't want him to be

in the playpen passively drinking a bottle when you are paying someone $2.50 an hour to amuse him. You let it pass. Before you know it, you're not communicating.

A: I'm surprised that many people use baby-sitters whom they have never met before. I interviewed a couple of people who came recommended from friends and found that only one of them was satisfactory. One woman had lots and lots of baby-sitting experience. She was a grandmother. And this, believe it or not, was part of the problem. She was very sweet and gentle with Jeanie, but fell asleep in front of the television when she was taking her nap and didn't wake up until I finally roused her. I worried about her stamina at keeping up with an active ten-month-old.

A: It is often suggested that you talk about your child-rearing philosophy with a housekeeper. Well, I didn't have one yet. Who knows, maybe I never will? What I found useful was to try to establish whether or not the person is rigid or flexible. If they're flexible, and you're flexible, you can accommodate each other. If you're rigid and they're flexible, it can still work. If you're both rigid, forget it. I asked questions like, how do you feel about the baby throwing his entire dinner on the floor and mushing the peas into his hair, and crawling around on the floor and eating the cat hairs, and pulling out the records, and standing up in the bathtub, tearing up your favorite magazine, and hating to take his nap? You know, all the things that can drive you absolutely nuts, but you're willing to put up

with because babies are babies and they enjoy doing these things, and you can't stop them anyway, and you love your own baby. All you can do is protect them from killing themselves and marvel at their energy because you hardly have any left yourself by the time five o'clock comes around.

A: Be sure to ask all those "what if" questions. What if the baby rolls off the changing table and bumps his head? What if there is a fire in the apartment building, and it starts to fill up with smoke? You feel quite foolish asking these questions, but you would be surprised what people don't know.

A: Tell people in your book never to underestimate the baby's likes and dislikes. I found a very qualified woman to take care of Andrew one afternoon a week. She had worked for a friend of mine who has a baby who is two months older than Andrew. I had used sitters before, and he was used to staying with them. I liked the woman, but he didn't. He cried when I left and he kept crying. She couldn't calm him down or get him to sleep. We tried again the next week, and it happened again. She agreed with me that they just weren't hitting it off. So she went back to work for Margie, and I had to find someone else, which I did, and he was fine. One other thing. I've had better luck with teen-age girls (fifteen or sixteen years old) than college students. They seem to be more conscientious about doing a good job.

WHO WILL TAKE CARE OF THE BABY?   147

A DOZEN CHILD-CARE RESOURCES

1. Word of mouth is one of the best ways to find someone. Talk to friends, neighbors, and local tradespeople. It's amazing how many people in your community your druggist may know. Also talk to friends about their teenage children as well.

2. Check bulletin boards in your local supermarkets, community centers, schools, day-care centers, Y's, churches, or libraries. Post your own notices at the same time.

3. If you live near a college, university, school of education, or nursing school, check with the student employment office as well as the foreign students' center, if there is one.

4. Read ads in local community papers, or place an ad yourself.

5. Visit the senior citizens' center if there is one in your community. Many elderly or retired people who are separated from their own grandchildren would love to be involved with your baby.

6. Baby-sitting agencies are a last resort. They are expensive, and usually will not send the same person to you each time you make a request. This is okay for older children, but very hard on a baby.

7. One resource commonly overlooked is your local state employment service. They often have a household branch and do some preliminary screening. They charge no fees to the employer.

8. For family day-care and day-care programs, check with the Department of Social Services or your local community zoning board. These agencies are often the licensing agents for day care. Also check under *Day Care* in your telephone book. Most programs do not serve infants, but your phone calls may lead you to one that does.

9. Check with your local women's organizations, including your local NOW office if your city has a chapter.

10. If you are part of a union, ask there about child-care resources.

11. If you are associated with a university, ask about child-care resources.

12. Also check with your local CETA (Comprehensive Educational Training Act) organization. Under CETA funding, new programs may be starting that you haven't yet heard of.

GENERAL SUGGESTIONS ABOUT BABY-SITTERS

1. Always plan to interview a caretaker in advance.

2. If you are enlisting full-time baby care, ask for references and take the time to check them. Prior experience is important and always worth striving for. However, for sporadic service, references are not as crucial. Qualities like dependability, flexibility, and warmth override anything else.

3. If you will be going out at night and the baby is asleep when the sitter arrives, make sure that he has become quite familiar with the caretaker on previous occasions. If the baby wakes up to find a total stranger, it may be a terrifying experience and may be the beginning of sleep problems that neither you nor the baby needs.

4. Leave the following phone numbers and information behind:

☐ Police

☐ Fire Department

☐ Poison Control Center

☐ Pediatrician

☐ Nearest hospital

☐ Friendly neighbor

☐ The number where you can be reached, and approximate time of arrival home

All of the above can be posted on a piece of cardboard with a slot for an interchangeable piece of paper listing the last two items.

5. Review how the stove, thermostat, locks, and burglar alarms work.

6. Review baby-proofing, and apprise the sitter of your baby's latest athletic abilities.

7. Go over feeding, bedtime rituals, location of clothing, diapers, bottles, etc. Don't hesitate to write copious notes if this makes you feel more confident.

8. Show the sitter where to look for first-aid information (see Chapter 21, Health Care, for instance) if she or he is not already familiar with it.

9. Make it clear from the beginning how you feel about visitors, television, food in the refrigerator, and using your phone and stereo.

10. Leave written instructions if any medicines need to be given to the baby.

EVALUATING CHILD-CARE ALTERNATIVES

Question: *What are your needs for child care, and what kind of arrangements have you made? What are some of the pros and cons?*

Answer: *I needed my sanity at the end of the day. I worked out an arrangement with a friend who has a twelve-year-old daughter. My friend works full-time and doesn't get home until six. Felicity, her daughter, has after-school activities three days a week. On the other two days she is more than welcome to come here if she wants to, and she is welcome to bring a friend, too. She doesn't have to play with the baby if she doesn't want to, but she always seems to want to, and she is wonderful with her.*

*When Caitlin was in the jumping stage, Felicity would put her in the Jolly Jumper and jump along with her. When Caitlin was learning how to crawl, Felicity got down and crawled with her through an elaborate nest of blankets and pillows she'd constructed. When the baby stood up for the first time, Felicity was there cheering her on. Now that's she's learning to walk, Felicity enjoys walking her back and forth and back and forth, something I weary of doing pretty quickly. It's back-breaking! I am always nearby, but am usually quite free to read a newspaper, cook dinner, talk on the phone, or take a bath. If I have to do errands, it is infinitely easier with a twelve-year-old along. In return for helping me with Caitlin, I am teach-*ing Felicity how to sew. In a year or two, when they are both older, I think I'll feel fine about trusting them alone in the house.*

A: I'm going to school three mornings a week. I have a friend with a baby near Mariah's age (thirteen months). I wanted someone who was really good with toddlers and who would stick with me if possible for the two years it would take me to finish my degree. I was able to pay quite a bit, but not as much as a professional housekeeper–nanny charges for full-time work. Here is a solution which worked perfectly for me: I share Lila with a friend who has a fifteen-month-old boy. She works for me two-and-a-half days a week and for Rosalie the other two-and-a-half days. We live near each other. Once or twice a week Lila gets the two babies together, at either my house or Rosalie's. It's great for the babies! Together we are able to pay her what she needs plus a little more. Separately neither of us could afford her, or use her for a full five days. Of course, she is a flexible person. Some women wouldn't be willing to work under these circumstances.

A: I met a househusband—yes, a househusband, one in a million—in the park. John lives in the same student-housing complex that we do. We trade off with each other once a week. It's a little tiring taking care of two babies (four months and six months), but all I can say is that it's worth it when it's my turn to be off. We also have an informal evening arrangement. His wife baby-sits for us about once every other week, and my husband for them about once every other week.

A: I didn't know it was called family day care. I leave Bryan with a neighbor who has five children of her own, three of whom are teenagers. She cares for one crib-age baby a day and one two-and-a-half-year-old every day for a woman on the next street. She charges us $1.25 an hour, which is the most I can afford. One of her teenage daughters helps out with a five-year-old and a seven-year-old who come after school. Mrs. Glen seems to know a great deal about children. What I like most about her is that she includes Bryan in her activities, the way I do when I take care of him. She takes the two little ones to the grocery store if she has to go. She reads him and Michael a book while she's waiting for the coffee to get made. The two-and-a-half-year-old, Michael, who is there every day, calls him **her** baby. It's like visiting his grandmother. Life goes on as usual, but he is special. I use her two days a week. On those days I work as a receptionist in a doctor's office, so that I can pay to go to night school. George, my husband, watches the baby at night.

A: I went back to work when Danny was nine months old, full-time. I spent three months looking for a housekeeper. I interviewed eleven people and finally found one through advertising in the community paper. She had prior experience, which I felt was important. She had been at her previous job for four years, until, as she said, the family had outgrown the need for her services. I had some reservations about relying on one person fifty hours a week, day-in day-out, so her job record was a big plus. But Mrs. Dale makes the job pleasant for herself. The first thing she asked about was where is the nearest park. She wanted Danny to get out every day, and she wanted to meet other people herself. She now has several new friends, and so does Danny. When I call home every day to talk to her, there are often four other people and babies there. She's getting the inside story on the nursery schools in the neighborhood for the future.

A: When Jesse was six months old, I had gone back to work. I am self-employed as a therapist and consultant and have to travel for my job all over the East Coast. Fred, my husband, works in our community in a nonprofit youth program. We wanted someone who lives near us because our work schedules are so erratic. We also wanted someone who would take care of Jesse outside our home, since we both use the house as an office.

Fred found the person—Mrs. Gonzalez, the mother of one of the teenage kids in the program, who had been providing child care for many years in her apartment to supplement the family income. She is a member of St. Bridget's Church, a strong community focal point in the neighborhood. This was a good recommendation to start out with. Anyone associated with St. Bridget's knows everyone else and is usually the kind of person who is community oriented. I also knew Alberto and his sister well, and they are creative people, which gave me confidence.

When I met Mrs. Gonzalez and visited her home, I knew she was the right person. She is very warm and generous. She wanted us to stay for dinner, which is something we now often do regularly. Besides being a much better housekeeper than I am, she already had everything a baby needed—a toy box, lots of books, and a crib. She doesn't belive in high chairs, a quirk I am certainly willing to tolerate.

Jesse started to stay with her when she was five months old for about three hours a day, two afternoons a week. We gradually built up so that she is there five afternoons a week from noon until five thirty. The one time that Jesse was sick, Mrs. Gonzalez came to our house, and when she had to go away for her daughter's wedding, her sister-in-law took over for three days. She has a huge family.

We have only had one minor run-in, over food. When I picked the baby up and took her home for dinner, she was never hungry, and I was getting worried. It turned out that Mr. Gonzalez arrives home from his work at four thirty for a big dinner, and Jesse is always included because this is the social point of the day. I decided this wasn't worth making a fuss over.

I sometimes felt very guilty about leaving her, particularly when I travel. If Mrs. Gonzalez wasn't such a sympathetic and supportive person, I know that I couldn't do it. Many people are critical of working mothers. Mrs. Gonzalez has always worked, even when her children were babies. She really understands Jesse and loves her. She seems to understand me, too.

A: Rachel is in an excellent cooperative day-care program in the teaching college where I teach three days a week. I have absolutely no reservations at all about the quality of the care she is getting. The staff, who are hired by the parents, are really great. The group she's in is small, six children ranging from five months to twenty months. There are two caregivers. The center is located right in the college. The rooms are set up to be like a home—cozy chairs and couches to sit on, and lots of toys and books. There's a separate "bedroom."

The program is very small, with a huge waiting list. It costs more than many people can afford to pay, but what can you do? You have to pay the teachers decent salaries for this kind of work. If you have a program that is really going to reflect the needs of babies and of working parents, you have to hire very special people who are willing to work with us as well as the kids.

The program is relatively new. We are still working out a lot of the policies. This is very time-consuming, and I sometimes resent this. It's like having a third job. First, I'm a mother. Then I'm a teacher who works with kids all day, and then I'm a member of the co-op and have to go to meetings at night and on weekends. This will ease up once things are settled.

I gripe a lot, but as I said, Rachel's really happy. Perhaps I'm biased, but her language development is quite advanced compared to some of the other children she plays with in the park. Already she talks about her friends, and seems to miss them on the days I don't work. I can visit her for lunch, pick her up early if I want and bring her in any time before ten and stay around for as long as I want to play with her and the other children. The only problem is germs. We have to have elaborate backup arrangements if she is sick, or Doug, my husband, who is a painter, usually has to give up a day of work.

A: My husband has recently started out as a self-employed dental technician and can keep his own hours. When Elizabeth was eight months old, I had to go back to work part-time to supplement our income, and my husband takes care of the baby in the afternoons. As soon as we are making a little bit more money, we're going to hire someone for at least one of those afternoons. It's hard right now. He has to work at night and on weekends to make up for his baby-sitting time. And he's pooped by then. But it's really an eye-opener.

A: My church has a mothers' morning-out program—for pre-school-age children over six months. It's only a couple of hours, but it has saved my life. It's in the Sunday-school room. We all chipped in and painted it, and brought in our extra toys. There are two cribs for the babies. Usually there are about six to eight children there, and one of us mothers and the pastor's wife. A local college girl is going to start working with us for course credit next month. Our only problem now is having to put everything away because of the Sunday-school class. We'd like to get our own space so that we feel a little freer about messing it up.

A: I use a college student one afternoon a week, so I can go out and do whatever I want to do. I started this when Melissa was about six months old. The first student I got left after a month, just when we were beginning to settle in. She took a waitressing job instead. Then I got another student, but she quit, too, during exam season. Now I have another college student, but summer vacation is coming up. They've all been nice with the baby, but none of them has stayed. Now I'm so used to my afternoon that I couldn't possibly give it up.

A: I take David to my mother-in-law's. She's not so great with him. She's a little nervous, and we don't see eye to eye on a lot of things—things that I wouldn't tolerate with a paid baby-sitter. Like what? Well, like breast-feeding and nutrition. She thinks he's not getting enough to eat and that he's too old for "that" now. She gives him ice cream. He's ten months old. I don't want him to have ice cream. She thinks he needs a haircut. I don't. She thinks he ought to be wearing shoes. I don't. She can't stand the "raggedy old clothes" I dress him in. Should I go on? My husband tells me to keep my mouth shut and not to look a gift horse in the mouth. So that's what I do. I know she loves him. And that's what's important. But now she's on me about having another baby, a sister for David. That's all I need!

BABY-SITTING CO-OPS

A baby-sitting pool or cooperative is a good solution for parents in need of experienced, free child care. No money changes hands—only time represented by play money, poker chips, IBM cards, or the like. Besides baby-sitting, a co-op offers many other fringe benefits as well. It is a means of getting to know other neighborhood parents with whom to share experiences, toys, clothing, and medical and educational information. It is also a source of playmates, who become increasingly more important as the baby gets older.

The disadvantages of a large co-op are that parents probably won't have the same one or two sitters all the time. But if you start your own co-op and keep it quite small, your baby can come to know all the parent-sitters. The following by-laws of the East Village Baby-Sitting Cooperative could serve as a model for starting your own co-op.

THE EAST VILLAGE BABY-SITTING COOPERATIVE

RULES AND REGULATIONS

The purpose of these rules and regulations is to enable each member of the cooperative to have a clear and simple understanding of the operation of the East Village Baby-sitting Cooperative.

1. A secretary will act as the record keeper for the cooperative.

2. Each month the duties of the secretary will revolve in the order of the roster of the members.

3. Each member in need of services will make her own sitting arrangements (with one exception: see cancellations below). Try to select a member with debits.

4. The baby-sitter will be in touch with the secretary and report the time as well as the family for whom the sitting service was performed.

5. The sitter will sit in his/her own home by day. At night the sitter will go to the member in need of services to sit.

6. A family may not incur a debit greater than 15 hours.

7. One hour is debited for the first child, and a half an hour for each additional child. (For instance, if you bring two children for one hour, you will be charged for one and a half hours.) Time will be rounded off to the half hour if a member returns after the quarter hour.

8. If you find that you cannot sit for a member who you have already committed yourself to, you must cancel at least twenty-four hours in advance. If this is not possible, then you must arrange for another sitter for the family in need of services.

9. At the end of the month, the secretary gives totals of debits and credits to each member, whether active that month or not.

10. Membership will be limited to 15 members. When a member has been inactive for a period of three months, the secretary will inquire as to the intent of the member family to remain in the cooperative. If a member wishes to withdraw, the family first on the waiting list will be invited to join.

11. When you receive your end-of-the-month statement, the next month's secretary's name and phone number will be at the top of the page.

-17-
Going Back to Work

THE DILEMMA: TO WORK OR NOT TO WORK

Many of us were unsettled about the job question because of conflicting goals our communities seem to set up for us. We're cued to cultivate our individuality while we're saddled with child rearing, which limits such cultivation. If we seek jobs, we must often accept boring ones in order to fit them into our family obligations. Or we're told to go back to careers after the child-rearing years have left us ignorant of recent professional developments. Or our professional effectiveness is diminished by our guilt about leaving domestic responsibilities unmet. Or we're told to demand equal opportunity though we're not allowed a male's long stretches of time for uninterrupted concentration. Society's conflicting standards leave us confused about where our major obligations lie.

—Virginia Barber
and Merrill Maguire Skaggs,
The Motherperson

To work or not to work is a decision no mother makes without considerable thought and, usually, some anxiety. Finding a balance between your personal needs—psychological and/or financial—and the needs of your baby is an issue we all face. But it can become a preoccupation for the working mother* of a young child who is in a "traditional" relationship, where the baby's care cannot be split down the middle with the father.

The dilemma is complex. The notion still prevails that the best and only place for the baby or young child is at home with his mother. Among other things, we are told about the importance of the attachment of the infant to the mother. This, the first love relationship, is felt to be the archetype of all future relationships. It is through loving contact with the mother, sensitive and tuned to her

*I hesitate to use the term *working mothers*, since all mothers work. But "mothers who work at jobs other than baby care for pay part of the time" is too awkward.

own baby's cues, that trust, communication, and learning develop. We almost need not be told. We feel this in our own hearts, and see our baby perform miracles daily as he grows, changes, expands his curiosity, and reaches out to us and the world around.

Will being away from the baby *x* hours per day or week diminish the special quality of this relationship? Will it interfere with this attachment? Several studies say no. Some experts say yes. Others say they just don't know. But nobody disagrees that the quality as well as continuity of substitute or "complementary" care is critical.

We have also to deal with the quality-vs.-quantity issue. Can we make up for quantity by spending "quality" time with the baby? We wonder exactly what "quality" time is. We wonder how much quality time a full-time mother spends with her baby. We wonder how much quality time a baby needs. We sense he needs as much as is available.

Everyone would like answers. But the

evidence is by no means in. We ultimately make the decision about work based on fact and feeling; based on the child-care arrangements available to us; based on the importance of our work to us personally as well as financially; based on attitudes that we inherit from our mothers, husbands, employers, and society as a whole. We do our best to perceive what will be best for the baby—what will harm him the least. And we often feel guilty.

The dilemma is further complicated. Controversy or no, the number of working mothers with pre-school-age children continues to grow rapidly. But the types of working arrangements that would benefit the entire family (flexible work shifts, job sharing, part-time jobs, longer maternity and paternity leaves, etc.) continue to lag far behind the need for them. The growing number of women who must work for financial reasons don't necessarily have the quality of child care their babies need and deserve. And the woman who chooses to work for "psychological" reasons is in a double bind. Besides having the normal problems with her children, she is often characterized as an ambitious malcontent chafing at the bit to get away from the confines of child care.

PART-TIME WORK

The woman who does not depend on work for financial survival and/or has a flexible job, particularly if she is a professional, is usually in a better position to opt for part-time work. Most people agree this is a comfortable solution for babies and parents. One reasons that any negative effects substitute care may have on a baby will be minimized if a parent works part-time. Though part-time work is usually a break-even financial endeavor, it does allow a woman to stay connected to her work or outside interests. For many this is the key to their own well-being as people and parents.

Given the choice, a lot of women and men would agree that for those who want it, creating a balance between work, home, and family during a child's early years is ideal. The logistics of balancing two demanding roles are infinitely easier if you work twenty hours a week as opposed to forty. Though it's by no means a fact, it *seems* to be easier to find quality part-time child-care arrangements than full-time—unless you luck into a jewel of a full-time housekeeper or a "demonstration quality" day-care program or a wonderful family day-care home. It *can* be easier for a caretaker to sustain the energy and interest that the job of caring for a baby requires and to provide the continuity we all are searching for, if her job is part-time rather than full-time.

ONE MOTHER TRYING TO THINK IT THROUGH

Before: *Right now I'm trying to decide whether or not to return to work. My six-month leave will be up in two months, and yesterday the woman I work under called to remind me that my job won't be there in September unless I make a decision soon. The possibility of part-time is an option, but I have some doubts about whether or not it will be worth it.*

After Carol was born, I was certain I would go back to the newspaper after my postpartum checkup. Those first weeks were very rough on us because she had colic, wasn't sleeping, and we were still renovating the house to make a room for her. In the midst of the plaster dust, the mounting carpentry bills, her crying, and our bickering over my resentment about the full responsibility for the baby and the supervision of the workmen as John went out to work in his nice, neat suit every day, my job was my ace in the hole if the going got too rough. I was, of course, ashamed to admit this, and was too busy and exhausted to look for a housekeeper then.

As the weeks went on the colic disappeared, Carol started sleeping through the night, and now at four months she is a delightful, smiling, cooing baby. I'm really enjoying her. The car-

pentry is done, and John and I have stopped arguing—most of the time, at least. I'm trying to make the decision about work more rationally.

I have discovered in the course of searching for a housekeeper that I have many more opinions about the kind of care I think our baby needs. I know I am a perfectionist and am quite critical of people who don't do things exactly the way I want them to be done. I have interviewed several women for the position. One woman was very nice and gentle, but she didn't talk. Another was so aggressive and opinionated that she literally pushed me aside when I was trying to pick up the baby. Another woman was terrific, but it turned out that she was pregnant herself and wasn't sure what she would do with her baby when it was born. John, who is much more flexible (and I think more easily satisfied than I am), points out that no one will seem good enough, and that maybe I don't want a job after all.

We could always use the money. But financially I will be making a great deal less if I work part-time and pay for a housekeeper as well. So I then try to evaluate what the job offers me personally. I've been there for six years and get tremendous satisfaction from the responsibility, the prestige, and the challenge, but of course every job has its negatives, too. Journalism does mean working late hours sometimes, and as a part-time worker I wonder if I will be taken seriously. Will I be given good assignments or stuck with the routine ones? And will the job provide me with the independence I enjoyed,

now that we have a baby?

But more to the point, I wonder why we decided to have a baby if the mere thought of leaving her with someone else makes me feel so guilty. How will I feel when I actually do it? How will the baby feel? Will she flourish the way she seems to be flourishing now? Can anyone else take care of her quite as well as I do even if I do make mistakes? But if I stay at home all the time, will I feel engulfed and trapped? Will I stagnate and turn into a housefrau? Will I be able to reenter the job market in a couple of years? I'm thirty-four now.

You asked me how I was going about thinking through the question of going back to my job, and I'm afraid I haven't answered the question very well. For me, at least, it's very complicated. I do know one thing, though: If I do decide to go back, I am determined to regard it as an experiment.

After: We were in touch when Carol was four months old. She's now a year, and I wanted to let you know what has been happening. In the first place, I'm a lot calmer now, and far less of a perfectionist than I used to be. I did decide to go back to my old job on a part-time basis. I now work three days a week and one late night instead of five days. I waited until Carol was nine months old. It turned out that my employers were more flexible than I thought, once I explained that I needed more time with the baby, more time to find a good

person to take care of her and some time for us all to settle in.

I did find a wonderful woman to come into our home. It may be useful to others to know that it does take a couple of months for everything to begin to work smoothly. After some trial and error, we have worked out what Mrs. Brown's job role is. We've both had to make some minor concessions in terms of the way we do things, but we do agree on the basics.

Her first responsibility is to take care of the baby and to have fun with her. Carol is now walking, and is very busy exploring. There isn't much time for Mrs. Brown to do anything but keep up with her, do a little of her laundry, and keep her room clean. The house is not as clean as I would like it to be. We can't afford cleaning help on top of child care, but I feel it's worth trading the sticky floors and cracker crumbs for the peace of mind I have knowing that Mrs. Brown really loves Carol. Somehow John and I share the cleaning when it gets unbearable.

I had been very worried about not spending much time with the baby on work days, but she somehow put herself onto her own crazy schedule, which works well for all of us. She's up until nine thirty or ten at night, then sleeps to nine in the morning. This isn't as exhausting as it may sound. Now that she walks, she's quite good at entertaining herself, and of course her father is home too in the evenings to help out. John and I don't have that much time together in the evenings because of her late bedtime, but we're surviving.

We do live even more simply than we did

after Carol was born. John does all of the grocery shopping once a week. We used to shop daily—a New York City syndrome, I think. For each meal that I cook, I often make a double portion and freeze the remainder. We very rarely entertain, and when we do, it's very simple. We never go out on weeknights. I also try to do errands during my lunch hour near the office. For instance, I've found a dry cleaner and a shoemaker near work. If I have to get my hair cut or go to the dentist, I also do this during lunch. I make it a point to get home at a set time every day to relieve Mrs. Brown. By a quarter to six, she's had it. This is the hardest part of the day. There's no time to wind down. I'm in the door and Carol's in my arms or pulling on my shirt as I try to make her dinner.

As for the guilt, probably my biggest concern before I went back to work, I'm still a victim, but not nearly as great a one as I had thought I would be. Some mornings when I leave her crying with her nose pressed against the window, and I'm late anyway, and the house is a disaster, and the roof is leaking and the roofer hasn't arrived as he said he would, and the heel on my shoe is falling off, and my skirt is wrinkled, I wonder why I'm doing this. The first month was hell. I fell into bed at ten o'clock every night. But my imagined guilt was far more severe than the real guilt. I have simply to look at Carol, myself, and John and see that though we're all a little crazy the way we live, we are pretty happy.

As for the job, I am doing my old job in three days instead of five, for less pay, of course. I had feared that I would not be taken seriously as a part-time worker, but in my case, at least, this isn't true. After three months back, I have actually gotten a promotion in terms of responsibility. I'm so damn efficient! The pay raise is yet to come, but it's been promised.

THINKING IT THROUGH: IS IT WORTH IT FINANCIALLY?

Every line in this discussion surely must disclose how intellectually and emotionally I am committed to the right of a girl and a woman to have her own career and the importance of this to her own sense of values and dignity. And surely my own life underlines how I have translated my beliefs into reality.

But you may want to calculate the advantages strictly in financial terms.

—Sylvia Porter,
Sylvia Porter's Money Book

To estimate your own costs, fill in this chart and weigh the total against your own paycheck.

Gross Weekly Salary	_____
Deductions:	
Federal income tax	_____
State income tax	_____
State disability	_____
Social security	_____
Group health insurance	_____
Group life insurance	_____
Pension plan	_____
Total Deductions	_____
Amount of take-home pay	_____
Weekly Expenses:	
Transportation	_____
Lunches	_____
Child care	_____
Personal grooming	_____
Extra clothes	_____
Dues (professional, etc.)	_____
Household help	_____
Added household expenses (convenience foods, paying for things you might have done yourself, etc.)	_____
Office contributions	_____
Other	_____
Total weekly expenses	_____
Take-home pay	_____
Minus weekly expenses	_____
Your real net pay	_____

CHILD-CARE CHOICES AND OPTIONS FOR WORKING PARENTS

Everyone agrees that working parents must find the best and most reliable child care, and that finding it usually takes more time than expected. Don't delay your search, even if you have mixed feelings about returning to work. These feelings are normal and are greatly diminished if you know you've made a thorough search of the options available before you make a choice. They are never minimized if you settle for an arrangement you aren't happy with. You and the baby and the caretaker will need to have an adjustment period of at least a week or two.

Needless to say, it is usually the working mother who is responsible for finding and evaluating child care so that she is free to work. Is this fair? The job is much simpler if both parents participate.

Before you go one step further, remember that there is (unfortunately) no perfect childcare arrangement. There are options, and each has its positives and negatives. You have to decide which arrangement suits you best, or which of the pros outweigh the cons.

There are two basic options with many variations open to parents: individual care or group care. It has been assumed that the best thing a working parent can do for a baby is provide the baby with a one-to-one relationship that most closely approximates the mother-child relationship. Some very interesting research from the
Educational Testing Center in Princeton may open your mind, however, to group alternatives. The center has discovered, after extensive observations of infants, that babies experience little stranger anxiety if there is another baby present. They have also found that infants become attached not only to their own parents but to other infants and young children as well. Babies do play together and begin to form friendships far earlier than three years of age—despite what many experts have said in the past (and still do in some cases). We are all aware of how much babies learn in the first year, but until recently it was never considered that babies learned from each other. It is apparent that they do—through play and imitation. By fifteen months of age, for example, babies can detect the sex of another infant from facial photographs, something few adults can do.

HOUSEKEEPER–BABY-SITTER: PROS AND CONS

The most convenient child-care arrangement is to have a caretaker come into your own home. The baby is already familiar with the environment, and it is set up and child-proofed according to his level of agility and curiosity. All his toys and equipment are there, which means you don't have to carry the baby plus his paraphernalia back and forth. It's comfortable. There are fewer complications if the baby has a cold, and certainly less exposure to germs from other children. A full-time caretaker's job often also includes some light housekeeping responsibilities, which makes it possible for working parents to spend more time with the baby when they are home.

But there are some distinct disadvantages to this child-care arrangement. It is, of course, very expensive. You must be able to pay the salary of a mature adult, and even then there is no guarantee that the person will stay. Being solely dependent on another person's physical and mental health, goodwill, and humor is a tricky business, especially in the beginning. Until you've developed a trusting working relationship, you have no way of knowing what goes on when you are away, and if difficulties do arise in communication, you and the caretaker are on your own. A caretaker can feel just as socially isolated as a mother, because she may not live in the community where she works. Unless she is outgoing—and unless there are places for her to go—the baby will miss out on valuable social experiences with other babies and young children.

The Live-In Housekeeper. A live-in child-care arrangement overcomes some of the live-out problems, but has several of its own. Obviously, having someone move in with you requires a big home or apartment. While a person who shares your space is more likely to become like a member of your family and your community and be available at night sometimes as well, it is a risk to invite someone in whom you don't know very well. Unless you are used to giving up some of your privacy, this can be a difficult adjustment.

If you have sponsored a young foreign woman from abroad, you may find that you are taking on the additional responsibility of helping her adjust to a new culture and a new language, overcoming homesickness, and developing a social life of her own. College and graduate students may have schedules that you will have to work around—which change with each semester. And because they are a highly mobile segment of society, they may "drop out." And there just aren't very many women who are willing to "live in" nowadays. Those who are willing are very expensive.

Some Questions You Can Ask to Overcome The Disadvantages of Individual Care

1. Prior experience is often but not always a good indicator of a caretaker's interest in and enjoyment of the job. Because you are looking for continuity, the length of each job is important. Find out why the person left.

2. Written references should be taken with a grain of salt. A telephone call, even if it is long distance, can give you a great deal of reassurance about a new caretaker. You can ask about reliability and what kind of relationship she or he had with the child, and how easy or difficult it was to communicate.

3. It is also important to ask the caretaker about her own family responsibilities. If she has young children of her own, who takes care of them while she is away? What happens if she gets sick? And is she in good health herself?

4. The logistics also have to be very carefully worked out in advance —salary, benefits, sick or vacation days, transportation costs. If the job involves housekeeping, it's not a bad idea to have a written description of exactly what you want that person to do.

5. Then come the questions that are sometimes more difficult to ask. What is satisfying about taking care of a baby? What are the rewards as well as the stresses? How does this person feel about schedules, about letting the baby explore the house and rub peas and mashed potatoes in his hair? How would she handle crying when you put your coat on to leave? How important does she feel socialization is? Is she willing to sit in the park or participate in a play group when the baby is older? And most important—how does she actually react to the baby? It is hard to tell in an interviewing situation. But does she seem warm, and friendly and interested in the baby, and relatively relaxed around him? Does she ask questions about the baby as well as the parameters of the job?

6. And how are you about talking openly to each other? Is this the kind of person who will let you know if too many demands are being made? Will she talk about the baby—share what he's doing—and be "straight" if she feels any problems are developing?

7. Is she willing to work for a trial period—a week or two, or at least a weekend, so that you can both decide if it will work on a long-term basis?

FAMILY DAY CARE

Many of us use family day care without knowing it. The term means simply that someone takes care of your baby in her or his own home—either alone or with a small group of other children. Some parents use relatives, friends, neighbors, or people who have put advertisements in the paper or notices on community bulletin boards. A very few homes (between 5 and 10 percent) are chosen and supervised by a social-service agency, church group, school, or day-care center. These are usually licensed, a procedure which varies tremendously from state to state.

The only general truth about family day care is that it defies generalization. *Usually,* however, a day-care person is a mother herself—young or old, or somewhere in between—who has gained her experience with infants and young children through on-the-job training, which usually has little to do with degrees or training in child development per se. And the quality of family day care obviously has a great deal to do with the mother—her enthusiasm for her work, energy, imagination, patience, and understanding of babies and young children; her connection with the resources in her community; and her work load.

If she is taking care of more than one child, she must also be able to divide her time, attention, and affection among different children, perhaps of different ages and different interests and needs. Her job may seem terribly difficult to those who find a single baby quite mind-boggling, but it is, after all, the challenge that all parents who have more than one child take on.

When family day care is small (no more than two children under the age of two) and the mother skilled, it can offer the same rich experiences a baby would get in her own home—and more. A day-care home can become an extended family, providing playmates and "older siblings"—perhaps a seven-year-old who arrives home from school in the afternoon or a grandmother who lives next door and drops by to visit. The flexible rhythm of home-based care—ringing telephones; neighbors or delivery people dropping in; dogs coming and going; trips to the bank, the grocery store, the park, or the zoo—can provide just the right amount and variety of stimulation that a baby needs.

The American home, assuming that it is safe, is a very stimulating place for a baby to be. It is full of educational "toys"—pots and pans, lids and strainers, spaghetti pots for water play, cupboards to open and close, footstools to climb on, tables to crawl under, pillows to struggle among and blankets to hide under—as well as quiet sleeping places removed from the bustle of household activity.

As with all types of child-care arrangements, there can be disadvantages to family day care. *Windows on Day Care,* a study done by the United Council of Jewish Women, is full of depressing horror stories about bad family day care —children in lethal settings, propped in front of televisions or even tied to cribs, no outdoor play, junk food, and harassed mothers. Just as often, however, the report talks about warm, loving women who provide excellent custodial care for infants and young children but few educational or other types of experiences. Many of these women expressed a desire for further training and support but did not qualify for it because their homes did not meet the (often outlandishly) rigorous licensing standards in their state.

Family day care is often the only economically feasible child-care arrangement parents can afford. The overhead for child caring in small groups in a home is much lower than in a day-care center. But a family day-caregiver usually makes very little money for the services she provides and the hours she works. If she feels isolated, overwhelmed, and unsupported in her work, she—like anyone else—won't be able to perform her job well—or she may quit. As with any other child-care arrangement, a parent is relying on the good health, goodwill, and good humor of one person. While it can be hard to articulate your philosophy and wishes and to communicate openly and straightforwardly to an in-home caregiver, it can be even more difficult to do so with someone who is used to functioning autonomously in her own home.

A licensing agency can help overcome these problems—by selecting well-qualified, warm, healthy people; by insuring that their homes are safe; by aiding in parent–day-caregiver communication, and by serving as an educational resource. One very positive development in the family day-care field is networks—loose associations of day-care mothers who exchange information through newsletters, attend lectures on children and the family, share toys and outings and practical information, and even take over for each other during illness or vacation. Being organized like this helps insure the continuity of care that babies and young children need, and also makes child care much more satisfying for the day-care mother.

If you are thinking about family day care for your baby, the day-care mother and home you choose may not be licensed or a member of a network. But we all need supports—people we can turn to if a problem or emergency arises. We need people to share time with or go out with if we're feeling isolated or are simply having a difficult day. Be sure to ask about this.

Besides asking a family day-care mother the same questions you'd ask someone who comes into your own home, here are some other suggestions.

1. Visit the home before you decide, and spend some time there. Is it a safe and comfortable place to be? Would you enjoy spending time there yourself?

2. Who are the other children, and how will your baby fit in? Who comes and goes during the day?

3. Can the day-care mother describe a typical day? Does this include getting outside when the weather is good?

4. What are her views on nutrition?

5. How can you work together to help the baby make the separation with the least anxiety?

INFANT DAY-CARE PROGRAMS*

If you are considering day care for your baby, your chances of finding a quality program that accepts children under one year old are exceedingly slim.

Group care for infants and toddlers is still a relatively new and controversial area in this country. Its critics stress that babies, in order to learn and develop trust, need an individual relationship with an adult who is completely sensitized to them, subconsciously in tune with them, and familiar with all their cues. They fear that this intensely per-

*This discussion is limited to nonprofit infant day care. In my readings and discussions with day-care professionals, it is clear, to me at least, that it is almost impossible to run a program that truly meets the needs of babies and parents for profit. The expenses of individualized care in a group setting are simply too high for profit making without cutting corners that have negative effects on babies.

sonal relationship cannot occur when a caretaker's attention is divided among a group of babies or toddlers.

These fears are well grounded. Good group care of any sort, be it in a day-care home or a center, has to have a low ratio of infants to caretakers (preferably three to one). The caretakers must be a small group of consistent people who truly come to know the babies and are sensitive to their nonverbal cues, and to whom the babies can become attached. A small group is also important to give a family feeling.

Tiny babies have a protective screening device with which they can block out unpleasant stimulation—loud noises, for example, and even physical pain. Older babies and toddlers don't. If there are too many people, babies, toys, activities, and noise, they simply become cranky, irritable, tired, lost, withdrawn, or overwhelmed.

A small, low-ratio center is also important for providing the flexibility that babies need. By nature, babies are not conformists. They don't necessarily nap, eat, play, or feel sociable at the same time. They have unique needs for individual attention—holding, cuddling, and quiet time in which to play, make messes, and explore, and to interact with each other.

Then, too, parents cannot afford to feel that they are handing their babies over to a group of child-development professionals. They must feel included. The book *The New Extended Family: Day Care That Works* (see page 162) presents an entire range of solid group-care alternatives. The programs and goals vary tremendously, but one common element stands out: parent involvement on some level (e.g., assisting at the center with the children, attending meetings, parent discussion groups, serving on the boards or on committees, helping with building and renovation, hiring staff, doing curriculum planning or fund raising, or being part of the administration). This kind of involvement takes more time than some parents may want to invest, but these centers reflect what parents want for their children.

Parent involvement also serves another important function: A working mother often doesn't have the time that a nonworking mother has to find and establish a community of friends who offer support and make the job of parenting easier, less lonely, and more fun. Parents working together for their center can form that peer group we all need. They can share general information and discuss problems and concerns unique to their situations.

Assuming that a center is small and that parents are involved, it becomes possible to look at many of the distinct advantages day care can offer a baby over other kinds of child-care arrangements.

It also becomes possible to look objectively at some of the difficulties. The following is a list of the pros:

1. Continuity of care can be achieved, because you aren't relying on one person to take care of the baby. A good center will respond to the baby's preferences for a particular caretaker and "assign" one, but if this person is sick or on vacation, other caring adults known to the baby will be there in a familiar setting.

2. There is usually a higher degree of professionalism in trained day-care-takers than in any other group. The staffs are usually carefully chosen by more than one person, and often by parents as well, for their warmth, interest in, and understanding of infants. Their working conditions are somewhat more pleasant than those of individual caretakers, because they have each other to talk to, to share experiences with, to help solve problems, and so on. Male caretakers are also much more likely to participate in a center than in any other kind of child-care arrangement. This can be especially important to the single working mother. It is good in general for babies and young children to get used to the idea that men as well as women can take care of them.

3. The spaces can be designed especially for infants and toddlers, and many of the dangers in a home can be eliminated (household-cleaning agents, sharp knives, unlocked windows, etc.). A safe outdoor space may also exist, with enough staff on hand to insure that the babies do get out every day in good weather.

4. Obviously, group care offers extensive opportunities for social play and interactions. Infants can form attachments to each other through play and exploration. It has also been observed that babies in the company of other babies experience less separation anxiety when a parent leaves, and that verbal communication appears earlier in infants who have socialized with each other at an early age.

5. Day care provides a more open environment for observation. One of the biggest problems with individual care in your home or family day care can be simply not knowing what goes on when you are not there. A good center will encourage parents to observe and comment. Policies tend to be articulated, and if a parent does have an objection or a complaint, there is usually a more clearcut method for dealing with it objectively.

6. A good day-care program will also take pains to insure that separations are made gradually and with sensitivity over a period of time. It's not easy for parents to leave their babies in someone else's care. We all feel ambivalent at times. A sensitive staff who have worked with many parents and have had some guidance, training, and experience in this area can be very supportive both to babies and their parents.

The following is a list of the possible disadvantages of day-care programs:

1. A center may not be conveniently located near your home or job. A center's hours usually are not as flexible as a family day-care home, nor are its policies on sickness.

2. Germs can be a real problem. Parents must have backup child-care systems if the baby is sick, in order not to miss a day of work.

3. Continuity of care is the most striking advantage of group care, but it can't be provided if the center isn't a fairly stable institution in terms of funding and licensing. Here enters another disadvantage, the largest for many parents: Infant day care is expensive. Many programs must charge between $50 and $60 a week, which is more than many parents can afford. More funding is gradually becoming available to underwrite some of the costs, but it appears it will be a long time before day care for babies is available to every parent who wants and needs it.

RESOURCES

Child Care

Benjamin, Lois, *So You Want to Be a Working Mother!,* Funk & Wagnalls, New York, 1966.

Curtis, Jean, *Working Mothers,* Doubleday & Company, New York, 1976.

Galinsky, Ellen and Hooks, William H., *The New Extended Family: Day Care That Works,* Houghton Mifflin, Boston, 1977.

Glickman, Beatrice Marden and Springer, Nesha Bass, *Who Cares for the Baby? Choices in Child Care,* Schocken, New York, 1978.

Olds, Sally Wendkos, *The Mother Who Works Outside the Home,* Child Study Press, New York, 1975.

Price, Jane, *How to Have a Child and Keep Your Job,* St. Martin's Press, New York, 1979.

Baby Sitter's Handbook for Emergency Action
National Fire Protection Association
470 Atlantic Avenue
Boston, Mass. 02210

Choosing Child Care: A Guide for Parents
Send a check for $3.00 to:
Stevanne Auerback & Linda Freedman
Parents and Child Care Resources
1855 Folsom St.
San Francisco, Calif. 94103

Day Care and Child Development Council of America, Inc.
1012 14th St. N.W.
Washington, D.C. 20005 (Write for their list of publications)

When Teenagers Take Care of Children: A Guide for Baby Sitters
No. 409-1964
c/o Superintendent of Documents
U.S. Government Printing Office
Washington, D.C. 20402

Part VI
PRACTICAL MATTERS

-18-
The Portable Baby

If nature had designed us for living in the modern world, we'd be like kangaroos with handy pouches for our babies. But alas, it's not so simple. By the time you've gotten the baby fed and dressed, zipped and buttoned into the snowsuit, found your keys and your own coat, the baby has had an "accident," which has gotten all over his clothes *and* the snowsuit, or the weather has changed, or the sun has set, or you're too tired to go out anyway. (It's easier in the warm weather or if you live in Florida!) But you have to get out. Getting out is your sanity. Besides, you have to get things done.

Although it sometimes seems easier to stay home, there are many positive reasons for taking the baby out. Fresh air is one of them. If we followed Dr. Spock religiously, our babies would be aired winter and summer for at least two hours a day. But more to the point, motion, a change of perspective, new people, sights, sounds, and smells are interesting to babies. They learn in myriad ways about how the world functions on those trips to the bank, the grocery store, and so on. And maybe—just perhaps—the despairing baby who has been fed, burped, bathed, held, rocked, and sung to may possibly forget his woes once he's out in the world.

But don't let anyone tell you that getting out the door isn't an exercise in logic. Besides carrying the baby, you must carry his world with him—food, clothing, and entertainment. In the beginning, at least, getting out the door seems to require the discipline of a drill sergeant. The following should make it easier.

Question: *When can I take the baby out?*

Answer: *If you've brought the baby home from the hospital, you've already taken him out. Next question.*

—Dr. Virginia E. Pomeranz
with Dodi Schultz,
The First Five Years

Q: When is the weather too bad for the baby to go out?

A: It is never too cold, too rainy, too snowy, too sleety, or too windy for the baby to go out, even though you may prefer not to go out; he will always be adequately protected from the elements. It may, however, be too hot and humid for him outdoors . . .

Dr. Virginia E. Pomeranz
with Dodi Schultz,
The First Five Years

I was quite nervous about taking her out the first time, but I knew I had to do it. For two days I planned a trip to the A & P, which is only two blocks from my house. I had fed her but was still afraid she'd get hungry at the store. As we walked along, I anguished over how I was going to breast-feed her as I waited at the meat counter, especially since I'd worn a dress that zipped up the back. What would people think of me subjecting my new, two-week-old baby to the ninety-five-degree heat, the air pollution, and the germs on the Bowery? What would happen when I took her into the air-conditioned store?

Maybe I should have brought a hat for her. And even worse, what if we both got hit by a bus on the way home? What would Charlie do without us?

WHAT TO CARRY

- [ ] A waterproof hand or shoulder bag (perhaps even made of see-through plastic so you can find what you're groping for). This bag should contain:
- [ ] A changing surface (a small towel or cloth diaper will do)
- [ ] Disposable diapers plus plastic bags to dispose of them
- [ ] Premoistened clean-up towels
- [ ] Plastic bottles and nipple covers, or a thermos and cup containing something to drink
- [ ] Special straws that fit into the standard nipple and ring are good for the baby who can sit up and hold his own bottle. The 8-ounce size can be cut in half to fit a 4-ounce bottle
- [ ] A nonmessy snack (if there is such a thing) might make the difference between being able to wait in a line or not

- [ ] A "busy" toy such as a set of measuring spoons
- [ ] A hat for when the sun comes out
- [ ] A sweater for when it goes in

Question: *Is there any such thing as a quick exit when you're taking the baby?*

Answer: *Not really, but the following things help:*

- [ ] *One place—a hook or shelf—near the door for the baby's things—her bag, shoes (if she wears them yet), snowsuit, mittens, hat, etc. They are so small and easy to lose.*
- [ ] *A safe place to put the mobile baby, while you get organized yourself. This is the primary function that a playpen often serves.*
- [ ] *Leave extra diapers, bottles, pacifiers, and clothes in the car.*
- [ ] *The last thing you do is dress the baby.*
- [ ] *Then you go out the door and let the telephone ring if it's ringing.*

Going out with a baby is like going to Europe. You practically need a suitcase and itinerary. First you size up the state of the baby. Is he in a good mood today? How long will he sit in the stroller—moving or stationary? Is it worth waiting at the bank, or better to send in the deposit by mail? I got pretty good at planning the route—before rush hour, making the most important stops first, where to go to avoid revolving doors with the carriage, which depart-

ment stores had a ladies' room with a chair where I could sit to nurse if we didn't make it home in time.

We took Allison everywhere. And yes, our circle of friends did narrow. We felt most comfortable with other couples with young children. They understood we might have to leave early if things got bad. Barbara and I always made an agreement beforehand about who would take care of her. She'd be "on" for part of the time, then it was my turn. That way neither of us was always stuck with walking her back and forth when everyone else was eating dessert.

We used to take Zack in his infant seat to Chinatown at about ten or eleven at night. It wasn't crowded then. If he'd sleep through our whole dinner, we felt like we'd really pulled off a great coup. It's the small things in life that count once you have a baby!

Sam and I just couldn't handle taking Joanne to social gatherings. Even if she slept, I found I was always aware of her—wondering when she'd wake up and would she feel strange in someone else's house when she did? What if she needed something that I'd forgotten? In retrospect, I think I projected a lot of this onto her. It was me who wasn't very flexible—much more than the baby.

Jake was born in June, and I remember taking him to all sorts of outdoor events—picnics and concerts. This seemed to work better than being in a strange environment, but maybe we felt freer ourselves outside and he picked up on this.

I delayed getting the work done on my teeth because I didn't know what to do with Vanessa. I didn't want to leave her with a sitter because she was still breast-feeding every two hours. I had all these complicated solutions worked out, like inviting a friend to come along to hold her. I also thought maybe my husband could meet us there at lunch hour. As I was explaining all this to the receptionist, she suggested that I bring Vanessa whenever it was best for me. I never would have thought to ask, but she said entertaining babies was one of the best parts of her job. It worked out really well. They had a fish tank in the waiting room, and she loved the lights and bubbles. We went every week for sixteen weeks. By the time I had finished the treatment, she was crawling, and the waiting room was completely baby-proofed.

USEFUL EQUIPMENT FOR THE PORTABLE BABY

There is a lot of equipment on the market for making the baby portable. But it's important to remember that everything costs money, has to be kept relatively clean, and takes up storage space. Some things are more useful than others because they are multifunctional and have longer lives. What you buy or even borrow depends on your own needs and the way you live.

When you shop for some items like backpacks that will be "worn," it's a good idea to bring your spouse and baby along. Don't buy anything that doesn't have clear assembling and how-to-use instructions unless the salesperson is willing to go over everything step by step.

If you are borrowing, you are not an ingrate when you inquire whether anything is missing or not functioning or ask how to use it. (With great difficulty and little satisfaction, I wore a borrowed Snugli baby carrier backward for three months and couldn't understand why everyone thought it was such a wonderful product.)

INFANT SEATS

An infant seat provides the baby with a welcome change of perspective and a larger view of the world from the newborn period to four or five months, or until the baby becomes too wiggly to tolerate confinement. The seat is very easy to carry, convenient for feeding the baby at home or away, and also fits easily into a shopping cart at the grocery store. Some parents use the plastic version of the seat to help bathe their newborns in the sink or tub. This way they don't have to hold onto the slippery baby. The seat can also be used in conjunction with an umbrella-type stroller to offer the very

young baby more back support. Be sure to strap it in securely, however.

Suggestions:

1. The very lightweight plastic models are quite tippy. You can help offset this by weighting the metal rod in the back with a heavy book.

2. Always strap the baby in. Even a newborn can startle, lurch forward and out. A baby in an infant seat is much safer left on the ground. If you place the baby on a table or countertop in the seat, get in the habit of keeping one hand on the seat if you must turn away.

3. The back of a newborn tires easily, so use the seat sparingly and for short periods at first. The younger the baby, the slighter the angle.

4. Never use an infant seat to replace an approved safety restraint in the car. There is no effective way to attach it securely to the car, and such seats are not designed to withstand the impact of a crash.

Infant Seat

HOW TO WRAP A SHAWL OR REBOZO FOR CARRYING A BABY

Step 1. Drape the shawl or rebozo out to its full width across your shoulders. Leave it shorter on the side where you will place the baby.

Step 2. Fold both edges of this short side over the baby, leaving his feet hanging uncovered. The bottom edge of the shawl may hang free, or may be wrapped around the baby.

Step 3. Lift up the long end, holding it away from your body, then lay it over the baby. Bring this end around under the baby as far as it will go and pull it up between the baby and your chest.

Step 4. What is left of the long end will now be inside and top-side of the baby. This can be tucked around the baby on the side away from your body.

SLINGS AND SHAWLS

A sling offers the baby a close and cozy view of the world and pleasant motion for the first two or three months. It's easy to get the baby in and out of and allows for convenient, discreet nursing while your other hand is free. Slings are also washable and easy to store. But in general a sling will not be useful for too long, because a wakeful baby soon prefers to be vertical and able to turn his head freely to see what's happening. Slings are also not useful for fathers because they don't have hips to rest the baby on.

Alternatives. Rather than buying a sling, make a *rebozo* (the Spanish word for "shawl") out of any three-yard length of nonstretch fabric. The *rebozo* can be used on your back as well. This is a great trick for travel. When not in use, the fabric can double as a sheet, cover, or play space.

FRONT (SOFT) PACK CARRIERS

One of the oldest, most comfortable, and convenient ways to transport a baby is by carrying her on your front or back. In a front carrier, positioned over your heart, rocked by the motion of your steps, a small baby can nap or observe the passing scene as you go about your work with both hands free. A soft front-pack carrier is also good for that transition period when the baby is still too young to sit up in a stroller, but parents have neither the funds nor the room for a carriage. And if you must get out on foot, rain or shine, there is no better way to travel in bad weather. You can both fit under the umbrella.

A front carrier is also lightweight and easy to store, but choose one that is washable. Some brands come in both summer and winter weights. As the baby grows larger and more active, it will be easier to carry him on your back. Though front carriers are often marketed for use on the back as well, it is hard to position them there without help.

Suggestions:

1. A pack should provide a newborn with head support.

2. Before you buy, check seams to make sure that they are well constructed.

3. Try the pack on for comfort. Make sure that it is easy to get on and off alone.

Front Pack Carrier

BACK (FRAME) PACK CARRIERS

A backpack is useful for the baby who sits up well. By this time she's probably getting a little heavy to carry comfortably on your front without straining your back. She'll also appreciate a better view and more freedom to move her head and arms than a front pack permits. Some packs come with built-in loading stands, which make loading easier and allow the packs to convert to free-standing seats. It's a good idea to practice and build up your carrying time over a period of days

Back Pack Carrier

when you first start out. If you don't use your backpack for a number of weeks, you also may have to build up your carrying time.

Suggestions:

1. Definitely try out a pack with the baby in it before you buy. A backpack might not be your style.

2. A pack must have a safety belt so that the baby can't climb up and out or topple out when you bend over.

3. The seat in the carrier should be located midway down your back. This is important for two reasons: This position is stable, and it places the weight on your back rather than on your shoulders.

4. Is there plenty of room for the baby's legs to rest in a normal position, out to the front, rather than to the sides? Make sure that the leg openings are not restricting.

5. Are the shoulder straps at the top adjustable and *well padded*? If not, a pack can be excruciatingly uncomfortable.

6. Look for a pack anchored to the frame at the top as well as the bottom. The shifting of the baby's weight in a pack which is not well anchored can be very bothersome and uncomfortable.

7. Look for a strong back bow. An active baby will bounce on this.

8. Is the pack easy to load and unload alone?

UMBRELLA-TYPE STROLLERS

I've nothing but praise for this wonderful invention. For the urban parent in particular, who has to negotiate on public transportation, this stroller is a lifesaver. It can be opened and closed with one hand and one foot and carried easily over an arm, fits into a car trunk or the carry-on baggage section of an airplane, and can be stored on a coat rack. There are only two drawbacks: In general, these strollers are rather unstable. They will tip backward if packages are hung on the handles. If the baby is under four months old, he will not have the back strength to sit comfortably in this kind of stroller, and will seem lost in it as well. You can help remedy this by strapping an infant seat to the stroller (see page 173).

If you are an inveterate walker and use a stroller every day, buy a good one. The very inexpensive models are tempting but will not last through your baby's toddlerhood. Wheels will have to be replaced, and the sling seat, unless it's made of sturdy canvas, will tear. The more expensive models, which offer firm back support, are somewhat heavier and

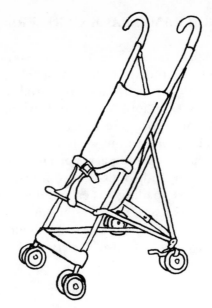

Umbrella-type Stroller

harder to fold, but probably provide the baby with a more comfortable ride. For bad weather, consider the optional bags to keep both the baby and stroller dry. A stroller with springs will give your baby a much smoother ride, and a stroller with a reclining back rest will keep the baby more comfortable if she falls asleep.

CARRIAGES

A carriage is a true luxury that only makes sense if you live in a building with an elevator, have plenty of room to store it, and shop in large stores with wide aisles and without revolving doors. There's plenty of room for the baby to sleep protected from the wind and rain or to play, and room for your packages as well. A carriage can also double as an extra bed. Some models convert to (bulky) strollers.

But carriages are very expensive. It is very tempting to buy one when you have a floppy newborn in the depths of winter. But try to borrow instead. Babies soon want to sit up and look out, and a stroller provides a quality view for about a third of the price. If you must buy new, though, here are some guidelines.

Suggestions:

1. Make sure the carriage is lightweight enough for you to maneuver, and that the handles are at the appropriate height so that you don't strain your back pushing.

2. Check the brakes. Are they easy to operate and secure?

3. Is the inside of the carriage well padded, with no metal parts exposed that might pinch or scratch the baby?

4. If the top of the carriage is removable as a portable bed, make certain the catches that lock it in place are strong and secure.

5. Is there a place to anchor a

harness—a necessity once the baby is able to pull herself up to stand?

6. Is the carriage deep enough for safety?

7. If you are using the carriage for shopping, a package shelf on the bottom is a worthwhile investment.

BICYCLE SEATS

Bicycling with a baby can be lots of fun, but don't attempt this until the baby can sit up well, otherwise his back muscles will not be strong enough for the upright position.

There are two kinds of bike seats—front mounted and rear mounted. The front-mounted seats make it easier for a parent to be in touch with the baby, but they have a few disadvantages. They are made only for open frame or "women's" bicycles, and they leave too little room for a parent to lean forward, partially dismount, and get a firm footing on the ground in order to balance the bike when stopped. Unless you adjust your seat to its lowest position or have very long legs, you'll have to swing your leg off the bicycle and get off each time you want to stop. Front-mounted seats are also useful only for children under thirty pounds and thirty inches tall.

A rear mount can accommodate a child up to forty pounds and be fitted to either an open- or closed-frame bicycle. On a closed-frame bicycle it's quite difficult to mount and dismount, because the baby is in the way.

But on a beautiful spring day, a true enthusiast can put up with these minor drawbacks in either type of seat.

Suggestions:

1. Whatever type of seat you choose, make sure it provides foolproof protection for the baby's feet as they straddle the wheel. A foot caught in the spokes can cause a serious injury. Some front mounts have no wheel guards, and some rear mounts have

Bicycle Seat

inadequate ones. What seems like adequate protection for a baby may well not be enough for a two- or three-year-old with longer legs.

2. A strong and reliable safety belt is a must.

3. I've seen toddlers sporting the smallest sized football helmets for extra head protection.

THE PORTABLE BABY IN THE CAR

If you buy one piece of equipment for your baby, make it an approved, crash-tested car safety restraint. This is one item which you cannot afford to be without or improvise. Car accidents are the leading cause of death in childhood after the early months have passed. Protection in the event of a crash is just as important as the immunizations that your baby receives, yet many parents either use no safety restraints at all, use inadequate ones, or use them improperly.

To date, government standards are not strict enough for this item, and some of the restraints on the market will not protect your baby as well as your safety belt protects you. Brands of seats are not discussed here because new products are constantly coming on the market. Instead, general guidelines for selecting

Question: *Why do we need to buy an approved car-safety restraint for the baby?*

Good Advice

It is vital that babies travel in automobiles in government-approved carriers. Children under 45 pounds in government approved seats.

—Benjamin Spock, M.D.,
Baby and Child Care
(208th printing, 1976)

Ordinarily a parent's arms are a very secure place for a child. But this is not so in a car. Even if you are wearing a lap and shoulder belt yourself, the child would be torn from your grasp by the violent forces of a collision.

—Physicians for Automotive Safety,
Don't Risk Your Child's Life! (1977)

Never put a belt around you and the child held on your lap. Your own weight, greatly increased by collision forces, would press the belt deeply into the child's body; this could lead to serious or even fatal injuries.

—Physicians for Automotive Safety,
Don't Risk Your Child's Life! (1977)

An adult lap belt isn't satisfactory for a child under the age of about four years or weighing less than forty pounds. In a crash, the lap belt could slip up over the child's underdeveloped pelvic bones and onto the abdomen, possibly causing internal injuries.

—Consumer's Union,
Guide for Buying for Babies

There are no safe car beds on the market. But if you must use one, strap it to the back seat with two safety belts, put netting over the top, and wedge something between the bed and the back of the front seat. For the baby who sits up, it is far safer to use a belt in the back seat, in the center of the car, than letting him ride loose.

Bad Advice

The leg space for the back seat for the car can be filled with luggage and covered with a pad so that the crawling baby will have room in which to roam or fall asleep.

—Benjamin Spock, M.D.,
Baby and Child Care
(168th printing, 1967)

I hold Jennifer in my arms. She's not a very good traveler. This way I can feed her easily and distract her with toys.

When I drive alone with the baby, I wear him in a front carrier and strap us both into the car with a safety belt.

Mark is a husky, 23-pound eleven-month-old. A grown-up seat belt contains him quite well.

The top part of our carriage can be lifted off and used as a car bed.

among four basic types of restraints are included. Please see the Resources section for a useful pamphlet, which is well worth looking at before you buy or borrow a car safety restraint.

Owning a restraint, however, is only the first step. Unless you install it properly and use it correctly each time you take the baby in the car, you are not providing your baby with the protection he needs should an accident occur. You may be a skillful and careful driver but others you are sharing the roads with may not be.

THE INFANT CARRIER

The infant carrier is a tub-shaped seat suitable for the baby from birth to about 20 pounds. It is designed to ride backward and *must* be used that way. The carrier is strapped to the seat of the car with a lap belt. The baby rides in a semi-upright position secured with a shoulder harness and cross strap.

This type of seat is easy to install and to get the baby in and out of. No permanent installation is necessary, which means the seat can be used in the front or back of the car. Some brands convert to accommodate a child over twenty pounds. Before you invest in any seat, check the length of your car's seat belts

and be sure to measure the space where you will be using the carrier.

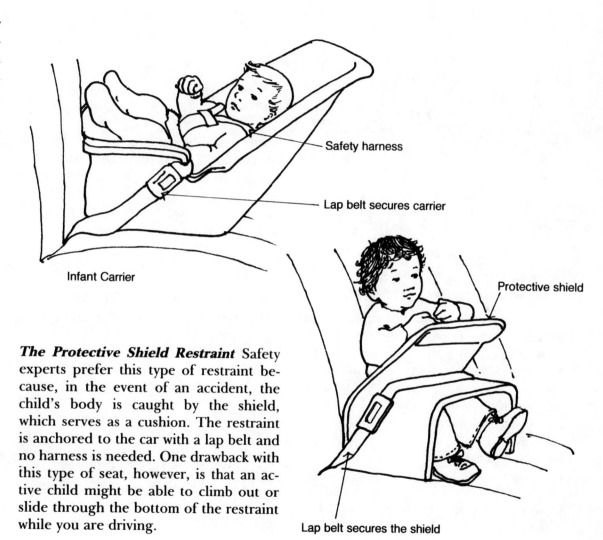

Safety harness

Lap belt secures carrier

Infant Carrier

Protective shield

Lap belt secures the shield

The Protective Shield Restraint Safety experts prefer this type of restraint because, in the event of an accident, the child's body is caught by the shield, which serves as a cushion. The restraint is anchored to the car with a lap belt and no harness is needed. One drawback with this type of seat, however, is that an active child might be able to climb out or slide through the bottom of the restraint while you are driving.

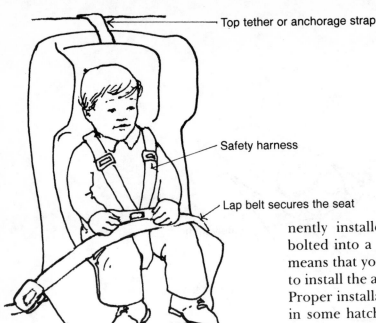

Top tether or anchorage strap

Safety harness

Lap belt secures the seat

Traditional car seat

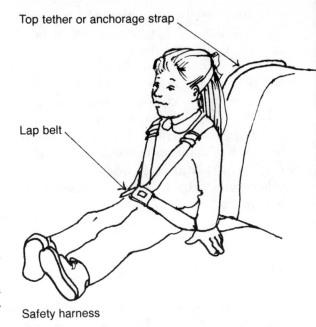

Top tether or anchorage strap

Lap belt

Safety harness

The "Traditional" Car Restraint This restraint is suitable for babies from about 15 to 20 pounds up to 40 to 43 pounds. The child is held by a harness which consists of two shoulder straps, a lap belt, and a crotch strap. The seat is then strapped to the car with a vehicle lap belt.

Many restraints of this design require additional anchorage to the car in the form of a tether strap secured at the top of the seat. This tether strap can be joined to a lap belt in the rear seat, or it can be clipped or hooked to a perma-nently installed ring or hook which is bolted into a metal part of the car. This means that you may have to pay someone to install the anchorage assembly for you. Proper installation can also be a problem in some hatchbacks and station wagons, so be sure to check into this before you buy. Extra anchorage assemblies are available for a second car.

It must be stressed that unless the tether is used properly, this seat will lose its protective value entirely. If you bor-row or rent cars, don't invest in a re-straint which requires additional anchor-age. One other seldom-mentioned buy-ing consideration is whether or not the restraint provides a good view. A baby might not care whether or not he can see out the window, but a two- or a three-year-old does. Make sure the restraint you choose is high enough so that an older child can see outside the car. These seats require top tethers.

The Safety Harness This type of re-straint is suitable for babies and young children between 15 and 50 pounds. It provides good protection at considerably less expense than the shield or "tradi-tional" designs. The harness is secured to the car with a vehicle lap belt, but must also be anchored at the top with a tether hooked to a permanently installed anchorage system. The harness should be used in the center of the back seat only. It can be used with a cushion to provide an older child with a view.

KEEPING THE BABY HAPPY IN THE CAR

Most tiny babies hardly notice they're in the car. The steady churn of the motor and the soothing motion puts them right to sleep. But as the baby gets older and more active and curious, sitting in a safety restraint for more than a magical amount of time can become sheer torture for everyone.

We soon learn what the limit is, and it grows ever shorter. A quick trip is tolerable because the end is in sight, but on a longer ride a "bag of tricks" is really a necessity. The following suggestions—gleaned from miles of experience and from the parents of many babies—are geared for driving under the worst possible conditions—alone in 95-degree weather, when you have to get there.

CAR TRICKS

1. Use an approved car-safety restraint correctly every time you take the baby in the car!
2. Remove all loose objects from the back window ledge of the car.
3. Dress the baby in comfortable clothing.
4. In hot weather take off the baby's shoes.
5. In hot weather line the restraint with a towel. Restraints are made of vinyl, which doesn't absorb the baby's perspiration.
6. Start out with a double diaper or an overnight disposable diaper. (Though we often mean to stop to change the baby, things might be going too well to rock the boat.)
7. Tie as many tried and true diverse toys to the restraint as possible (using a *short* length of string in which a baby cannot get dangerously entangled), and so that they won't interfere with your driving if the baby decides to throw them.
8. An older baby might enjoy a "surprise bag" of small, manipulatable toys he has not seen before (paper cups that nest, measuring spoons, baseball cards, a harmonica, a small hand mirror, etc.).
9. Music is a wonderful distraction—the car radio or your own voice.
10. If possible, tie a bottle of juice or water to the restraint. Otherwise, bring two or even three bottles, so that you won't have to pick up the castaways every two minutes. There is now a product on the market for attaching a bottle to a safety restraint.
11. Bring food—anything that works which is easy for the baby to chew and swallow. (If appearances are important, cover the baby with a large bib.)
12. Leave a little before naptime or travel at night or plan to stop often.
13. Decide before you leave when and where you're going to stop. You'll be less tempted to take the howling, furious baby out of the restraint if there is a concrete goal in sight.

TRAVELING WITH THE PORTABLE BABY

PLANNING

When you have a baby along, you deserve to travel in style. If you've never used the best accommodations you can afford, now is the time to start. The baby doesn't know that you're trying to get where you're going and has the same needs as always—to eat, sleep, play, and fuss. If you're taking a long trip, try to fly. After that, a train is preferable to a bus.

Any kind of travel requires some planning, but if you're going *alone* with the baby, it's wise to prepare with care.

Until "people movers" are standard equipment at airports, train stations, and bus terminals, you may find yourself walking as far as a mile to get to your seat—an exhausting project if you're juggling a baby, your coat, a pocketbook, and the baby's bag as well as luggage. You'll also want to get to the departure point early enough to change the baby before boarding. Take what you need for a short outing—diapers, pacifiers, and food as well as some toys of the highest distractability value. Travel on public transportation is one of the few situations in which there is no exit if the baby does fall apart.

FLYING WITH A BABY

If you have to travel more than a couple of hundred miles, flying is certainly the easiest way to get there. If you fly, the chances are good that you won't have to think about eating more than one meal out or sleeping somewhere overnight. Whatever anxieties you or the baby experience will be over very quickly.

Making a Reservation The baby is a free passenger until age two on domestic flights. On international flights her ride will cost 10 percent of your fare. You will have to hold her on your lap unless you are lucky enough to have a free seat next

to you. Travel on slow days and off hours for the best chance at this.

Airline personnel are almost as harried as you are and sometimes forget to mention the array of services they provide for parents traveling with children. To get the best accommodations you must ask point by point about what they offer. The following are some questions you might go over with the ticket agent when you make your reservation.

Questions to ask the airline when making a reservation:

1. Can I make seating arrangements now? If so, request the "bassinet row," the first row of seats in tourist class, where no smoking is permitted. There is more legroom here, and a small space to put the baby on the floor. If you can't arrange seating in advance, get to the airport early. You'll probably be allowed to board the plane ahead of everyone else.

2. Does the airport provide strollers? Many do. If strollers are available, find out exactly where you will have to go to get one. However, your own umbrella-type stroller can be very useful in an airport and can be carried onto the plane and stored with the carry-on luggage.

3. Does the flight carry baby food? Airlines usually do, but it's typically

some jarred stuff; they usually don't have formula. The attendants will warm up a bottle for you if you make your request before they start serving a meal.

4. Does the plane stock disposable diapers? This applies to international flights in particular. Don't use yours if you can use theirs.

5. Does it have bassinets? Some do. They lock onto a bulkhead and are very convenient for the baby who doesn't yet sit up or crawl.

6. If you want to bring a car seat for use at your destination, it can be checked through with your luggage, unboxed, because it is crash proof. You also can often ship larger equipment as "oversized packages" (playpens, etc.) for an extra charge.

A Bag of Tricks for Flying

1. During takeoffs and landings have the baby sucking on a bottle, a pacifier, or your breast. Swallowing helps clear the ear passages, which become blocked when the air pressure in the cabin changes as the plane changes altitude. But if the baby won't drink anything, and cries, don't be too upset. Crying helps clear the ears, too.

2. If you are in the bassinet row with a fairly active baby, place him on the floor on an airplane blanket and give

him some toys. The blanket defines a spot from which the baby may be less apt to wander.

3. If you have a free seat next to you, request a tray for the baby who can sit up fairly well. The tray is good for playing on, banging on, and eating from—at least for a little while.

4. If earphones are available, take advantage of them (and hope your fellow passengers do, too). Even an eight-month-old enjoys trying to tune in the channels and listening a bit.

5. Everything in the seat pocket should be of interest to a baby—the reserved seat cards are good for teething, the flight magazines for looking at and tearing up.

6. Food! Bring some snacks for the baby and indulge her. For those with teeth the usual bland airline dinners are very appropriate, and so are the spoons and cups wrapped in plastic. (You, however, might not have time to eat.)

BUS TRAVEL

If you can take a train, a plane, or drive instead of riding on a bus, do so. Buses have fewer amenities, less space, little "action" to divert the baby, and no one to help you. You'll need to bring everything in one bag—bottle, lunch, diapers, and a pad to change the baby on your lap. A "surprise bag" of toys will also help. You won't necessarily be able to replace used-up items at rest stops, except for whole cow's milk and snacks. A harness or infant seat can be useful if there is a free seat next to you. But if the baby is into the creeping, crawling stage, make your trip as short as possible. A couple of hours of peace is all you can expect before you and the baby begin to deteriorate.

TRAIN TRAVEL

The train is somewhat better equipped than the bus because of room to walk around in, drinking fountains, restrooms, and club cars to visit. An overnight trip is not difficult with a baby who still sleeps in a basket. Put a net over it and wedge securely. But there is no room for a crib on a train even if you're traveling in a drawing room. There are also no high chairs, though Amtrak claims that if you are on a train with a dining car, it will be well stocked with commercial baby food.

SHIP TRAVEL

Aboard a luxury ocean liner you might actually be able to have an (expensive) vacation with a baby. Passenger ships are equipped with cribs and high chairs. Food is no problem. If you find the dining room too trying, you can feed the baby in your cabin. A true luxury liner has baby-sitters for the evenings when you want to go dancing, and nurseries where you can drop the baby off while you go for a massage. On some ships you can even have your laundry done while you sleep. Should the baby get sick, a doctor is nearby.

HEALTH NEEDS AWAY FROM HOME

What are you going to do without the pediatrician's call-in hour at seven in the morning? Who but your doctor knows whether or not cork is digestible, how many bowel movements make diarrhea, what the strange crust is on the baby's eye, or if the blotches on his back are prickly heat or roseola? A sick baby is so helpless. Caring for one is nerve-racking no matter where you are. Should the baby get sick, though, you will probably find your intuition and common sense sharpened when the doctor is a hundred or a thousand miles away.

MAKE YOUR TRIP MORE PLEASANT...

Dear Frances,

We actually found ourselves looking for parks for Anna to play in instead of visiting museums. Next time I think we'd do it differently. It might be better to go camping. It's more informal. There are other people with young children, and we wouldn't have to worry about eating in restaurants all the time. I'd do that or settle in one spot for the summer. You see, originally we'd planned to stay at a Yugoslavian resort for two weeks, but we kept going down the coast looking for the ideal place and never found it. My husband, though, has a totally different view of our trip. It was a novelty to him — not working nine to five, and spending lots of time with Anna. He actually thinks he had a vacation. It was interesting, but not a vacation for me at all. My expectations weren't unrealistic, though. My mother had warned me! She said she didn't have a real vacation until my sister and I went to camp at ages ten and twelve. Do you think we'll have to wait that long?

Cynthia

Dear Frances,

Wish we hadn't loaded up the car with all that stuff—high chair, playpen, and walker. When we got to St. Louis, my mother had rented a crib and borrowed the rest from a family down the street.

Mary

Suggestion.

For equipment, including a car seat, ask your hosts to borrow if possible or look in the Yellow Pages under Baby Rentals or Rentals.

Dear Michael,

I'm sorry we didn't warn you about an eleven-month-old's expertise at getting into everything. I feel terrible about the broken china and torn paperbacks.

Barbara

Suggestion.

See page 193 on baby-proofing the house. A few simple devices, which are very portable, might make a trip more enjoyable. Strapping tape is more portable than baby-proofing devices.

SCHEDULING A VISIT WITH THE DOCTOR OR TALKING BY PHONE

If you haven't traveled with your baby before, you might want to schedule a visit or phone call to your pediatrician or clinic at least a week before you leave. You will be assured that the baby is in good health and will have a chance to go over any concerns you might have. If the baby needs shots, the reaction (if any) will be over by the time you leave. You will also be able to find out if there is anything you need to take along.

If the baby is prone to ear infections or stomach upsets and has been treated regularly for these before, you might consult your doctor about taking the proper drugs along, particularly for travel outside of the country, or about getting a prescription which can be filled once you get there (check the country or state's regulations, though, because they may not honor the prescription of an out-of-town doctor). Miracle potions to soothe the baby on the airplane or in the car should always come from your doctor. Don't rely on anyone else's advice or anything you have in the medicine cabinet for adults. Also, if you are still sterilizing bottles and your baby is over three months old, ask your doctor if it is still necessary. This way there will be one less thing to think about.

TRAVELING WITH MEDICINE . . .

1. Make sure "old" medicine will still be good by the end of the trip.
2. Make sure it doesn't need to be refrigerated.
3. If it's not already in plastic bottles with good child-proof caps, have your druggist transfer it (as well as the directions).

WHAT TO TAKE FOR HEALTH CARE

- [ ] Rectal thermometer.
- [ ] Baby aspirin.
- [ ] Favorite health-information book.
- [ ] Vitamins.
- [ ] Quick-drying sun shield if you will be outdoors in hot weather.
- [ ] Something for diaper rash (new foods, changes in weather, and fewer diaper changes in transit can bring this on).
- [ ] Your doctor's phone number (long distance is not an outrageous possibility!).
- [ ] Medical-insurance card and numbers.

IN A FOREIGN COUNTRY

- [ ] Medicine for diarrhea.
- [ ] Medicine for a bad cold.
- [ ] Centigrade rectal thermometer with formula for conversion to Farenheit taped to thermometer case. (See health care chapter, page 203, for conversion to Farenheit.)

HEALTH CARE RESOURCES WHEN YOU ARE AWAY

1. Experience, intuition, and common sense.
2. Health-information book.
3. Long distance call to your doctor, or call to a local doctor.
4. Emergency room at nearest hospital.
5. Police, fire, ambulance, etc.
6. Nearest poison control center (also take the number of the one in your home town).
7. Most motels and hotels have doctors on call.

IN A FOREIGN COUNTRY

8. American Consulate or embassy.

9. Through the largest and best hotel, if you're staying there or not, you can contact medical help.

I didn't really worry about health care when we went to Italy last summer with Anna because I think there are good doctors everywhere. The only medicine I took with me was baby aspirin. They actually had better drugs over the counter in Europe. She did get a bad cough, and the pharmacist there gave us cough medicine in suppository form. It was great. No battles. I just slipped it in when I changed her diaper and she hardly noticed it . . . . No, I didn't take a thermometer because I can tell when she has a high fever by feeling her. Her eyes look dull and she is very listless and whimpery.

Jessica did get diarrhea—a day after we got to San Francisco. I did all the logical things I'd done when it happened before—taking her off fruit, giving her rice, etc. But I think what really helped was using bottled water instead of tap water.

I absolutely panicked when he rolled off the bed. I can still remember the sound of his head hitting that cold, hard Mexican tile floor. I wrapped him up and ran downstairs to the desk. As I was trying to explain "broken head—concussion" in my terrible Spanish, Jake

stopped crying, but I still insisted on taking him to the nearest hospital for an X ray. By that time he was very cheerful and I felt a little embarrassed. I'm sure they though I was absolutely nuts at that hospital, but they were very obliging.

EATING AWAY FROM HOME

The best approach to feeding the baby away from home is not worrying if the baby isn't as hungry as usual. A baby who normally eats three meals a day might prefer four or five snacks. Also, if you know that the baby eats better at one meal than another, no one will report you if you serve the veal for breakfast and the oatmeal at dinner.

Dear Frances,
Have been in Los Angeles with Jessica for a week and she's holding up really well. But I'm not. Meals are a real struggle. What a drag it is to hold a wiggly ten-month-old on my lap three times a day. If we weren't coming home tomorrow, I would beg, borrow, or steal a high chair.

Ethel

Suggestion.
Portable alternatives: car seat, backpack with loading stand, circular walker which folds up flat, baby chairs with suction cups which will stick to the bottom of any table.

FOOD FOR TRAVEL

LIQUIDS

1. If you're breast-feeding, don't stop. Breast milk, the ultimate portable food, is sterile, warm, and easily digestible as well as a familiar, soothing comfort and sure continuity on a trip. Remember to keep up your own fluid intake.

2. Proprietary formulas are convenient in bottle, can, or powder form. Try the baby out on other brands in case your usual brand is not available.

3. Powdered skim milk is very convenient because it is lightweight and

needs no refrigeration. It can also be mixed up one bottle at a time as needed.

4. In transit, it's wise not to let your baby drink the water which comes out of the tap on trains or buses or in gas stations. Bring your own water or purchase bottled water along the way. Water in a foreign country can be risky, too. If you want to sterilize water a bottle at a time, bring along an electric immersion coil (for travel abroad also bring a voltage converter) and let the water boil for at least three minutes.

5. Juice travels well and comes in a variety of small cans. Orange juice is the least desirable, unless your baby has done well on it before. It can cause diarrhea and, unstrained, it plugs up nipples.

SOLIDS

1. Yogurt is a good food to introduce before a trip, if you haven't already. It helps establish strong bacteria in the intestinal tract, and it is available in most large and small stores throughout this country.

2. Commerical baby food in jars requires no refrigeration until it is opened, but if the baby doesn't eat all the food in the jar, throw the remainder away—especially if you have fed her directly from the jar.

3. Make your own baby food a meal at a time from your own plate with a small baby-food grinder. The grinder also serves as a dish.

4. Dried cereal, rice, eggs, and bananas are all bland foods, available everywhere.

MISCELLANEOUS

1. A large, smock-type plastic bib (which covers the baby's arms as well as his front) is invaluable for travel away from a washing machine.

2. A clothespin or sweater clip will convert any large napkin or cloth diaper into a bib.

EATING IN RESTAURANTS

If you have never taken the baby to a restaurant, screw up your courage and try. If you haven't been in a couple of months, try again before you start traveling—things change rapidly. The baby who is still happy in an infant seat can be a wonderful dinner companion.

The eight-month-old can be a perfect guest, cooing and playing quietly with a spoon. But an eleven-month-old can be an absolute horror.

It was six o'clock and Caitlin was really hungry by the time we pulled into a restaurant called the Chicken Stop. A huge plastic chicken on the roof made us think it was a fast-food place. It wasn't. All the guests were dressed up on their way to a concert. We waited for twenty minutes for a table. She'd already had her bottle in the car and was delighted with the mints fed to her by the cashier. When we were finally seated, I took one look at the high chair and knew we were in for trouble. It had no strap, which was fine for a while. She sat quietly, shredding up the paper napkins, opening the cellophane packages of oyster crackers, stuffing them in her mouth and blowing them out at us. Then she ate a few ice cubes, but when I turned to cut up the chicken which finally came, she stood up, lunged for the ice water, and knocked it over. The waitress slipped and almost fell with her tray. By that time Caitlin's only interest in the chicken and mashed potatoes was rubbing them into her hair. We asked for the check, left a huge tip, and ran.

By the third baby, I finally figured out that breakfast is the most successful meal to eat out when you're traveling. The baby is still relatively fresh and hungry, and breakfast food—french toast, scrambled eggs, and *juice—is perfect for a baby. For lunch we usually stop for a picnic by the road if the weather is nice, and for dinner I feed Benjamin a jar of baby food in the motel room, while the others go out to eat. Then I go out, happily, alone.*

SOME SUGGESTIONS

1. Choose an appropriate restaurant.
2. Go early.
3. Bring a harness if you are unsure about the high chairs.
4. Bring a healthy hors d'oeuvre such as carrot sticks.
5. Bring several good toys or a book to look at.
6. Request a table out of the main traffic flow, so the mess will not offend or endanger waiters and waitresses.

CLOTHING FOR TRAVEL

1. Dark clothing *looks* cleaner longer than light clothing.
2. Any clothing will stay cleaner longer if the baby is covered with a huge waterproof bib or smock that goes over the arms as well as down the front.

3. Lightweight clothing, rather than denim or corduroy, is easy to pack and carry. It also dries more quickly if you have to wash it out by hand at night.
4. Babies grow very quickly. If you're going away for more than a few weeks, take clothing and shoes that will fit by the end of your stay.

DIAPERS

Though disposable diapers are a logical choice for most travel, they can become a real bother if you have to carry a whole trip's supply through a foreign country or into the wilderness on a camping expedition. Here are some things you might not have considered.

1. You can purchase disposable diapers without the plastic backing and use them with rubber pants. These are not as good as the real thing, but they are biodegradable and less bulky than regular disposables.
2. Retired cloth diapers from a service are almost as inexpensive as disposables, and they can also be thrown away as you go. The advantage of cloth is that it is less bulky than paper and can be wedged into the infinite corners in a suitcase or camping gear.

3. A cloth diaper aided by a disposable paper diaper liner on the inside and rubber pants on the outside will last much longer than a cloth diaper alone. The diaper liners are lightweight and not too bulky to pack. But practice first.

The diaper scene in Greece was a pain. We took a duffel bag full of Pampers, four a day to last for eight weeks. The baby was lighter than the diapers, and I think Terry actually carried her most of the time while I pushed the Pampers around in the stroller. I wouldn't ever do this again. I would bring a dozen cloth diapers, rubber pants, and diaper liners. I'd wash them out by hand if I had to.

I figured out how many Susanna used a day—eight—and threw in two for good measure in case she got diarrhea. Do you have any idea what the volume of 300 Pampers is? We paid $70 in overweight. Then it turned out that she only used five a day. She lost her special bottle with a straw and refused to drink out of a regular bottle. She would drink very little from a cup, and just wasn't urinating as much. I certainly hadn't planned on coming home from Europe with 150 Pampers, but we did. Even so, the security of having them was worth it.

SLEEPING AWAY FROM HOME

Tiny babies can sleep just about any-where. During the short, golden phase, before they can move around, improvisa-tion really works. A well-padded laundry basket, a humble cardboard carton, a dresser drawer, or the center of an adult bed is fine. But when the baby starts to move, you'll have to think about contain-ment. A lightweight aluminum and mesh portable crib or playpen are good choices for travel, and so are crib sides which strap on to any regular bed. They weigh less than ten pounds. Wooden portable cribs are heavy and expensive.

Just like adults, it takes babies a while to adjust to sleeping in a new place. The same bedtime ritual you use at home will make going to sleep easier for the baby and so will a familiar blanket or stuffed animal.

RESOURCES

The Portable Baby

Fales, Edward D., *Belts on Buttons Down,* Delacorte, New York, 1971.

Don't Risk Your Child's Life!
Write to:
Physicians for Automotive Safety
50 Union Avenue
Irvington, N.J. 17111

Backpacking with Babies and Small Children
Write to:
Goldie Silverman
Signpost Publications
16812 36th Avenue
W. Lynnwood, WA., 98036

-19-
Saving Money

There is no getting around it: Having a baby is expensive. The price of delivery, health care, clothing, food, basic equipment, and child-care services goes up every day along with the cost of living. At the same time, the pressures to buy grow and multiply. We are besieged by magazine and television ads urging us to own myriad "new improved" baby products, from educational "crib environments" to plug-in bottle warmers for the car and rolling toys designed to aid a baby in learning to crawl. Even if parents do stick to the basics and resist the frills, most have to make some financial adjustments during the first year, particularly if one parent no longer works or if the family had to renovate or move to make room for the baby.

On the brighter side, wouldn't you agree, even if you didn't know in advance what the expenses would be, that your baby is worth every penny and more? The expenses, in fact, need not be overwhelming. Friends, relatives, and even strangers are truly generous when it comes to a baby—quick to help, give, lend, share, and trade. There is the tax deduction, for whatever it's worth. And to some degree, there is a self-correcting tendency to reduce overall living expenses. Many new parents go out less, entertain on a more informal basis, and take simpler vacations. Most often, they do so mainly to simplify their lives, which have suddenly become more complex, and make more time available for parenthood. In the process, though, the savings recapture many of the extra costs of the baby.

Following are some ways to analyze expenses (if you can bear to) to save money. The format for calculating expenses is adapted from Sylvia Porter's *Money Book*. With all you save, be sure to treat yourself to something special; you honestly deserve it.

One of the biggest adjustments we've had to make is being broke. I'd given up my job. We'd renovated to make room for Dana, and were paying off the home-improvement loan. And then there are the surprises—the washing machine that decides to bite the dust just when you need it the most. You can't affort to wait for the sale that's coming up to replace it, so you buy whatever they have, which happens to be the luxury model that has more knobs and dials and options than you want. When I actually sat down to figure out why we were so much broker than we'd expected, I realized it was mostly the insidious buying: two $40 car seats, because the first one didn't give the baby a view once he was old enough to want one; two folding strollers in fifteen months, because the first one was a cheap piece of junk that wore out in eight months; an unusual backpack which didn't fit properly; a walker which he used for a month; a fancy Danish-modern high chair that he won't sit in anyway; puzzles that he is too young to do anything with but chew on; two mobiles that are in pieces. Oh, that's another thing. The more you own, the more you have to clean, store, pick up the pieces of, and protect from damage. And then, of course, you pay a baby-sitter, if you can find one, to go out for the evening to get away from it all. But then, it's either that or the psychiatrist.

HOSPITAL AND HEALTH CARE COSTS

YOUR COSTS

Hospitalization _____
Delivery-room charge _____
Nursery charges _____
Pediatrician's visit in hospital _____
Circumcision setup charge _____
Circumcision fee _____
Obstetrician's fee _____
Pediatrician's fee for 6–12 visits first year, plus _____
   cost of immunization program and tests
Additional cost for health insurance _____
Rectal thermometer _____
Vaporizer _____
Miscellaneous drugs (vitamins, antibiotics) _____
   Total $ _____

Ways to Save Money

☐ Leave the hospital as soon as you feel able.

☐ A private room can cost up to $40 more per day than a semiprivate room.

☐ Review your health-insurance plan to make sure you are getting the best deal.

☐ Be aware of several deductions when you do your income tax (see box on page 189), particularly those relating to health care.

☐ Ask pediatrician for and/or accept all sample vitamins or "starter" drugs. They often have free samples from drug companies for just this purpose.

☐ Shop at a discount pharmacy.

☐ Ask pediatrician to prescribe the baby's medicines by their generic names.

☐ Take the baby to the doctor regularly. These visits, along with good nutrition, are the best form of preventative medicine.

CLOTHING COSTS

YOUR COSTS

Undershirts _____
Nightgowns _____
Sleeping bags _____
Stretch suits _____
Receiving blankets _____
Diapers _____
Diaper pins _____
Sweater, hat, booties _____
Waterproof pants _____
Bunting _____
Snowsuit _____
Mittens _____
Overalls _____
Shirts _____
Socks _____
Shoes _____
Pajamas _____
Miscellaneous _____
   Total $ _____

Ways to Save Money

☐ Don't buy everything all at once. Common gifts are blankets, sweaters, hats, booties, and sacque sets.

☐ Accept all hand-me-downs (see page 103 for revitalizing them).

☐ Patronize discount stores, thrift shops, and the Salvation Army. Mail order can also be cheaper than department stores.

☐ Clothing sales are often held in the following months: January, March, April, and July.

Ways to Save Money on Clothing Costs

☐ When you buy new, start with six-month sizes. Then go by your baby's weight and height rather than age.

☐ Skip the bunting. Put the money toward a good snowsuit instead (see page 96).

☐ If you sew, knit, or crochet, and have time, do so for your baby.

☐ Figure out the cost comparisons in your area for owning your own diapers, or using a service or disposable diapers.

☐ If you use disposables, try out supermarket brands for very young babies. Always buy by the case at a discount drug store (see diaper section for more suggestions).

☐ Don't buy shoes until the baby needs them.

NURSERY AND EQUIPMENT COSTS	YOUR COSTS
Fitted crib sheets	_____
Waterproof pads	_____
Crib blankets	_____
Comforter or quilt	_____
Mattress pad	_____
Bassinet, cradle, or carrying basket	_____
Crib	_____
Crib mattress	_____
Crib bumpers	_____
Diaper pail	_____
Infant seat	_____
Changing table and drawers	_____
Nursery lamp	_____
Miscellaneous decorations	_____
Baby carriage	_____
Baby stroller	_____
Front pack or sling	_____
Backpack	_____
Port-a-Crib	_____
Playpen	_____
Total $	_____

Ways to Save Money

☐ Make your own changing table out of an old dresser (page 100).

☐ Even if you don't sew, wait until the gifts come in before you buy receiving blankets.

☐ Consider buying a secondhand crib if you can't borrow one. The cost of replacing the mattress is less than buying the whole works new.

☐ Skip the nursery lamp. Any lamp with a low-wattage bulb will do.

☐ Don't buy a carriage—borrow one. Few people have room to store them anyway.

☐ Do not buy a wooden portable crib if you really want a portable bed. They are very heavy and do not fit easily into the trunks of small cars. Buy or borrow a lightweight aluminum and mesh crib or playpen instead—or crib sides.

FEEDING EQUIPMENT AND FOOD COSTS | YOUR COSTS

Bottles	_____
Extra nipples, rings, caps, etc.	_____
Bottle brush and nipple brush	_____
Sterilizer	_____
Hot plate	_____
Bottle warmer	_____
Warming dish	_____
Formula for 3–5 months	_____
Bottled baby food (6 months' supply)	_____
Baby spoon, cup (tip-proof)	_____
High chair or feeding table	_____
Baby-food grinder, food mill, etc.	_____
Total	$ _____

Ways to Save Money

☐ Breast-feed your baby.

☐ If you bottle-feed, forget the sterilizer. For the short amount of time you will be sterilizing (if at all), a spaghetti pot will do the job (see page 41).

☐ A bottle warmer is not really necessary either. A sink or coffee can full of hot water will do the job. And infants don't need warmed bottles anyway.

☐ Introduce solids between 4 and 6 months, then make your own baby food. Commercial baby food is ten times more expensive than homemade.

☐ Borrow a high chair or, if you buy, choose a high chair over a feeding table. Without the tray, the child can sit at the table with you when he's older.

☐ Hot plates and electric warming dishes are expensive. Any plastic dish will do for the baby to eat out of. Food can easily be warmed in a four-egg poacher or Pyrex dish (see Feeding section).

☐ Read labels for the best nutritional buys.

☐ Do not buy an elaborate electric baby-food grinder. For the short amount of time a baby eats pureed foods, a hand grinder or a blender works just as well.

MISCELLANEOUS EQUIPMENT COSTS | YOUR COSTS

Baby-care books	_____
Baby record-keeping book	_____
Diaper bag	_____
Bottle bag	_____
Brush and comb	_____
Crib mobile	_____
Car bed or seat	_____
Birth announcements	_____
Baby-proofing devices, e.g., gates	_____
Baby toys, ad infinitum	_____
Baby swing	_____
Jolly Jumper	_____
Baby walker	_____
Riding toy	_____
Total	$ _____

Ways to Save Money

☐ For record keeping, see the back of this book.

☐ See page 232 for a mobile you can make.

☐ A good car seat—not a car bed, which is dangerous—is an investment well worth making. See page 171 for ideas on choosing the seat which will last the longest, be easiest for you to use and install, and offers the baby the most interesting ride once she reaches the age where distractions are absolutely necessary.

☐ Child-proofing devices are important but are often available secondhand. Read pros and cons on page 195 to get the best safety gates.

☐ Your house is full of baby toys. See page 229 for ideas. If you buy new toys, do not rely on manufacturer's suggestions for the appropriate ages.

☐ Bigger toys—swings and slides—can often be found at tag and garage sales. Also consider a hammock instead of a swing.

☐ Special bathtubs are a luxury.

MISCELLANEOUS SERVICE COSTS	YOUR COSTS	TOTAL COSTS	
Baby nurse and/or household help	_____	Total hospital and health care costs	_____
Baby-sitters	_____	Total clothing costs	_____
Day-care centers	_____	Total nursery and equipment costs	_____
Family day care	_____	Total feeding equipment and food costs	_____
Larger telephone bills to announce birth and	_____	Total miscellaneous equipment costs	_____
long-distance calls to keep you from feeling		Total miscellaneous services costs	_____
isolated		Grand Total $	_____
Baby photographers	_____		
Legal services, e.g., updating will	_____		
Increased life insurance	_____		
Total $	_____		

Ways to Save Money

☐ Do you really need a baby nurse? If friends, relatives, and husband can't volunteer to help you out in early weeks, consider a part-time housekeeper 2 or 3 hours a day to take care of the house and you, not the baby.

☐ Don't scrimp on child care! It's not worth it.

☐ Birth announcements will save on initial news of the baby. But as far as I'm concerned, bigger phone bills for local calls are part of a new mother's sanity.

☐ Take advantage of free photography offers from large discount stores. But stop there.

THE CHILD-CARE TAX CREDIT

The Tax Reform Act of 1976 lets working parents offset their income tax with a credit for child-care and housekeeping costs. The credit allows you to deduct 20% of such costs (up to $2,000 a year—$400—for one child, or $4,000 a year—$800—for two or more children) from the total tax you would otherwise have to pay. Now with the credit, those who choose the standard deduction as well as those who itemize, may have tax relief for child-care expenses.

The maximum credit of $400 for one child or $800 for more than one child replaces the itemized deduction for child-care expenses allowed under prior law. The basic requirement for eligibility is: the working parent must maintain a household for at least one dependent child and pay for child care or housekeeping help in order to be available to earn a living.

Under this law, there is no income limitation in the child-care provision. Whether you earn more than $100,000 or less than $10,000, you get the same $400 or $800 tax credit, provided, of course, that you've spent at least five times that amount for child-care fees.

Married persons, whether part-time or full-time workers, are eligible for the tax credit as long as the child-care expenses upon which the credit is based don't exceed the amount earned by the lower-paid spouse. Married people are also allowed a credit when one spouse does not work but is either enrolled as a full-time (five months or more during a year) student or is disabled. Such a student or disabled spouse is deemed for these purposes to have an income of $166 per month for purposes of earned income limitation.

Married taxpayers, except those who live apart, must file a joint return to claim credit for child-care expenses. Those who live apart from their spouses may have the credit if they have lived apart for the last six months of the taxable year, instead of for the entire year.

Among the divorced or legally separated, the parent who has custody of a child for the longest period of the year may now have a credit, whether or not she or he is entitled to a dependent exemption for the child.

As for the type of child care covered, the law no longer makes any distinction between home and outside care. Nor does it disqualify baby-sitting provided by close relatives if the relative is not the parent's dependent.

These costs may be claimed up to the child's fifteenth birthday.

TAX DEDUCTIONS

Apart from the $1,000 standard deduction for each dependent, there are numerous other child-related deductibles buried in the fine print of your tax manual. Here are some of them:

1. The cost of medicine and drugs, whether or not prescribed by a doctor, is deductible.

2. The cost of a vaporizer and thermometer is deductible.

3. The cost of orthopedic shoes or similar devices for a baby is deductible.

4. The cost of vitamins, iron, and other food supplements, if prescribed or recommended by the doctor, is deductible. The cost of special formulas for allergies is not deductible because such formulas are substitutes for regular foods that the baby would eat anyway.

5. Hospital, nursing and laboratory fees, X rays, therapy treatments, and fees paid to doctors are deductible.

6. The cost of hospitalization and medical insurance is partly deductible. The cost of life insurance is not deductible.

7. Accident and health insurance premiums are partly deductible.

8. Travel expenses to and from the doctor's office (carfare or 7¢ a mile, plus tolls and parking) are deductible if you are going when the baby has a cold, an injury, or other illness. (If you are going for a well-baby checkup, travel expenses would come under preventive care and should be deductible.)

9. With a new baby there are many items that must be purchased at one time (clothing, furniture, car seats, etc.). The total cost of all these is very high, but if you elect to pay for them with credit cards and to pay in installments, the finance or carrying charges are deductible.

10. A mother who quits her job to have a child may, when she decides to resume working, deduct the cost of an employment agency to help her find a job *in the same field*. The Internal Revenue Service may disallow these deductions if it finds a "sub-stantial" lack of continuity between the past job and the new job; unfortunately the IRS offers no guide-lines for what is "substantial."

11. Child-care expenses and house-keeping costs if you work. (See note on page 156 for more details.)

There are also many items that are *not* deductible. Here are some of them:

1. Maternity clothing

2. Diaper service

3. Baby nurse or household help during postpartum (unless you are working)

4. Cost of caring for baby if you are sick or recovering from an illness

5. Baby toiletries

6. Refresher courses to better qualify you for returning to your job

7. Entertainment expenses incurred while maintaining business contacts from your old job with the intent of reentering the same profession

RESOURCES

Saving Money

Ashley, Paul P., *You and Your Will*, McGraw-Hill, New York, 1975.

Consumers Union, *Guide for Buying for Babies*, Warner, New York, 1975.

Porter, Sylvia, *Sylvia Porter's Money Book*, Doubleday, New York, 1975.

The New ABC'S of Health Insurance
Write to:
Health Insurance Institute
277 Park Avenue
New York, N.Y. 10017

Part VII

SAFETY AND WELL-BEING

-20-
Baby-Proofing the House

For your baby's safety and your sanity, take your first safety tour of the house *before* he learns to crawl. At this point you can still move faster than he can (you often can't with a toddler) and can calmly remove many of the dangers for the baby and frustrations for yourself. A baby has no discrimination or "taste" when it comes to sampling furniture polish, lighter fluid, aspirin, or the contents of your button box. What he lacks in taste, he makes up for in imagination. "Water play" in the toilet bowl, teething on the frayed toaster cord, testing paper clips in electrical outlets, and tasting beautiful bits of sparkling glass from the garbage all have infinite appeal and can be lethal for the curious baby.

FANTASIES AND FEARS

The baby-proof house has padding which covers the floors and runs up the wall for about three feet. The furniture is low, made of foam, and nailed to the floor. An elbow-height shelf runs around every room for precious objects. And, of course, there is professional vacuuming service on call twenty-four hours a day.

My fear is that I'll never be able to be careful enough. When Jason was tiny, we came home one night and discovered that the baby-sitter had put the pacifier on a string around his neck. I was horrified and felt terribly guilty that I'd hired someone who would do such a stupid, dangerous thing. When he learned to crawl, the mouth battle began. No matter how clean I thought the floors were, he could find the nastiest, rustiest old carpet tack and put it in his mouth. Then he learned to stand and kept slipping on the hardwood floors. I was sure he would be permanently brain damaged. Two weeks ago it seemed preposterous that some parents actually remove the knobs from their gas stoves. Not so now. . . . On bad days I sometimes wonder how the human race has survived.

When Sara was eleven months old and not even walking yet, my worst fear was realized. She somehow climbed up on a low bookcase under our bedroom window, which won't open more than six inches in damp weather, and got out onto the fire escape. She is still alive to tell the tale, but I hardly am. Words can't describe the panic or my guilt. Since I couldn't fit out the window, I had to coax her back in.

REALITIES

Nothing is more fundamental to solid educational development than pure, uncontained curiosity.

—BURTON WHITE,
The First Three Years of Life

Parents cannot prevent all accidents. If they were careful enough to try, they would only make their child timid and dependent.

—BENJAMIN SPOCK, M.D.
Baby and Child Care

More children die from accidents than the total of the next five most frequent causes of

childhood death (cancer, congenital malforma-
tion, pneumonia, gastritis and meningitis).
—BOSTON CHILDREN'S HOSPITAL
MEDICAL CENTER,
The Children's Hospital Medical Handbook

USEFUL SAFETY DEVICES

The following safety devices are helpful, but don't let them seduce you into a false sense of security. A watchful eye and a quick hand are still *absolutely* essential.

DRAWER SAFETY LATCHES

Safety latches consist of long, flexible, plastic hooks which fit into catches. A drawer can be opened enough for an adult to slip two fingers in, press down, and release the hook from the catch.

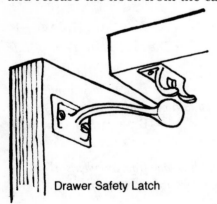

Drawer Safety Latch

CUPBOARD LATCHES

These are useful for cupboards with handles no more than 10 inches apart. Adult dexterity is required to slide the latch bar while pressing down on a release button. In a pinch, strong strapping tape can also be used.

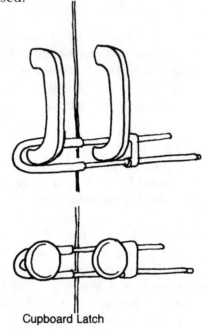

Cupboard Latch

DOORKNOB COVERS

These will make it quite difficult for the baby or toddler to open a door. (A sock held in place by a rubber band works almost as well.)

BLANK OUTLET PLUGS

Blank electrical outlet plugs can be purchased at most hardware stores. They should go in all unused outlets.

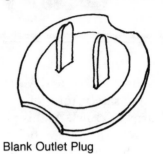

Blank Outlet Plug

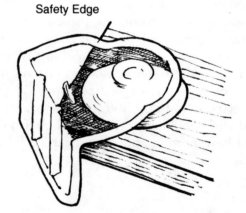

Safety Edge

SAFETY EDGES

Made of soft plastic, safety edges are useful for softening sharp corners on coffee tables and other low furniture.

FOAM TAPE

Foam tape, sold in many hardware stores, is helpful for covering long, sharp expanses such as the edges on a glass coffee table.

STRAPPING TAPE

This incredibly strong tape is a good standby if you don't have safety latches. It can be bought at any hardware store and can easily be replaced once you cut it to open an off-limits cupboard.

SAFETY GATES

Safety gates are useful for closing off high-risk areas such as the tops and bottoms of stairs. Unfortunately, neither of the existing types are totally safe (see below). The most effective gate is one that you can make yourself out of plywood.

Folding Gate. The traditional accordion-type folding safety gate is attached to screw-mounted hinges on one side of a door frame and hooks to a screw eye on the other side. The portable counterparts (which look very much the same) are held in place with a pressure-bar system. The folding gate has many pros and cons as outlined below.

Pros:

1. Permanently mounted gates can be bought to fit openings up to nine feet in width.
2. They are also hard to push out of place.
3. Both the permanent and the portable folding gates are less expensive than the portable mesh gates.
4. Permanently mounted gates are relatively easy for adults to open and close.

Cons:

1. The diamond-shaped openings can entrap arms, legs, and small heads.

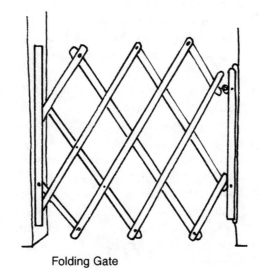

Folding Gate

Such latticework also provides a foothold for a climbing toddler.

2. When they are not in use, these gates become a tantalizing hinged toy that can pinch small hands and fingers.
3. Eventually a dexterous toddler will figure out how to open this gate.
4. The portable type will yield if pushed hard.

Suggestions:

1. Choose a gate with good, strong hardware.
2. Consider a gate which is wider than necessary for the opening. (A five-foot gate for a three-foot opening will be taller and closer to the floor on the bottom, and the diamond-shaped openings will be smaller.

Portable Mesh Gate. The portable mesh gate consists of two overlapping wood frames screened with plastic mesh. It locks in place within the door frame with a pressure bar. Plastic or rubber bumpers at each side help hold the gate in place. The pros and cons of the portable mesh gate are listed below.

Pros:

1. Small hands, feet, and heads cannot poke through the mesh.
2. These gates have aesthetic and practical appeal, and can be stowed away

or moved about the house or packed up for a vacation.

Cons:

1. These gates will yield if pushed hard enough.
2. They are suitable only for openings from two to four feet in width.
3. They are twice as expensive as the accordion-type gate.

Suggestions. Don't take a chance with this gate at the top of your stairs, unless you install wood channels on the sides of the door frames to hold it securely in place. If it is fitted to wood channels, this gate will be as effective as a plywood gate you build yourself.

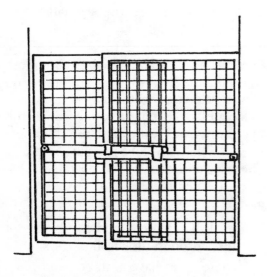

Portable Mesh Gate

ACCIDENT PREVENTION

Most accidents to children are caused by a chain of events, not by a single event. Although most children are exposed regularly to dangerous situations, it is seemingly ordinary conditions—such as a minor family illness, a parent who is overly tired, a child who is very hungry—that set the stage for accidents. Any one of the following factors might not, by itself, cause an accident; but two or three together greatly increase the chances.

ACCIDENTS OCCUR MORE OFTEN . . .

1. when a child is hungry or tired
2. when any hazard—a sharp knife, a busy street, a bottle of aspirin, etc.—is too accessible or too attractive to resist
3. when a mother is ill, about to menstruate, or pregnant
4. when a child has no safe place to play
5. when a child is considered hyperactive
6. when the relationship between parents is tense
7. when a child's surroundings change, often at moving or vacation time
8. when other family members are ill or the center of the mother's attention
9. when the family is rushed—particularly on days when many activities are being planned
10. when parents lack understanding of what new activities to expect at each stage of a child's development
11. when a child is in the care of an unfamiliar person or a brother or sister too young to be responsible

POISON PREVENTION

DON'T TRUST CHILD-PROOF CAPS!

"Poisoning is now the most common medical emergency among young children that exists in pediatrics today. It has been documented that 75% of all poisonings are caused by *IN SIGHT* drugs or household agents."
—CHEMICAL SPECIALITIES MANUFACTURERS ASSOCIATION, INC., *Your Child and Household Safety*

POISONOUS PLANTS

Many common house and garden plants are dangerous and can cause various injuries. The numbers that follow plant names are keyed to the four different reactions listed below.

1. skin irritation,
2. mouth- and throat-lining irritation,

3. stomach and intestinal irritation, and
4. poisoning of the system.

Houseplants

Angel's Trumpet	4
Caladium	2,3
Castor Bean	3,4
Dieffenbachia	1,2
Elephant's ear	1,2
Mistletoe	3,4
Philodendron	1,2
Poinsettia	1

Ornamental

Bleeding Heart	1,4
Daphne	1,2,3
English Ivy	3
Mountain Laurel	4
Oleander	4
Rhododendron	4
Wisteria	3
Yew	3

Forest Growth

Baneberry	3,4
Bittersweet	3,4
Bloodroot	3,4

Deadly Amanita	4
Fly Agaric Mushroom	4
Jack-in-the-Pulpit	2,3
Mayapple	3
Moonseed	4
Poison Ivy	1
Poison Oak	1
Rosary Pea	4
Snakeroot	3,4
Yellow Jessamine	4

Flower Garden

Autumn Crocus	4
Belladonna Lily	3,4
Christmas Rose	1,3
Daffodil	3
Four O'Clock	3
Foxglove	4
Hyacinth	3
Hydrangea	3,4
Iris	3
Larkspur	4
Lily of the Valley	4
Monkshood	4
Morning Glory	4
Narcissus	3

Snowdrop	3
Sweet Pea	3

Vegetable Garden

Asparagus (unripe shoots)	4
Flax	4
Potato (eyes, stems, spoiled parts)	4
Rhubarb	4
Tomato (leaves)	3,4

Field Plants

Buttercup	2,3
Death Camas	4
False Hellebore	4
Lupine	4
Milkweed	4
Nettle	1
Nightshade	4
Poison Hemlock	4
Poison Ivy	1
Pokeweed (Inkberry)	3,4
Snow on the Mountain	1
Sour Dock	4
Tobacco	4

Trees

Apple	4
Black Locust	3,4
Box	3,4
Cherry	4
Chinaberry	3
Elderberry	4
English Holly	3
Fig	1,2
Golden Chain	3,4
Horse Chestnut	3,4
Lantana	3,4
Oak	3,4
Osage Orange	1
Peach	4
Privet	3

Marsh

Cowslip	3
Lady's Slipper	1
Skunk Cabbage	2,3
Sneezeweed	4
Water Hemlock	4

BABY-PROOFING YOUR HOUSE ROOM BY ROOM

If you are renovating—to adapt the house to the baby or for any other reason—remember that renovation requires very special precautions. Besides the obvious dangers, plaster and old paint are full of lead. Paint removers, turpentine, and the like have deadly fumes.

THE BATHROOM

LOCK UP! Aspirin, eye and heart medicine, tranquilizers, pep drugs, rubbing alcohol, hair dye, permanent-wave solution, perfume, iron pills and syrup, some douche preparations, paregoric, iodine, corn and wart removers. Razor blades, nail scissors, toilet bowl cleaners, mirror cleaners, drain cleaners. All medicines. First-aid preparations.

SUGGESTIONS

1. Bathrooms should be off bounds when the baby is alone (drowning can occur in a toilet bowl!).
2. Put all medicines on a high shelf (with no counter underneath) or in a locked box.
3. Never leave electrical appliances such as space heaters plugged in while the baby is in the bathroom.
4. Dispose of razor blades carefully.
5. Never leave baby alone in the bathtub. If the phone rings, take the baby with you to answer it.
6. Don't let the baby stand up in the tub or touch faucets.
7. Hot tap water can cause a severe burn. Babies are notoriously interested in faucets. Keep water temperature below 130°F or 55°C. As the temperature rises, severe burns occur in a shorter and shorter period of time. At 124°F what is called a full-thickness burn can occur in three minutes. But at 140°, it only takes five seconds. And from 158° and up, only a second is required.

WINDOWS

1. **Open windows from the top or place guards at bottom.**
2. **Make sure screens are in good repair.**
3. **On blinds, cut open loop cords that can cause strangulation.**

THE KITCHEN

LOCK UP! Ammonia; bleach; drain cleaner; oven cleaner; furniture polish; metal polish; grease remover; carbolic acid disinfectants; roach, ant, rat, mice poison; washing soda; vitamins; beer; and liquor.

SUGGESTIONS

1. *Make poisonous household cleaners and sharp objects inaccessible.*
2. *While cooking, simmer on the front, boil on the back burners. Turn pot handles in.*
3. *Avoid tablecloths and place hot dishes in the center of the table.*
4. *Keep high chair, playpen, etc. at least two feet from counters.*
5. *Unplug appliances with long cords after use.*
6. *Remove all ant, roach, mice, or rat poison. It's too dangerous.*
7. *Keep pails of hot, soapy water off the floor.*
8. *Pick up broken glass with vacuum.*
9. *Elevate or securely lid the garbage.*
10. *Make matches inaccessible.*
11. *If necessary, remove knobs from gas stove.*
12. *Post Poison Control Center and emergency numbers by the phone, with information on what to do in case of poisoning or other accidents.*
13. *Remember many accidents occur when baby is tired and hungry—between four and seven P.M.*
14. *Dispose of empty containers.*

OUTSIDE

Fence in play yards, swimming pools, wells, and cisterns.

STAIRS

1. Block stairs at top and bottom.
2. Teach baby to negotiate stairs.
3. For everyone's safety, don't wax stairs. If stairs are carpeted, make sure tacks are firmly in place.
4. Put railings on open stairs. Your toddler might well be very careful, but will her friends?
5. Be aware that existing railings are often the right size to entrap a small child's head.
6. Light stairs brightly.
7. Check for objects.

WHILE CARING FOR THE BABY

1. Never leave him alone in the house.
2. Don't use a pillow in her crib. This can cause suffocation.
3. Do not prop bottle or leave him alone to eat. Liquids can be aspirated and cause suffocation.
4. Make sure you use a safe crib and playpen with slats 2⅜ inches apart, painted with lead-free paint.

SUGGESTIONS FOR ALL ROOMS

1. **Check floors for small objects: coins, tacks, pins, paper clips, etc.**
2. **Check every room for matches.**
3. **Plug all unused electrical outlets with blanks.**
4. **Fill all empty light sockets with bulbs.**
5. **Block radiators, fireplaces, and riser pipes with furniture.**
6. **Soften hard edges and corners on low furniture.**
7. **Elevate plants—they often have residues of poisonous plant food.**
8. **Elevate precious objects.**
9. **Wedge books and records tightly in their shelves.**

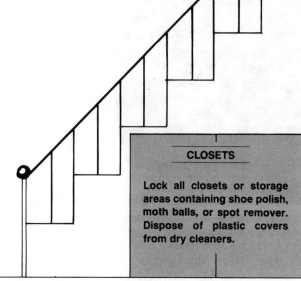

CLOSETS

Lock all closets or storage areas containing shoe polish, moth balls, or spot remover. Dispose of plastic covers from dry cleaners.

THE GARAGE, BASEMENT, AND UTILITY ROOM

1. Declare these areas off limits to the unaccompanied baby or toddler
2. Lock up all power tools, sharp objects, car cleaners, paint thinners, weed killers, etc.

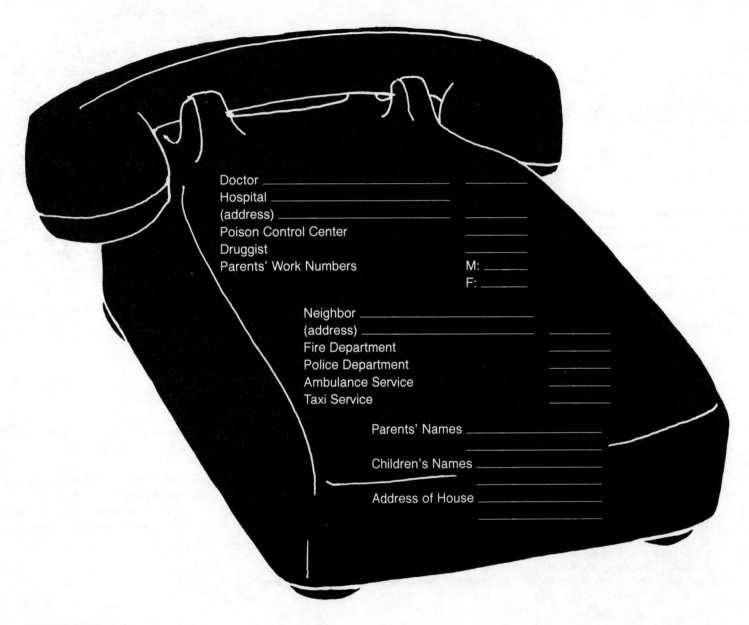

Doctor _____

Hospital _____

(address) _____

Poison Control Center   _____

Druggist   _____

Parents' Work Numbers   M: _____

F: _____

Neighbor _____

(address) _____

Fire Department   _____

Police Department   _____

Ambulance Service   _____

Taxi Service   _____

Parents' Names _____

_____

Children's Names _____

_____

Address of House _____

_____

TO PREVENT POISONING

1. Get in the habit of reading labels when you buy household cleaners.

2. Keep all medicines and household cleaners on a high shelf, out of sight, with no counter underneath—or locked up.

3. Keep all medicines and cleaners away from food.

4. After using medicines and cleaners, recap them immediately.

5. Keep all medicines, drugs, and cleaners in their original containers. (Many deaths have occurred when the last bit of turpentine, stored in a

Coke bottle, was mistaken for a drink.)

6. Clean out the medicine cabinet periodically. Throw out all drugs from past illnesses. They may not be good any longer anyway.

WHAT TO HAVE ON HAND IN CASE OF POISONING

1. A half-ounce bottle of ipecac syrup as well as a can of activated charcoal.

2. Emergency telephone numbers, posted by your phones.

LEAD POISONING

The severe consequences of acute or chronic lead poisoning have been known for many years; they are anemia, mental retardation, convulsions, and death. Now researchers have linked low-level lead ingestion to less visible but still insidious effects. These include hyperactivity, retardation of brain growth, slow learning, and increased susceptibility to viral disease.

If you have a hand-me-down crib, playpen, or other furniture from the '50s or early '60s that the baby is likely to chew on, and you suspect they were painted with lead paint, sand them down and repaint them with paint bearing the label "Conforms to USA standards Z66-1-064 for use on surfaces that might be chewed by children."

BABY SAFETY LESSONS

1. There is *nothing* you can do to prevent your baby from putting anything and everything in sight into his mouth. Teach your baby to say "ahhh" very early on. An "ahhh" will give you the chance to see what's in the baby's mouth and grab it.

2. Teach the baby the meaning of the word *hot*. One *supervised* experience with a radiator, stove, or light bulb is usually all it takes.

3. You probably won't need to teach your baby how to climb *up* the stairs, but do teach her to climb down back-

ward. If you can, mount a safety gate a few steps up, put a pillow below, and let her practice.

4. The administration of medicine and vitamins should be low-key and rather serious. The Consumers Union suggests that parents *not* buy flavored children's aspirin because the candylike taste is too tempting. It is very simple to quarter or halve an adult aspirin. This can be made quite palatable if mixed with applesauce, peanut butter, or jelly.

5. An easy way to release something from baby's tight grasp is to stroke the back of his hand lightly. No struggle.

P.S.: By providing maximum access to the safe home, you have also gone a long way toward making possible the preservation of a balance of interest. Just think for a moment of the contrasting situation, where to avoid danger, the extra work, the stress, and so forth, you routinely prevent your child from moving about the home by using a playpen. You may in the short run have an easier time of it, but in the long run the negative effects of such confinement on a child's curiosity and on the growth of his capacity to play alone far outweigh the short-term returns.

—Burton White,
The First Three Years of Life

CONSUMERISM AND YOUR CHILD'S SAFETY

If any piece of baby equipment or toy proves to be unsafe in any way, do not hesitate to contact the U.S. Consumer Product Safety Commission. Their address is 1750 K Street N.W., Washington, D.C. 20207. Write with the following details:

1. The brand name of the item.
2. A brief description of what the article is and how it functions.
3. Any numbers appearing on the product.
4. The country where the item was manufactured.
5. The store where you purchased it.
6. Describe how the item proved dangerous.
7. Do not forget to include your name, address, and phone number.

You might also be interested to know that the Safety Commission has a free hotline during the busy toy-buying seasons. Not only can you complain about faulty items, but you can also get information on safe toys and furniture. Here is the toll-free number:
800-638-2666
800-492-2937 (Maryland residents only)

RESOURCES

Baby-Proofing

Contact your local fire department and ask for a ''Tot Finder'' sticker to go on your child's bedroom window.

Home Safety Checklist
Write to:
The Travelers' Insurance Co. of Hartford
Hartford, Conn. 06101
(This is an excellent, free checklist. On the reverse side is a place for emergency phone numbers).

The Children's Hospital Accident Handbook: A New Approach to Children's Safety
Send 35¢ and a self-addressed, stamped envelope to:
The Children's Hospital Medical Center
Department of Health Education
300 Longwood Avenue
Boston, Mass. 02115

-21-
Health Care

PEDIATRICIANS

Excellent medical credentials are only the minimum to expect of a doctor. The right pediatrician for you and your baby must be someone with whom you can communicate—someone who will never make you feel more ridiculous or insecure than you already may feel for having so many questions. While she or he may have cared for a thousand newborn babies, yours must interest him or her and so must your concerns, as routine as they may be.

A pediatrician should be not only a good listener but also a willing explainer and sharer of information. Even though you may be lacking an M.D. degree, you should never feel condescended to, or be uninformed about decisions a doctor is making.

You really need to have a doctor who is compatible with you, because the relationship is not a passing one. During the first year you will meet regularly, and there will be times when you may talk on the phone daily. There is enough newness to deal with when you have a baby without having to shop around for another doctor, whether during a crisis or just when you are in need of some reassurance or advice. This is why it's so important to meet the doctor—or at least talk to the doctor on the phone—in advance.

WHERE TO FIND A PEDIATRICIAN

1. The best way to find a baby doctor is through people who use them most —other parents, preferably those who know you as well as the doctor. Comments like "A little crisp or efficient," "Rather rushed," or "Not specific enough or too vague" can be useful clues. Friends are also likely to know how easy or difficult a doctor is to get in touch with, how the office operates, and how the pediatrician reacts in emergencies and deals with older children.

2. Your obstetrician is also a good source. After eight-plus months, he ought to know you pretty well.

3. You can also make inquiries at the nearest accredited (preferably a teaching) hospital. Request a list of pediatricians on the staff as attending physicians, and choose a few to talk with who are conveniently located.

4. Or, if you live near a medical school, you can get a list of doctors on the faculty who practice in your community.

5. The *Directory of Medical Specialists*, found in the medical sciences section of the library, or the county medical society, listed in the phone book, will also list qualified pediatricians in your area.

Once you have assembled a few names and addresses (convenience is important), you can make phone calls in advance.

On the phone you can find out several bits of pertinent information from either the doctor or his or her nurse. You can ask about training (see box) and hospital affiliations, as well as fees and the cost of the immunization program during the first year. This is usually an additional cost which can come as a shock if you aren't prepared for it. You can also ask if she or he thinks it's a good idea to meet with you in advance. If the doctor doesn't feel this is necessary, you might at least ask why before you consider going elsewhere. You may or may not have to pay for an advance visit, but if you do, it is well worth the cost.

MEETING THE DOCTOR

If it's at all practical, both parents can benefit from meeting the pediatrician in advance. Two opinions are always better than one. More importantly, though, a father who has met the doctor has established some sort of relationship and may be more comfortable when calling with questions or taking the baby for a visit in the future.

An advance visit should be as important to the doctor as it is to you. The better sense he has about what kind of people you are, your history, and your particular concerns, the easier it will be

---

WHAT THE TITLES AND INITIALS STAND FOR

Board certification. The American Board of Medical Specialties is responsible for establishing training requirements and qualifications, and for giving certifying exams in a particular specialty area. A doctor who passes the American Board examinations within a specialty area becomes board certified, and is known as a *diplomat* of that board. Board certification is important because any doctor who wants to have hospital affiliations usually must be board certified. You definitely need a doctor who is connected with a hospital. If your doctor is board eligible, you might inquire about when she is going to take the exam.

Additional certification. In many of the board specialties, the doctor may also be a member of a "college" or honorary society whose main concern is continuing medical education within the special-ty. Once certain qualifications have been met, the doctor may be elected a fellow of the college. The initials FAAP stand for Fellow of the American Academy of Pediatrics, and mean that the doctor is a fellow or very probably a diplomat in that specialty.

Hospital affiliations. It's always good if your doctor is affiliated with a teaching hospital. Because continuing education is very crucial to the professional standing of many doctors, these positions on the staffs of teaching hospitals are sought after.

P.C. These initials, which often come at the end of a string of initials after the doctor's name, have nothing to do with medical standing. They mean Professional Corporation, and are useful for the doctor's tax and legal purposes.

---

for him to interpret your needs and put you at ease.

While you are waiting in the office, you can also get a feeling for how it runs, perhaps what the nurse's role is, or how incoming phone calls are handled.

QUESTIONS YOU CAN ASK THE DOCTOR

Some of the suggested topics cover areas in which you might not yet have opinions. But the purpose of asking the questions is not just to get the answers; it is to see how the doctor goes about answering them.

1. *This is very important.* What system does she have for answering routine questions? Is there a morning call-in hour when the doctor can be reached? Or does the office accept routine calls all day, and then have the doctor get back to you at her convenience? The first system is easier for parents.

2. Ask about the role of your doctor's nurse or receptionist. Some nurses act as intermediaries between you and the doctor. For instance, they may take the routine calls and questions, make suggestions, and so on. This may or may not make you feel comfortable. Interestingly enough, at least one study has shown that parents working through a nurse or nurse-practitioner feel more comfortable asking questions, and that the nurses in question spent more time providing answers than did the doctors they worked for.

3. How do you reach the doctor in an emergency? Who takes his calls and how are messages relayed to him? What procedures does he have for seeing a sick child? Does he ever make house calls?

4. How does she feel about breast-feeding? Does she consider problems with breast-feeding her province, or will she refer you to your obstetrician? (You want someone who knows quite a bit about this, who will be supportive and helpful if you run into difficulties.) When does she usually suggest introducing solid foods, and why?

5. An introductory visit is also a good time to go over your own medical histories. The doctor should be asking you some questions. This is also the time to go into your own quirks, if you have any. If you have theories out of the mainstream, assert yourself. If you are a vegetarian and plan to raise your baby this way, tell him. Or if you don't want to feed your child anything but breast milk for the first year, tell him. If you're against immunizations, mention this.

6. If paying bills promptly will be difficult, it's better to get this out in the open right away.

Question: *How did you choose a pediatrician?*

Answer: *"I only had one friend with children when I was pregnant, but she had four of them at the time and had been through almost every childhood illness in the book, many trips to the emergency room, and one hospitalization for a minor operation. Over ten years she hadn't had any complaints about her pediatrician. He had never failed to return a phone call or to explain what he was doing—either to her or to her children, once they were old enough to understand. This seemed like a good enough recommendation for me.*

A: I chose our pediatrician because she was affiliated with the hospital where Muffy was born, had an excellent reputation, but also because I'd heard that she was very supportive of working mothers. When I met her, she seemed to sense right away that I was very anxious about the whole thing. She spent a lot of time talking to me about this, and was generally very reassuring.

A: As a child I had lots of allergies, so I wanted a pediatrician who was also an allergist. I wanted to find out whether, if the baby did have any, they could be dealt with in a natural way. I remember my childhood as being full of painful trips to the doctor, and hours of waiting to see him. I met with two doctors in advance. One was willing to talk with me at length about my concerns, update me on a lot of advances in the field, and dispel some of my own misconceptions. The other dismissed the subject by pointing out that I didn't have a baby yet and shouldn't make problems before they actually existed. It's obvious who I chose.

A: When I was waiting to meet the doctor, I noticed that his nurse was taking most of the phone calls and giving out a lot of advice. I didn't like this, and asked him about it. He said that his nurse was capable of handling most routine questions, that he was usually very busy, and besides, many of the women he dealt with felt more comfortable talking to a nurse who was not an authority figure. This attitude totally turned me off.

***A:** A pediatrician who is supportive with breast-feeding can really make a difference. I chose mine because he'd written a book on the subject, which of course is very unusual. I met him in advance, and so did Doug. He gave me some excellent suggestions about dealing with hospitals and breast-feeding. He was also very reassuring about the birth and labor.*

***A:** I use a small neighborhood clinic. It's quite special as clinics go. There is a pediatrician on call every night, as well as a nurse-practitioner during the day to handle routine questions. But what I like about it the most is that the people who work there are very friendly.*

***A:** My O.B. recommended our pediatrician. She is very easygoing, which, since I'm not, makes for a reasonable balance.*

CLINICS

You may have been seeing references to *well-baby clinics* lately. This is a collective term for any clinic treating infants from birth to one or two and a half years. Most are operated in connection with a hospital or social-services agency and don't ever seem to be listed in the phone book under "Well-baby." To find out about clinics you can call the hospitals in your area as well as the Department of Health or Social Services, or the county medical society office.

A clinic can provide good medical care at less expense than a private doctor. Fees are usually based on a sliding scale adjusted to income. While qualities like warmth, smallness, and lack of red tape don't necessarily influence the quality of medical care a clinic offers, these things can make a tremendous difference in the baby-parent-clinic rapport.

If you are living in a large metropolitan area and are in the position to choose, it is well worth your while to make phone calls to several clinics in advance and plan to visit those which sound good to you. The closest may not be the best. Those which see only well babies for routine checkups and inoculations and assign you to a different doctor each time you come are obviously less desirable than those that will see your baby well, sick, or during an emergency and make an effort to assign the same doctor to you each time you visit. Following are some questions you can cover on the phone, which may save hours of waiting and red tape.

1. Not all clinics will accept all babies. Some require a referral by a hospital-affiliated doctor. Others require that the baby be born in their hospital; and still others will treat only children who live within a certain geographical area. Ask about this.

2. What kinds of services does the clinic provide? Do they see only well babies? If so, who sees a sick baby? Is there a way of dealing with routine questions over the phone?

3. Are there walk-in services, or do they require an appointment in advance?

4. What are the fee scales? What proof of income, if any, is required?

5. Will you see any one of a number of staff doctors, or is an effort made to assign the same doctor to you each time you visit?

WHEN TO CALL THE DOCTOR

It's hard enough to be responsible for your own health, and harder still to be responsible for the health of a tiny baby who can't even talk. There will be times when you'll wonder whether or not to "bother" the doctor. Is the baby really sick? Can it wait? Are you just overreacting? You may not have any hard evidence to go on.

We often agonize too much about this when what we should do is call. The ability to discriminate between what is normal and abnormal, sick and healthy, trivial and major, may well have something to do with instinct, but it does not come immediately. A doctor can help you develop these instincts, though, if you can support your sense that something is wrong by giving some details or observations when you call.

If you make a mistake, you'll feel better knowing that nothing is wrong. And in many cases you probably will be right, because you know what is typical of your baby better than anyone else.

As a pediatrician, I feel more harm than good comes when parents don't call when they are worried about something. I expect new parents to call me often. I'm well paid for what I do.

It takes time to get the right perspective in the beginning. I didn't want to be a pest, so I tried to limit myself to things that I considered life-and-death issues (which was almost everything at first). For instance, I knew diarrhea could kill a tiny baby. I once actually arrived at the doctor's office with one of Sean's dirty diapers. The doctor was very nice, but said that he would have been willing to trust my descriptive powers over the phone. In the case of a diaper rash, I was so casual that I let it go for two weeks. When I finally did get him to the doctor,

he had a very bad fungus infection.

You do make mistakes. I'd been trying to feed Elissa for two hours. Every time I stuck the bottle in her mouth, she'd suck, then scream frantically. I was frantic myself. I called the doctor, described each of my attempts. I was sure that there was something wrong with her throat that he hadn't noticed when he examined her. It turned out that I'd been using a blind nipple.

OBSERVATIONS YOU CAN MAKE—AND NOTE—BEFORE YOU CALL THE DOCTOR

Before you call, organize your thoughts. Be as specific as you possibly can. Following are some observations you can make before you call.

1. Is there a change in the amount that the baby has eaten as well as the vigor with which he eats? The doctor may also want to know what the baby last ate and when.

2. Is there a temperature? Do not trust your touch to determine whether the baby has a fever. Sometimes you can tell if you're two feet away before you even pick up the baby; other times the baby may have a temperature of 103° and feel perfectly normal to you. Tell the doctor if you took the temperature rectally or axillarily (in the baby's armpit).

3. Is the baby persistently irritable? For how long? If she is still a newborn, you might think this is colic. Parents should not diagnose colic without the help of a pediatrician. It could be something more serious.

4. Is the baby more lethargic than usual? Are her eyes dull or glassy? Does she feel floppy or heavier when you hold her?

5. How is her skin tone? Is she pale or flushed?

6. What is coming out both ends? How frequent have his bowel movements been, or infrequent, and what is their consistency? Is he spitting up more or less than usual?

WHEN YOU CALL THE DOCTOR

1. Get a pencil and paper, and write down beforehand some of the significant details based on the observations you've made.

2. Have the name and number of your drugstore handy.

3. When you place the call, give the child's full name, age, and weight before you start talking.

4. If you do not reach the doctor direct-

ly and must leave a message with the answering service or the nurse, after you hang up stay off the phone so that your line is free.

5. Write down exactly what the doctor says. It's very easy to get rattled and forget numbers, times, and amounts. Repeat it back if necessary.

CALL THE DOCTOR IMMEDIATELY FOR THE FOLLOWING EMERGENCIES:

1. any serious accident or injury (for poisoning, call your Poison Control Center)

2. bleeding that cannot be stopped

3. unconsciousness

4. severe breathing difficulties such as croup—a loud, deep, dry cough often coupled with breathing difficulties characterized by a "crowing" sound

5. severe diarrhea: frequent loose stools, watery stools which may smell fishy or worse than usual (with infants under two months consider three or four such stools in one day "frequent")

6. black or bloody bowel movements

7. convulsions: limbs stiffen and jerk, eyes roll upward, breathing is heavy or labored, baby is unconscious

8. head injury, particularly if there are symptoms of a concussion or skull fracture—bleeding from the nose, mouth, or ears; unconsciousness; an odd, unequal look to the pupils; or vomiting

9. projectile vomiting, particularly in a baby under two months. This is vomiting so forceful that the stomach contents will fly through the air and land a few feet away. This could be indicative of pyloric stenosis, a condition where the valve leading from the far end of the stomach into the intestine will not open up satisfactorily to let the food through. If pyloric stenosis is diagnosed, immediate surgery is required.

10. a marked change for the worse in a baby who is already sick

11. fever of 104°F or 40°C rectally (or 100.5°F or 38°C if baby has never been sick before)

12. two or three unexplained symptoms, whatever they may be

13. signs of dehydration: prostration or sunken eyes, which may accompany severe intestinal infection (very loose or watery stools, pus or blood in the stools, or vomiting and fever)

MEDICINE

A WORD ABOUT ANTIBIOTICS

Question: *What are antibiotics?*

Answer: *These are substances produced naturally by microorganisms which kill bacteria or prevent their multiplication, and thus lower the number of bacteria in an infection, so that your own antibodies can handle the remainder and cure you of the infection. There are over 100 different antibiotics on the market. The first recorded use of an antibiotic was over 2500 years ago when people in China learned that they could reduce boils by dressing them with fermented soybeans.*

—HAL BENNETT, and MICHAEL SAMUELS, M.D., *The Well-Body Book*

Some mothers are uncomfortable unless the pediatrician prescribes antibiotics at the first sign of illness. If the doctor suggests eardrops and aspirin instead of the "pink stuff," you may wonder why the baby and you have to remain in what seems like agony at the time. There's a very good reason, though, why a careful doctor avoids using these drugs as freely as we may sometimes wish.

The indiscriminate use of antibiotics

Do

1. Follow the exact dosage.
2. Give antibiotics for the exact time period the doctor recommends. Symptoms often seem to disappear very quickly, but it's vital to follow the full course of the treatment.
3. Ask for the name of the antibiotic. According to Dr. Virginia Pomeranz, you should be watchful for allergic reactions with penicillin or streptomycin. Signs of allergy are: a rash; unusual drowsiness; headache or dizziness; unexpected pain of any kind,

anywhere; any gastrointestinal discomfort or change in frequency or consistency of bowel movements. Report these to the doctor immediately.
4. Ask whether antibiotic should be given on an empty or a full stomach, or whether it matters.
5. Be sure to throw away the remainder of medicines you are finished using, unless specifically told to do otherwise.

Don't

1. Ever buy over-the-counter antibiotic preparations unless your doctor has specifically advised you to.
2. Ever administer any kind of medicine to a baby or child in the dark.
3. If you must leave the baby with someone else when he's sick, fail to leave *written* instructions regarding medicines.
4. Ever renew an old prescription for a new illness without consulting your doctor.

---

can result in the propagation of new strains of particularly hearty bacteria resistant to that antibiotic. What can happen with the overuse of an antibiotic is that the entire population of nonresistant bacteria within the child will be killed off. The remaining resistant ones will multiply and be spread about. If used with caution, however, an antibiotic will deal with the illness and leave the nonresistant bacteria to multiply in the future.

HOW TO GIVE MEDICINE TO YOUR BABY

It's always easier to administer medicine if two people are around—one to hold the furious baby, and the other to measure accurately and get it in. Following are some tricks to make it easier —especially if you are alone.

1. For administration, hold the baby with her head up and tilted slightly

back. It's easier to swallow this way.
2. A plastic medicine dropper or a flexidose spoon rather than a teaspoon can be easier for giving medicine by mouth. With a dropper you can squirt the stuff onto the inside of his cheek. He may be less likely to spit it out. For younger babies mix the medicine with applesauce, ice cream, or yogurt. Don't mix it with milk—this doesn't fool them. Cran-

berry juice is also a good cover-up.

3. Ask your pharmacist to dispense nosedrops in a plastic spray bottle. With one hand you can turn the bottle upside down and dispense, drop-by-drop, to control the dosage.

4. Eardrops are very simple. They will feel better in the baby's ear if you warm the bottle slightly under hot water.

5. Eyedrops are a two-person job (unless the baby is drowsy or asleep): one to hold, the other to spread the eyelids apart. Put the drop into the lower lid, then pull the upper lid down as far as you can.

6. Suppositories should be kept in the refrigerator and removed about an hour in advance. Dip in petroleum jelly, then guide it as far up into the rectum as you can by giving a firm push. Hold the baby's buttocks together for about five minutes.

STOCKING THE MEDICINE CABINET

1. Aspirin or equivalent liquid such as Tempra.
2. Rectal thermometer.
3. Petroleum jelly.
4. Absorbent cotton.

5. Calamine lotion for itching bug bites.
6. A good sun shield containing para-aminobenzoic acid (PABA).
7. Bandages: Band-Aids or Curads, adhesive tape, sterile gauze squares, butterfly bandage, Ace bandage.
8. Rubbing alcohol.
9. Baking soda.
10. Tweezers.
11. For poison treatment: syrup of ipecac (to induce vomiting) or activated charcoal (to absorb the poison), depending on source of poison.
12. Rubber nose syringe (optional), for suctioning out baby's stuffed nose.
13. Hot water bottle or heating pad (optional).
14. Vaporizer (optional—see page 212 for suggestions on choosing one).

HOW TO TAKE THE BABY'S TEMPERATURE

There are two ways to take a baby's temperature—rectally and axillarily (under the arm). The rectal method is preferred because it is considered more accurate. However, if you have access to only an oral thermometer, use the axillary method (see illustration of different thermometers).

1. Take the baby's temperature in a well-lighted room. You'll need good light to read the thermometer.

2. Shake the thermometer down. Take the end opposite the bulb and shake by snapping your wrist quickly two or three times, until the mercury is below the normal body temperature mark.

3. Place the baby over your knees with head down and gently insert the thermometer (dipped into petroleum jelly for easier insertion) about an inch into his rectum (see illustration of how to hold baby). The temperature will register within about a minute. Normal by this method is 99.6°F or 37.6°C.

4. If you are taking the baby's temperature under the arm, you can use either an oral or a rectal thermometer. Place it in her armpit and hold her arm firmly against her side. Wait four full minutes. Normal is 97.6°F or 36.7°C.

If you wish to convert Fahrenheit to Centigrade or vice versa, here are the correct formulas:

Fahrenheit = (9/5 × Centigrade) + 32°
Centigrade = (Fahrenheit − 32°) − 5/9

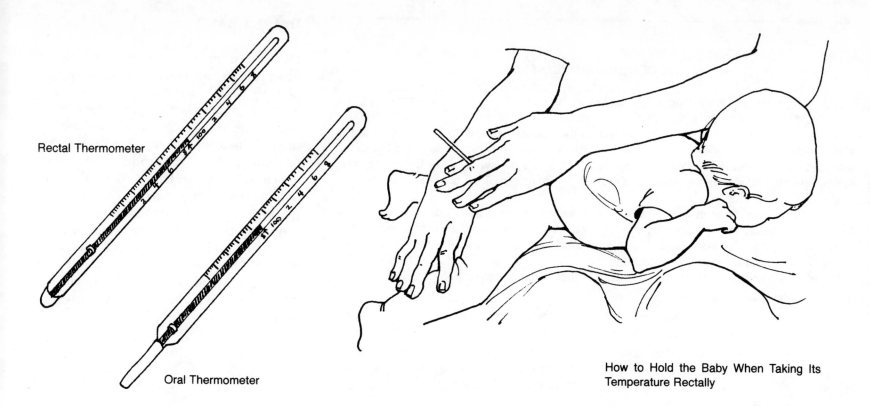

Rectal Thermometer

Oral Thermometer

How to Hold the Baby When Taking Its Temperature Rectally

COMMON SKIN PROBLEMS YOU CAN TREAT AT HOME

CRADLE CAP

Cradle cap, a yellow, flaky crust on the baby's head, is more of an embarrassment than a health hazard. It occurs when the oil glands have been stimulated by the mother's hormones in utero. It can be a persistent problem, returning just when you think you've gotten it under control. If you don't keep on top of it, it will get worse and worse. The baby may also have scaling behind the ears.

To treat cradle cap, you'll need baby oil, a soft brush, a fine-tooth comb, and for persistent cases a dandruff shampoo such as Sebulex, Subucare, Ionil, or DHS.

Mild cradle cap can be treated by vigorously scrubbing the baby's head with a soft brush. If the cradle cap is very thick, rub the spot with warm baby oil and—if you can—wrap her head in a towel for ten or fifteen minutes. Remove as much of the scaling as you can with a fine-tooth comb, then shampoo with a dandruff shampoo.

VAPORIZERS/HUMIDIFIERS

If your baby can't breathe through his nose because of a cold, or can hardly eat or drink his dinner without suffocating, and can't sleep comfortably, your pediatrician may prescribe the use of a steam vaporizer to help relieve some of the congestion. Before you hang up, ask if a cool-mist humidifier will do just as well. Vaporizers generate steam through boiling water and can cause bad burns when they are accidentally tipped over—either by you or your child—late at night in a darkened room. Once he can climb out of the crib, the chances of a spill rise.

A cool-mist humidifier is much safer than a vaporizer because it operates on room-temperature water, which is sprayed into the room. Another pro for many humidifiers is that they operate longer between fillings than vaporizers. A minor drawback is that the mist will lower the temperature in the room slightly.

If the doctor insists on steam, here is what to look for in a vaporizer:

1. A low, extra-wide base for added stability.

2. A cover that is locked to the water reservoir, rather than simply resting on it. If the unit is tipped over, the water will trickle out slowly rather than gush out.

3. Double-wall construction—this creates an insulating air trap between the heating cylinder and the water supply. The result is that the water temperature remains at about 130°F, rather than the 170° to 190° of a single-wall design.

Safe Usage

1. Place the vaporizer on the floor or below bed level with the cord well out of the way and at least four feet away from the baby.

2. Don't move it while it's plugged in.

3. If the mineral content of the water is very high, it can cause the vaporizer to steam too rapidly and raise the temperature to unsafe levels. To avoid this, use tap water mixed with distilled water.

NOTE: It's important to clean both vaporizers and humidifiers. Cleaning tablets are available at most drugstores.

DIAPER RASH

Diaper rash may be triggered by, among other things, infrequent diaper changes, plastic pants, disposable diapers, improperly rinsed cloth diapers, and orange juice. The rash is usually caused by the urea in the urine combining with bacteria or soap residue. This produces ammonia, which irritates the baby's skin. You can help minimize the chances of your baby getting a rash by washing the baby's bottom frequently and applying a thin layer of petroleum jelly, zinc oxide, or Desitin. You can also use Ammens or Caldesene powders, which are mildly medicated. The treatment is the same as the prevention.

HEAT RASH

A heat rash, or prickly heat, is caused by the blocking of the pores that lead to the sweat glands. The sweat is trapped under the skin and forms little red bumps. The treatment is to provide a cooler environment, fewer clothes, and a little powder, but no ointments. Ointment blocks the pores even more.

WELL-BABY VISITS TO THE DOCTOR

Monthly well-baby visits during the first year are extremely important for the baby's sake and your own. These visits insure that the baby has several thorough physical examinations, all the routine tests, and those very important immunizations. They also provide parents with an opportunity to ask questions, get answers, learn a little bit about medicine along the way, and, not least important, receive the much-needed reassurance that the baby is progressing well, and so are we.

Don't be shy about asking your doctor questions. Write them down and take them with you if this makes you feel more comfortable. My pediatrician, Dr. Irwin Rappaport, was kind enough to elaborate about what goes into a well-baby examination.

Question: What are you looking for in a well-baby examination?

Dr. Rappaport: *The most important thing in any well-baby examination is not, at first, to touch the baby, but rather to look and observe.*

We are first looking for growth and development—that is, what the baby is doing and how the baby has changed since the last visit. There are many things to look for, and these vary according to the age of the baby and whether or not the baby is full-term or premature. The lag time between the baby's development and the actual gestational birth are factors. If the baby is truly only eight months when born, it will be a month behind in development as opposed to a baby who has had a nine-month gestational period. The catch-up period occurs during the first year.

Beyond the actual age of the baby, though, growth and development is a very individual matter. There are wide margins of normalcy. You simply can't expect to compare your baby, with your limited exposure and experience, to your friends' babies and know what is normal and what is not. It's very important that a parent not get uptight about small differences that may appear to be larger.

Then, again, rather than touching the baby, you look at the baby and see, for example, the color of his skin, how he breathes, and how responsive that baby is. Responsiveness is most important. We see this in the interplay between the mother and the baby, or the effectiveness of stimulation between the parent and the infant. If you say, for instance, to the mother, "That's a beautiful baby," does she turn and look at the baby? A vast majority will turn to the baby on that question. You also can get a good idea about whether or not there is emotional interplay—if the baby smiles or starts to respond to visual observations from the mother. In the later months of the first year, we look to see if this interplay includes opportunities for the baby to mimic, because this is most important to learning.

Some mothers are very good at this, and it seems to come naturally. But some others are not very expressive. They feel as much love as anyone else for that baby, but they just don't stimulate the baby as much. In this kind of situation, you try to encourage the parent to play more with the baby, to make some extra time available—perhaps stop during a feeding or a diaper change or take a few extra minutes giving the baby a bath. You encourage them to take the baby outdoors, and get the baby to see the world a little bit.

Me: *I am amazed. You can really tell during a visit that a parent is not stimulating the baby enough?*

Dr. Rappaport: *You certainly can. You can see very clearly if there is good rapport between mother and child. This is extremely important. It's also important to get a father involved because there are two parents. We're really much more concerned about the nonphysical parts of a well-baby examination than anything else.*

Me: *Again, I never would have guessed that.*

Dr. Rappaport: *Then we're going to want to know a lot about nutrition. This, of course, is a very individual matter. Breast-feeding, for instance, is great. We encourage it because it is the finest of all feedings. But there can be many problems that relate to the diet of the baby that usually have to do with current trends or food* fads. In Manhattan, for example, parents seem to be readers. They read about the need for natural proteins, natural vitamins, low cholesterol, and so on. We have to be a little concerned that there is plenty of room for the expression of these feelings. A parent has a right to such expression within reasonable bounds. But, on the other hand, I've seen some mothers who give nothing but sixty-four ounces of milk a day, so that the child is simply wetting and bloated. This is why we always ask about the diet, then do a routine blood test for anemia to insure that the diet is adequate for the baby.

Then we turn to the physical part of the examination. The baby must be completely undressed, no diaper, not a stitch of clothing, in order to observe the skin color, activity, and breathing. Then we take the weight and height, and the head and chest circumferences. There should be a reasonable relationship between the head and the chest. We're looking for a child who has about one and a half inches difference between head and chest. If the head is too large in proportion to the chest, then we may suspect hydrocephalus, and if it's too small, microcephalus.

There should, of course, be a proportion in height and weight gain which is related to that particular baby's body structure. Body structure depends on the baby's genetics. We use those percentile charts for height and weight gain as a check. If, for instance, there is any dropping off in the baby's height percentile, we would look for other clues as to whether or not the baby was developing normally.

Genetics are also extremely important. On the first visit we take a complete family medical history and continue to look for any implied difficulties. Then, after measuring and weighing the baby, we check the eyes. We want to make sure that both eyes are present, and that they move in unison, and that both eyes have a good ability to converge. This will be very important when the child is learning to read. If there are any problems, we want to start with corrective measures soon.

We also watch for symmetry of the ears—of the auricles. They should be quite similar, though not necessarily absolutely identical. We do this because we know that if there is malformation of the ears, this occurs at the same embryologic time as the development of the kidneys. If the baby does have a malformed ear, we do a urinalysis and culture to make sure that he doesn't have something else going on.

We're also looking for the fontanels—checking to make sure that both are present and open before four months, and after that, that the posterior one is closing. As far as the neck is concerned, we check to make sure it is supple, that it moves well, and that the mouth can open and has an intact palate. Sometimes you have to be careful here and feel with your finger for what is called "skin covering" over an opening in the palate. We also check for any kind of masses in the thyroid area. And we check, on the first visit, to see if the clavicles are intact because these are the bones most frequently fractured at the time of a vaginal birth.

As far as listening with a stethoscope—this is one of the least important things you do. With most babies you can tell about their breathing by observation and by the color of their skin. It should not be blue. You can also tell by the speed of the respirations, the retractions, whether a baby is having difficulty. Then you listen to make sure, to verify your observations. As for heart murmurs—yes, many babies have them. Most of them go away. After checking the heart you feel the abdomen for any enlargement of the liver and spleen as well as for any masses. You also check for intactness of the spine to make sure that you feel all of the vertebrae and that there is no malformation which could allow the spinal cord to protrude out.

You also check the genitals, male or female, and check for any hip dislocation. Here, if dislocation is the case, it is best corrected before three months. We are also looking for neurological abilities—the so-called Moro, or startle, reflex, as well as the ability to suck and to cry. Beyond these, most neurological reflexes are not very important.

Me: *Do you look for all this every time you see the baby?*

Dr. Rappaport: *Yes, absolutely. For example, the first time I saw one particular baby, he was crying. The examination seemed fine. The next time I saw that same baby a month later, he wasn't crying, and his eyes were open. On that visit I found bilateral cataracts. When a child is crying, it's very difficult to open the lids.*

You try, of course, to examine everything as thoroughly as you can without great difficulty or discomfort to the baby, and sometimes you cannot. It takes a lot of practice, for instance, to tune into a heart examination or a chest examination on a child. Sometimes a pacifier is a way of trying to get around that, or holding the baby on your lap. But you must check for each and every thing, hoping that you have not missed something in the past, and if you have, that you will pick it up this time. The repetition of this is not only for the baby's security and the parent's, but also for the doctor's. Repetition is necessary in order for a doctor to be as thorough as he possibly can, to eliminate human errors, which you cannot predict in any examination. No one is infallible. And so the only way is to double-check, and triple-check and quadruple-check.

Me: *That's why regular well-baby visits are so important.*

Dr. Rappaport: *Exactly.*

ALLERGIES

An estimated 23% of American children under fifteen are allergic to something or other. If you suspect that your baby may have allergies, it's important to work closely with your pediatrician. You can be very helpful by keeping track of everything the baby has eaten or worn, and plants or animals that she may have touched, before you call.

IMMUNIZATIONS

It is terribly important to have your baby immunized against certain diseases: This is one more reason why regular well-baby visits to your pediatrician are essential. Because of the widespread use of vaccines, we tend to assume that most diseases are practically nonexistent. This is not true. There are some five million pre-school-age children who are not protected, and the latest statistics from the Public Health Service of the U.S. Department of Health, Education and Welfare show just how careless some parents have been. In 1974, for instance, there were 272 cases of diphtheria reported; 22,094 of rubella; 59,128 of mumps; 2,402 of whooping couch; 7 of polio; and 30,210 of tuberculosis. Knowing that all of these diseases can be lethal, why take a chance?

Following is the schedule, recommended by the American Academy of Pediatrics, which is followed by many pediatricians. There is, of course, room to deviate from these recommendations, but generally speaking, your baby should be fully immunized by the time she is two.

Age	Immunizations
2 months	Diphtheria, Pertussis, Tetanus (DPT), Trivalant Oral Polio
4 months	DPT, Trivalent Oral Polio
6 months	DPT
1 year	Tuberculin test (not an immunization)
15 months	Measles, Mumps, Rubella
18 months	DPT, Trivalent Oral Polio
4–6 Years	DPT, Trivalent Oral Polio

Question: *How can you tell if your baby might be allergic?*

Answer: *Look at your family history, because the tendency to allergy is usually hereditary. If one parent has a major allergy, the child may or may not be allergic. The chances of his being allergic are one in four. If both parents are allergic, chances are that most of their children will be, and their allergies will develop at an earlier age.*

—ALLERGY FOUNDATION OF AMERICA PAMPHLET

A: *It seemed to me that our second baby, Emily, was grumpy from the moment I stopped breast-feeding her (at six weeks because I had to have a gall-bladder operation) until she was seven* *months old. There was nothing obviously wrong with her. She was a very picky eater, spit up a lot after her bottle, and had a slightly runny nose a good deal of the time—which I blamed on David, our three-year-old, and his friends. I never put it all together—until I had finally had it. When the doctor had a total list of complaints, he suggested that she might have a milk allergy. After a week on the soybean milk, the change was so dramatic that I couldn't believe Emily was the same baby. I just wish we'd figured it out sooner. I hope her psyche wasn't too damaged.*

COMMON SOURCES OF FOOD ALLERGIES

☐ cow's-milk–based products
☐ eggs
☐ wheat
☐ cod-liver oil
☐ citrus fruits
☐ corn
☐ pineapple
☐ fish
☐ strawberries
☐ tomatoes
☐ chocolate

There are several symptoms that may indicate that your baby has a food allergy. The tip-offs are:

1. Frequent spitting up of large amounts of formula, cow's-milk products, or other foods—or frequent moderate intestinal upsets.

2. Chronic stuffy nose and/or chest congestion.

3. Eczema—irritated skin patches on the cheeks—as well as other frequent skin rashes.

4. General crankiness and irritability.

FIRST AID

ARTIFICIAL RESPIRATION

1. *Never administer artificial respiration to a baby, child, or adult who is breathing.*

2. In the case of drowning, turn the baby on his stomach with his head lower than the rest of his body to drain water from the lungs.

3. Then place the baby on his back.

4. Quickly use your finger to remove mucus or other matter from his mouth.

5. Open the air passage by gently raising the neck and tilting the head back. Make sure to keep the chin up

and jaw forward to keep the air passage wide open.

6. With a baby or small child, place your open mouth over the baby's nose and mouth to form an airtight seal.

7. Take a breath. Exhale only part of the breath into the baby's nose and mouth. His lungs are too small to hold your entire breath.

8. Remove your mouth and listen for the return of air. If you hear nothing, check head position again. Press on the abdomen to release air and try another shallow breath.

9. If there is still no return, turn the baby on his side and slap him between his shoulder blades several times to dislodge foreign matter that may be blocking the respiratory tract.

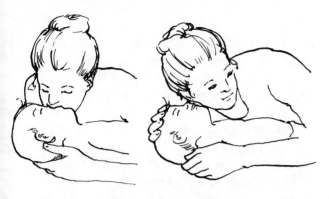

10. Quickly get baby back into position and continue resuscitation. Try to establish a regular rate, about twenty shallow breaths a minute or one every three seconds.

11. Keep this up until the baby is breathing regularly by himself or until medical help arrives.

FEVER

1. Call doctor if the baby has a fever. Don't use medications until you talk to the doctor.

2. If you can't reach the doctor immediately and the fever is over 103°F or 39.4°C, begin gently cooling the baby as follows:

3. Undress the baby in a draft-free place.

4. Place the baby in a partially filled tub or sink of lukewarm (not cold) water. Keep most of the baby's body exposed to the air.

5. Sponge her entire body with a washcloth, using light, brisk strokes. The purpose of this is to bring the blood to the surface by rubbing and to cool it by evaporation of the water off the skin.

6. Dry baby vigorously. Continue watching her temperature closely. Don't overdress her or cover her with heavy blankets.

BITES AND STINGS

Insect Bites or Stings

1. Scrape out stinger, if present, with a scraping motion of the fingernail. Do not pull it out.

2. Apply cold compresses.

3. Consult physician promptly if there is any reaction such as hives, generalized rash, pallor, weakness, nausea, vomiting, or breathing difficulty.

Animal or Human Bites

1. Wash with soap and water. Hold under water for two or three minutes if bleeding is not profuse.

2. Apply sterile dressing.

3. Consult pediatrician immediately.

BURNS AND SCALDS

Heat Burns of Limited Extent

1. Immerse extremities as quickly as possible in cold water, or apply cold, wet compresses to areas on the trunk or face. Cooling must be constant until the pain disappears.

2. Gently blot dry with sterile gauze or a clean towel.

3. Cover loosely with a nonadhesive dressing. If this is not available, use plastic film (Saran Wrap, etc.).

4. Do not break blisters. Do not use antiseptic sprays or salves, or ointments, greases, or powders.

Chemical Burns

1. Flush thoroughly with water. If necessary, place baby in the shower or under a hose.

2. Then remove all clothing which has come in contact with the skin.

3. Continue flushing with cold water until all traces of the chemical are gone.

4. Contact pediatrician immediately.

CHOKING

1. If the baby can breathe, let him try to cough the obstruction out. Don't interfere! Any attempt you make to

manually dislodge an object which is partially obstructing the baby's breathing *may* lead to complete obstruction. If the baby does not cough the obstruction out but can still breathe, go to the nearest emergency room.

2. *If the baby can't breathe,* place her face down over your forearm or knee and forcefully slap her back between the shoulder blades in an effort to propel the object from the windpipe.

3. *If the object does not come out,* and the baby still can't breathe, place your arms around the baby, and with your fist against the stomach between the navel and rib cage and your other hand over the fist, make four thrusts upward.

4. If the baby has stopped breathing, administer artificial respiration (see page 216).

CONVULSIONS

Symptoms: unconsciousness, stiffening of the limbs, violent jerking. The eyes may roll upward. Breathing may be heavy. There may also be frothing or drooling from the mouth.

1. Do not give the baby anything by mouth.

2. Place baby on a bed or soft rug. Clear area of dangerous or hard objects. Loosen tight clothing, if you can, particularly anything around the neck.

3. Do not restrain the baby as the convulsion takes its course.

4. When the convulsion is over, lay the baby on his side with head lower than hips. Again, give nothing by mouth.

5. As soon as the baby is calm, call pediatrician immediately.

FALLS AND HEAD INJURIES

Most babies will have at least one fall—off the changing table or a bed—as well as countless little falls when they learn to pull themselves up to stand. The bigger falls are almost harder on the parents than on the baby—you feel so guilty for having been careless. However, an infant's head is quite soft, and the fontanels, or soft spots, serve as a type of safety mechanism to help diminish head injuries.

Symptoms of serious head injuries include: loss of consciousness; vomiting; fluid or blood from the ears, nose, or mouth; unequal pupils; pallor; and difficult breathing. Call the doctor immediately and give the baby nothing by mouth if any of these symptoms appear.

HOW TO SPOT EARLY SIGHT AND HEARING PROBLEMS

Parents spend the most time with their babies, and if a baby does have any health problems, they are often the first to spot them. The earlier any visual or hearing problems can be detected, the more quickly a child can receive corrective help. Following are a few signs to be aware of.

SOME SIGNS OF POOR VISION IN INFANTS

1. The baby is visually very unresponsive.
2. He holds things very close to see them.
3. He often bumps into large objects.
4. He cannot pick up small objects with accuracy.
5. He constantly favors one eye when looking at an object.
6. One or both eyes turn in or out for noticeable periods of time.
7. The baby squints or closes one eye frequently.

(Adapted and reprinted with permission from the "Parent's Guide to Children's Vision" by James R. Gregg, O.D., Public Affairs Pamphlet No. 339, copyright 1972, Public Affairs Committee, Inc.)

SOME SIGNS OF POOR HEARING IN INFANTS AND YOUNG CHILDREN

1. A newborn does not act startled when someone claps sharply within three to six feet.
2. At three months the child does not turn his eyes toward the sound.
3. At eight months to one year, the child does not turn toward a whispered voice, or the sound of a rattle or a spoon stirring in a cup, when the sound originates within three feet behind him.
4. At two years the child cannot identify some object when its name is spoken, cannot repeat a word with a single stimulus, cannot repeat a phrase, and does not use some short phrases while talking.
5. The child is not awakened or disturbed by loud sounds, does not respond when called, pays no attention to ordinary crib noises, uses gestures almost exclusively instead of verbalization to establish needs, or watches parents' faces intently.
6. The child has a history of upper respiratory infections and chronic middle ear trouble.

(Adapted and reprinted with permission from "Helping the Child Who Cannot Hear" by Samuel Moffat, Public Affairs Pamphlet No. 479, copyright 1972, Public Affairs Committee, Inc.)

TEETHING AND TEETH

Teething is a very individual matter. The first tooth (often the lower central incisor—see illustration) usually comes in between six and eight months. Occasionally, however, a baby is born with a fully formed tooth. Others go toothless into the second year.

There is no reason to expect teething to be a continuously miserable experience for the baby (or you). If the baby who seems out of sorts is too old for colic, teething can become the catchall diagnosis for all sorts of otherwise unexplainable behavior. It is true that some babies have a difficult time cutting a new tooth—particularly the first one, and the molars. They become irritable, or uninterested in food, or wakeful at night, or all of the above. Others will simply drool, put everything into their mouths, gnaw on tables, and even bite their parents, but they manage to produce all twenty baby teeth without a whimper.

SIDE EFFECTS OF TEETHING

Miseries aside, some side effects of teething can be loose stools (not diarrhea) and diaper rash. The loose stools may be caused because the baby produces more saliva when teething and swallows a great deal of it, diluting the material in the intestine. When a baby is teething, she may also sleep for shorter stretches at night and stir in her sleep enough to wake up and wet. The diaper

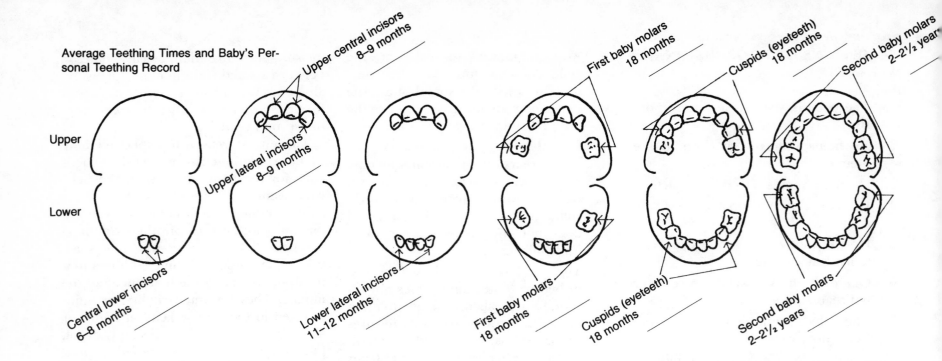

Average Teething Times and Baby's Personal Teething Record

Upper

Lower

Upper central incisors 8–9 months

Upper lateral incisors 8–9 months

Central lower incisors 6–8 months

Lower lateral incisors 11–12 months

First baby molars 18 months

First baby molars 18 months

Cuspids (eyeteeth) 18 months

Cuspids (eyeteeth) 18 months

Second baby molars 2–2½ year

Second baby molars 2–2½ years

becomes progressively wetter with each waking, and by morning she may have a rash. If this is the case you can put an extra protective layer of petroleum jelly or zinc oxide on her bottom before she goes to bed. Any other symptoms, such as true diarrhea, vomiting, or fever, should be reported to your doctor.

SUGGESTIONS FOR TEETHING BABIES

1. A simple, old-fashioned, hard, bumpy rubber teething ring for the baby to gnaw on will relieve some of the discomfort. Use rings filled with "nontoxic jellies" at your own risk.

2. A chilled carrot (with the tip cut off), a chilled apple slice, or an ice cube wrapped in a handkerchief will also soothe sore gums.

3. Cold liquids help.

4. You can also massage the baby's gums with your finger.

5. If it gets really bad, ask your doctor about using baby aspirin or its liquid equivalent—sparingly.

PROCEDURES THAT ARE NOT RECOMMENDED

1. A lot of teething biscuits and toasts—especially if they take the baby hours to consume. The continual exposure to the sugars in these foods can cause tooth decay. They also have less nutritional value than fruits and vegetables, and are fattening.

2. Paregoric, because it contains barbiturates which can make the baby drowsy, and because it can become habit-forming.

PREVENTIVE DENTISTRY

Many children have cavities by the time they become toddlers with full sets of teeth. Most of us have neither the time nor the patience to swab our baby's gums and teeth with gauze and water after every meal, a procedure recommended in some child-care books. But the "baby teeth" are very important in terms of the development of the baby's jaw. These teeth maintain space for permanent teeth, and if they become decayed, they can close together as the six-year molars erupt. This crowding, which can be due to weakened, decayed baby teeth, can also lead to infection, considerable pain and future orthodontic problems.

There are, however, some simple preventive measures that parents can take.

1. Good nutrition. In most respects the nutritional needs for maintaining healthy teeth and gums are similar to those for maintaining good health in general. Adequate amounts of calcium and phosphorus are definitely necessary for normal tooth and bone growth. Both vitamin A and vitamin D help the body absorb and utilize these minerals. Vitamin C is important for healthy gums and tissues. Fluoride, however, is thought to be the single most important element in relation to dental care. If your water supply is not fluoridated, by all means ask your pediatrician about supplementation.

2. Limited snacking. The second preventive measure is to limit the frequency of eating, particularly of foods that contain sugars and starches such as teething biscuits and sweetened juices. (Even milk contains the least sweet of the sugars, *lactose.*) Try to fill in with nutritious snacks. Apples, carrots, and green peppers, for example, have a scouring, cleansing effect on teeth. One bottle of milk or juice at night won't hurt the baby's teeth, but several a night can lead to "nursing-bottle syndrome" (teeth that are literally rotted away to small brown stumps). If your baby requires several bottles at night for his comfort and your sanity, dilute the contents with water. Gradually decrease the milk or juice until only water remains.

Question: *Will thumb-sucking affect the placement and development of the baby's teeth?*

Answer: *Yes, but. Thumb-sucking can push the baby teeth forward and out of place. This will* not, *however, affect the second teeth, if the child has given up the habit by the time they come in. Parents should not try to prevent thumb-sucking during early childhood, because it is an important and autonomous source of comfort for many babies and young children.*

RESOURCES

Health

Graedon, Joe, *The People's Pharmacy,* St. Martin's Press, New York, 1976.

Green, Martin I., *Sigh of Relief: The First-Aid Handbook for Children,* Bantam, New York, 1977.

Newton, Niles, *The Family Book of Child Care,* Harper & Row, New York, 1957.

Pomeranz, Virginia and Schultz, Dodi, *Mother's Medical Encyclopedia,* New American Library, New York, 1977.

Spock, Dr. Benjamin, *Baby and Child Care,* Pocket Books, New York, 1977.

A Primer on Medicines
(no. 74-3014)
U.S. Dept. of Health, Education and Welfare
Public Health Service
5600 Fishers Lane
Rockville, Md. 20852

RESOURCES

123 Most-Asked Questions by Parents About Their Children's Teeth
Write to:
Healthcare, Inc.
P.O. Box 94
Waterville, Ohio 43566

Better Teeth for Life
Send 25¢ and self-addressed, stamped envelope to:
Department of Health, Education and Welfare
c/o Superintendent of Documents
U.S. Government Printing Office
Washington, D.C. 20402

Appealing Recipes Using Prosobee Isolate Milk
Write to:
Mead Johnson and Co.
Evansville, Ind. 47721

Good Eating for the Milk Sensitive Person
Write to:
Ross Laboratories
Columbus, Ohio 43216

Allergy
Write to:
Department of Health, Education and Welfare
No (NIH) 74533
c/o Superintendent of Documents
U.S. Government Printing Office
Washington, D.C. 20402

Part VIII
PLAY AND LEARNING

-22-
Stimulating the Baby

A generation or two ago it was considered appropriate, if not essential, to run a tight ship where the baby was concerned. Keep him clean, quiet, and protected from noise, overhandling, and overstimulation. Feed him on a strict schedule, exercise and "sun" him regularly. Otherwise leave him to play quietly alone in the playpen or crib with a few well-scrubbed toys. The object, one guesses, was to foster independence. This philosophy suggests that the job of the parent, specifically the mother, was to create or mold the baby into a predictable being who exercised "good habits," and who would not grow up to be spoiled or an embarrassment to the family.

Nowadays we feel differently. Through the growing amount of research on infancy and—more to the point—our own observations, we know that babies thrive on being held, cuddled, and talked and sung to, and that they respond early to the human face and voice, to action and bright colors. The nursery of today may well be the most colorful room in the house, even if it is the least utilized. The baby spends her waking hours moving around the house on a parent's back or at a parent's side or out in the world. She may take in a few cultural events, such as a museum or concert, before her first birthday. She may also have a social life of her own by the time she's walking, particularly if her mother organizes a play group.

All this reflects our understanding of the baby as tough rather than fragile, a highly adaptable, alert, sentient, curious, communicative being. And as parents, we cannot help but marvel at our baby's imagination, curiosity, drive, and determination to practice, discover, master, and control the world around her. In fact, never again, as he strives to reach, turn over, grasp, creep, sit, crawl, stand, and finally walk and talk, will her strides in development be quite as dramatic as they are in the first twelve to sixteen months.

As knowledge about the capacities of the infant grows, more and more attention is being paid to stimulation techniques with a capital *S* and toys that teach with a capital *T*. An awareness of what is happening in terms of motor, speech, and social development is both fascinating and useful. But not surprisingly, when asked, "Are you concerned about stimulating your baby enough?" many parents will answer yes a bit nervously.

We really need not be as intimidated as we sometimes are. Books or no, studies or no, parents who are involved with their own babies know a great deal about stimulating them, precisely because they are involved and delighted with each step or bit of progress in the baby's development. Without thinking too much about it, we tend to play the games that the baby is physically and developmentally ready for, and these are the games that teach. Most parents do not coop their babies up in playpens. The baby has access to the best laboratory for learning, the (baby-proofed) American home, and encounters a variety of simple objects of different colors, textures, and weights that make different sounds—or "toys that teach" and stimulate curiosity. When the baby goes out with us, she learns, on the most basic level, how the world operates. Most parents know—though we may sometimes wish otherwise—that babies seldom play quietly alone with the expensive toys purchased to enhance learning, and that people are really the best toys. We talk to the baby, perhaps not consciously to stimulate language or speech development, but because it's fun and satisfying. And it's evident that the baby enjoys this.

Some of the most fascinating research on language development suggests that babies move synchronously with adult speech as early as the first day after birth. Videotapes of the baby's movements and gestures form a distinct pattern in response to the speaker's movements, gestures, rhythms, pitch, and stress patterns. This suggests that the baby communicates immediately through body language and is not an isolated being who slowly develops such skills after many months.

What we need to hear a little more often is not how to teach the baby, but the simple advice to relax, to trust our own instincts a little more, and to *enjoy the baby*. We also need to remember that comparisons of our baby with another baby or with the archetypal baby in the developmental books are tempting to

make, but a little odious. Babies and parents are individuals who learn and develop at their own rates. Eventually everyone succeeds. All the babies learn to walk, and all the parents can be classified as experts.

Question: *Do you worry about stimulating your baby enough?*

Answer: *No, not with this baby, at least not in a self-conscious way. I feel learning is a spontaneous occurrence. It takes place in the course of taking care of a baby in a warm, responsive way—every day. With my first child I did worry about it somewhat. I wondered why she wasn't interested in playing with the nesting toys I bought her when she was a particular age. I compared her constantly—and I must admit somewhat competitively—with other babies. She wasn't the kind of baby who ever sat still, and my efforts were fruitless to get her involved in using the toys the way I thought she should use them. She was far happier opening and closing the cupboard where the toys were, and knocking them onto the floor, or wearing a cup on her head like a hat. So she was learning about physics and using her imagination and discovering her own strength, rather than how objects fit together, at that point. She didn't enjoy books very much either, and I thought, Oh God, she'll be illiterate. She's the only baby in the world who hates* Pat the Bunny. *But she preferred going around the house, playing peek-a-boo be-*

hind the curtain or opening a real drawer and pulling out all my clothes, or terrorizing the cat. I talked to her, but I wondered if I talked enough.

My second baby, Paul, is totally different. He takes his time doing everything. He really enjoys dropping his colored beads into his bucket. He drops one in, then pauses and looks where it went. So I get down on the floor, and he hands me beads, and I drop them in the bucket—then he drops them in the bucket and he has a wonderful time. He tries to put one block on top of another. He's almost ten months, but doesn't crawl yet, but if he really wants something, he wiggles over to get it—even if it takes him ten minutes. He's a plugger, and we give him a lot of praise. He really enjoys books, so I spend time showing him books. But his idea of bliss is a trip to the grocery store. He loves to look at everything. He squeals when he sees the Pampers boxes, and is ecstatic when we pass the cat-food section. Sara would have been jumping out of the cart—in fact, she did once.

I think what stimulating a baby is all about is being sensitive to who that baby is and providing outlets for their interests and their energies as you go along. They create their own challenges if you let them, and don't coop them up. If he's bored, he'll let you know it. Then you use your imagination, too. One other thing I discovered—boredom and frustration are two very different things. You can attempt to keep a baby from being bored, but a certain amount of frustration is inevitable, and I know I took this a little too seriously when Sara was a baby. If she cried because she couldn't do something, I'd jump in and fix it. I don't do that as much with Paul.

Question: *Please describe your baby—besides age and sex, tell me what she's doing now, what games she likes to play, toys or nontoys which are interesting. If you've made any simple toys for your baby, please describe them and tell me how you did it. Is there anything particularly hard about this stage of your baby's development—for her or for you?*

Answer: *Peter is two weeks old. He likes to be held and rocked and to eat and sleep and cry. We don't play any games yet. We've been out once, and so far I can report that he is an excellent traveler. I can't ever imagine having time to make toys. I'm exhausted.*

A: Lucinda, age five weeks, just started smiling. I tickle her toes, and blow on her stomach, but those are about the only games we play. She does watch her mobile that David made out of a coat hanger. I also put a happy face on the headboard of her crib, so that it would be less boring. I put her in the infant seat. What's hard still is being tired because she doesn't sleep much at night—yet.

A: At nine weeks her hands are fascinating and in the mouth. She also likes the puppet my older child shows her. My older child, by the way—age 3½, is the best toy, when he's not feeling threatened! I learned with the first one that elaborate toys are a waste of money.

A: At twelve weeks there are a few games Caroline likes to play—or rather can play. She does love it when I clap her hands together or sing to her. She's just beginning to reach out and to touch and grasp things. She coos when alone or when spoken to. As for toys, she enjoys her mobile, a beautiful colored rainbow. The musical mobile holds her attention much less. It plays Brahms' "Lullaby." I think the repetition of the melody bores her quickly. She also likes her rubber squeaky toys. She tries to roll over, but can't make it yet. I think this lack of mobility frustrates her.

A: At four months, Ellie loves to bat at her crib gym. I made it out of a strong piece of red cord with different objects tied securely on to it. I used measuring spoons, an old toothbrush, a bell, a squeaky toy, and two curtain rings. I like this because it was easy to take down at night and transfer to the playpen. She loves to roughhouse. Her father or I hold her up in the air and twirl her around like an airplane.

A: At four months Emily's just beginning to be able to hold onto things now. Her favorite thing to hold is what I call her ameba, a wiggly shape which I made with felt on one side and taffeta on the other. She puts it in her mouth. I stuffed it with pillow stuffing. She enjoyed it so much that I made her another one, in different colors and fabric, and stuffed it with crinkly paper. She can almost turn over, but not quite, and I think this frustrates her. She also coos, wiggles, kicks, blows bubbles, and is generally a delight to be around.

A: Birch is almost five months old—and huge—too big for the infant seat so I use the car seat instead, but still not able to sit up. I think he's dying to be vertical, and is frustrated because he can't be. He turns from stomach to back—but can't get back to his stomach. When I prop him up with pillows, on the floor, he's happier, until he tips over. His favorite game is to lie in my lap and press his feet against my stomach, while I pull him up to a standing position. There are no toys in particular that he likes—everything goes in the mouth.

A: Alexis is five months. She loves people more than anything else, especially her two older brothers who are ten and twelve, who carry her around, tickle her, and really dote on her. She also loves anything and everything that goes into her mouth.

A: At six months Samantha is terrific fun. She's a real ham. Her favorite game is "Here are your eyes, here is your nose, your mouth," etc. She loves to be thrown up in the air, and tickled. Her favorite toys are the mirror and the cat. She has a plastic book with squeakers in the pages. I can't say that she looks at it, but she loves to chew it and poke it.

A: Zack is six months old, but doesn't sit by himself yet. He loves to be held standing up, adores peek-a-boo, likes to try to turn the pages of books. He loves crinkly paper, my pierced earrings, tin cans to bang, aluminum foil, and bells. He loves to go for walks as long as we keep moving. He also plays with his toes for hours and babbles.

A: Ann is six months old. She can finally sit up, which has relieved a lot of frustrations on her part as well as mine. She enjoys toys she can put into her mouth and chew on, and loves her musical toy that rattles. She sort of crawls backward, but not forward, and sort of waves bye-bye backward, too. She used to sleep two or three hours in the afternoon. Now she sleeps for one if I'm lucky.

A: Molly at six and a half months has mastered the Busy Box, and now wants the real thing—the kitchen cupboards. This is the best toy of all—her own cupboard, with aluminum pie plates, plastic containers, pot lids, sponges, small cans, things that rattle and clatter and are fun to chew on and roll. I'm looking forward to the stage where they want to put things back instead of pull them out. When does that happen? She's not interested in any real toys in particular, but loves her bath, finally!

A: At seven months Sara still doesn't crawl, but loves it if we throw her in the air, play peek-a-boo, or tickle her. She loves the rattle at last, and anything she can chew on. Most of all, however, she likes the cat and dog. I feel she gets plenty of stimulation because I take her with me wherever I go most of the time.

A: My eight-month-old is fascinated with everything, but especially with picking up dirt off the floor and putting it into her mouth. She likes books, and loves it when I put a dish towel over her head or over mine.

A: My eight-month-old girl does nothing but

pull herself up on the handles of my dresser and cruise from one piece of furniture to another, knocking things off surfaces as she goes. She's thrilled. I'm thrilled, too, I suppose, but she keeps bumping her head, and I feel like I have to watch her a lot more now. We've baby-proofed the house. Her favorite game, when she's not cruising, is following Mommy around the house—and getting Daddy to let her crawl up the stairs, bring her back down, and start all over. She also loves to crawl into cardboard boxes and play patty-cake.

A: Stephanie is eight and a half months old. She started walking two weeks ago. Yes, walking, unhelped! She loves to play peek-a-boo around a corner, and loves her kitchen cabinet full of Tupperware and small metal bowls. She dislikes the playpen after a few minutes. I think she needs to explore, and I let her.

A: At nine months he eats everything by himself—including dirt, marigolds, and garden mulch.

A: At nine months Matthew loves to sit inside a cardboard box. He also likes books—but especially those that I make myself out of cardboard. He can turn the pages himself.

A: At nine months he likes the walker for a while. He doesn't like any of his toys, except the pots and pans in the kitchen, and the telephone—the real one, not his play one.

A: Elissa is ten months old, pushes herself around in the walker, squirms, and rolls, but

still doesn't crawl. She sits up and drinks very well from a cup, though.

A: At ten months Anna loves nesting paper cups. She also loves patty-cake, and likes to knock things down, waves bye-bye, and wants to walk. My back is killing me from bending over!

A: She's eleven months old, walking a lot. Toys are of no interest right now—in fact they never really have been. All she wants to do now is go around and around, and around and around and around the dining room table."

A: At eleven and a half months Jake crawls unbelievably fast—dragging the pull toy as he goes—in his mouth.

A: Tara is a year. Her favorite toy is a coffee can with a plastic lid with slots cut in it, and lots of jar tops to fit into the can.

A: Becky is a year, walking, babbling, and opening the safety gates! She loves to put her face in the water. She loves to play with a beach ball. She likes her toy telephone, and is obsessed with opening and closing doors. She likes books, especially ones which have raised surfaces that she can feel.

A: She's a year and likes to push the dining room chair around to practice walking. She has a lot of falls and bumps, which don't seem to deter her. I do wish, though, they made crash helmets for babies.

A: Emma is fifteen months old and is still trying to walk. All of her toys are homemade, and the toys we have bought for her have generally been an enormous waste of money. Right now she spends most of her time exploring, climbing up on the footstool, and trying to catch the cats. She also likes to play ball.

A: She can't walk yet at twelve and a half months, but boy can she climb stairs and gets mad when I decide it's time to stop.

A: Elliot is thirteen months old. He crawls, but doesn't walk yet. He has quite a vocabulary and chatters constantly. He smiles a lot, eats everything in sight. He loves peek-a-boo, only he covers his ears instead of his eyes. His favorite toys are nontoys—pots and pans, plastic spoons, ice trays, books, paper, car keys (watch out). His only favorite real toy is his Fisher-Price mailbox. He can put all his nontoys in it. He also adores paperbacks because he can chew them up the best. At first we tried to help him roll over, sit, crawl, whatever, but it never helped. He figured it out for himself.

A: Jeramie Seth is thirteen months old. He rocks his body to the tune on the radio. He loves to carry around the popcorn popper for some reason. He likes to climb, loves wooden spoons, cups, clothespins, plastic bottles, pots and pans. He tries to turn the pages of books by himself. It doesn't seem to matter if the books have pictures. He just wants to turn the pages. He also loves to turn the light switch on and off. I don't worry about stimulating him. I can't even keep up with him myself.

A: At thirteen and a half months she loves a shopping bag full of junk. She also loves to tear up paper and did a great job unwrapping her birthday presents. At this point, as they say, the box was of more interest than the contents.

A: Tommy is fifteen and a half months old. His favorite toys are our coffee pot and a large plastic jar with a screw top, as well as a piece of strong elastic thread with a bell and a wooden thread spool with the ends tied together. He loves magazines with pictures of cars, animals, and people. He likes Who Lives Inside *books that have simple, direct language with familiar everyday things.*

A: At fifteen months Louise's favorite occupation is emptying my dresser drawers. I've given up! She's also gotten quite bossy. She tells me when she wants her book or bottle. She says "baby" when she sees one. When she has a bowel movement, she says "doody!" My mother points out that I was toilet trained at fifteen months and wants me to start training Louise. My reply is simply, "Oh, that's why I'm so neurotic!" She can walk now, but only if she has her shopping bags. She's like me. I need my pocketbook to hold onto, and she's got to have those shopping bags.

WHAT'S IN A TOY?

When babies reach the point of discovering toys, it seems the process is almost more important than the toys themselves. Finding a rattle under the blanket is as much a part of the fun as shaking the rattle and mouthing it. Throwing it on the floor and hearing it crash is even more fun. When you pick it up and hand it back to the baby so that he can throw it on the floor again, this is probably the best part of it all. He's not only manipulating the rattle, but you as well, which is tremendously satisfying.

A toy is nothing to a baby unless she can do something with it—make an impact on it with her mouth or hands or her bodily strength, or make it move or change or surprise her. Because babies are so imaginative, almost any manipulable object they can hold becomes a toy. One quickly discovers that a baby is almost certain to get far more entertainment from pulling the paperbacks off the shelves, tearing up an old magazine, banging a spoon on a pot lid, turning off a light switch, uprooting a potted plant, or emptying your ashtrays or Kleenex box than from some nine-dollar plastic Busy Box.

One also discovers that no matter how well designed or clever or humble a toy may be, it will seldom hold a baby's attention for more than a few minutes at a time. Most of us make the mistake of loading up on too many toys which are overwhelming for everyone. We always hope that something new will interest the baby, so that we, the tired parents, can have a few moments of peace and quiet. We end up with baskets of toys, or parts of toys, spread all over the house to pick up and sort through by the end of the day. In this respect, a good rule of thumb seems to be less is more. It's a good idea, if you own a lot of baby toys, to put some away. Trade with a friend, then bring out one or two "new" ones at a time.

Our homes are full of nontoys, but this is not to say that "real" or bought toys don't have some value. A well-chosen toy which is appropriate for the baby's age can teach and delight. The best buys, of course, are those that are versatile and will interest the baby over the longest period of time.

The large, brightly colored pop beads, for example, are simple, inexpensive, and enormously versatile. They are safe to chew on, and too big to swallow. For the very young baby, they can be strung across a carriage or a basket like a cradle gym. For the baby who can sit up, they make a wonderful toy. They float, they can be filled with water and emptied. They can be worn as a necklace or played with separately. An eleven-month-old may enjoy dropping them into a coffee can with an appropriately sized hole cut in the plastic lid. Once they're in the coffee can, they rattle. Eventually, the baby will also master pulling the beads apart. And at some future date, when he

becomes much more coordinated, he will master sticking them back together. For a walking baby, a string of these large plastic beads is a simple but satisfying pull-toy. For a two-year-old who is involved in imaginative play, the beads can become a snake or a tail. They can also be used to learn about color and eventually about counting.

Following are some suggestions for buying toys as well as for making or discovering some simple toys yourself.

POINTS TO LOOK FOR WHEN YOU BUY BABY TOYS

1. Is the toy unbreakable?

2. If it is a stuffed toy, is it well made, so that the stuffing won't come out?

3. If a stuffed toy or doll has eyes, are they embroidered or well sewn with strong plastic thread?

4. Is the hair on dolls well attached and not so long that the baby could choke on it?

5. Is the toy free of sharp edges? (You'd be surprised how many made by leading manufacturers aren't.)

6. Are toys such as cars, with movable parts, well constructed, so that none of the small parts will come loose and go into the baby's mouth?

7. Are toys made of brittle plastic? These break easily into sharp, jagged pieces.

8. Are toys operated by batteries? The batteries can leak toxic chemicals.

9. Are wooden toys well sanded and free of splinters?

10. Are cloth toys flame-resistant and washable?

11. Are any toys too heavy for the baby at this stage of the game? And can they be grasped with one hand?

12. Are any strings more than a foot long attached to toys? A long string could strangle the baby. If there is a loop or ring on the end, is it large enough so the baby can't swallow it?

13. Are painted toys labeled nontoxic?

14. Are the ages suggested by the manufacturer realistic? A toy that is too advanced will frustrate the baby.

15. Can the baby have fun with the toy himself, or is it so complicated that a parent must be involved to make it work properly?

A DOZEN GOOD BOOKS FOR BABIES

From about the time they are crawling, some babies really do enjoy books and,

Materials Needed

☐ sturdy poster board in a variety of bright colors for pages

☐ colored pictures and photographs of familiar objects, animals, people—especially those in the family—and actions

☐ clear Con-Tact paper (to keep the pictures intact and insure that the baby doesn't chew or eat four-color illustrations that contain poisonous lead dyes)

☐ nontoxic glue or paste

☐ hole puncher

☐ yarn for tying pages together or looseleaf rings, or a small looseleaf binder (address-book size is perfect) so that the baby can easily turn the pages himself

How to Make It

1. Cut the pages to desired sizes and round the corners.

2. Paste or glue pictures on both sides.

3. Cover with clear Con-Tact paper.

4. Punch holes.

5. Tie together with yarn or use rings, or place in looseleaf binder. Change the pictures often for variety.

A What's-Inside Book

For the older baby an "envelope" book can be more fun and challenging. Instead of using posterboard for the pages, use office-sized manila envelopes. Paste a picture on the outside, and cover with clear Con-Tact paper. For the inside, you can make cutouts of objects mounted on posterboard and covered with clear Con-Tact paper.

What's on the envelope can correspond with what's inside it. For instance, you might have a baby carriage on the envelope and a baby picture inside, a tree on the envelope and an apple inside, a hen and a chick, and so on. The baby will enjoy opening the envelope, taking the picture out, and putting it back.

of course, the holding, cuddling, and attention that go with reading. The first books should be simple, with brightly colored, familiar objects that are depicted realistically. But also don't underestimate a baby's interest in action and love of slapstick humor as well. Nothing is funnier to a baby than a picture of another baby trying to feed herself or an adult falling down or dropping something, catastrophes that are second nature to babies. Following are a dozen good books for babies and toddlers.

BROWN, MARGARET WISE, *Goodnight Moon*, Harper & Row, New York, 1947.

FLACK, MARJORIE, *Angus and the Cat*, Doubleday, New York, 1939.

GEISMER, BARBARA PECK and SUTER, ANTOINETTE, *Very Young Verses*, Houghton Mifflin, Boston, 1945.

KENT, JACK, *Jack Kent's Hop, Skip, & Jump Book*, Random House, New York, 1974.

KUNHARDT, DOROTHY, *Pat The Bunny*, Western Publishing, Racine, Wisc., 1962.

KUNHARDT, DOROTHY, *The Telephone Book*, Western Publishing, Racine, Wisconsin, 1975.

MATTHIESEN, THOMAS, *ABC: An Alphabet Book*, Platt & Munk Publishers, Bronx, N.Y., 1968.

OGLE, LUCILLE, *I Spy with My Little Eye*, McGraw-Hill, New York, 1970.

PORTER PRODUCTIONS, *Who Lives Inside?*, Grosset & Dunlap, New York, 1976.

SCARRY, RICHARD, *Richard Scarry's Best Word Book Ever*, Western Publishing, Racine, Wisc., 1963.

REY, H. A., *Anybody at Home?*, Houghton Mifflin, Boston.

REY, H. A., *See the Circus*, Houghton Mifflin, Boston, 1956.

BEAUTIFUL JUNK—HOMEMADE BABY TOYS

Toys that you make for your baby are special in many ways. Ideally, they come about almost organically from our own observations of what our babies delight in seeing, feeling, hearing, and manipulating. If your creations are ruined from overuse, you should be flattered. And, of course, homemade toys are inexpensive, biodegradable, and replaceable.

None of the following toys, with the exception of the texture blanket and perhaps the cardboard house, should take you more than half an hour to make, assuming that you have the needed materials on hand—and a sleeping baby.

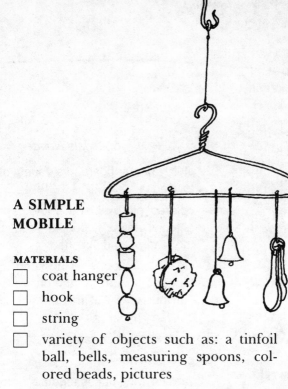

A SIMPLE MOBILE

MATERIALS

- [ ] coat hanger
- [ ] hook
- [ ] string
- [ ] variety of objects such as: a tinfoil ball, bells, measuring spoons, colored beads, pictures

Simply tie the objects to the coat hanger, install the hook in the ceiling, and hang the mobile up from a piece of string. Newborns focus best when objects are eight to ten inches away and to one side (since they rarely lie on their backs looking straight ahead). Turn the baby from back to stomach often. This way he can look at the mobile from different perspectives and exercise different muscles. For variety, change the objects periodically. And of course remove the mobile as soon as you notice the baby is beginning to take an interest in batting at objects.

A HAPPY FACE

MATERIALS

- [ ] white paper plate
- [ ] nontoxic Magic Markers or crayons
- [ ] yarn
- [ ] glue
- [ ] tape

A newborn baby prefers the human face to any other sight. Draw the features on the plate and glue yarn on for hair. Tape the face to the side or end of the crib or cradle.

A HAPPY-FACE PUPPET

MATERIALS

- [ ] happy face constructed out of a paper plate (see previous instructions)
- [ ] another paper plate of the same size
- [ ] dowel
- [ ] glue
- [ ] tape

A face in motion is more interesting to a baby than one that doesn't move. To make a simple puppet, glue the plates together with undersides facing out. Then cut a wedge-shaped slice large enough for the dowel to go through. Insert the dowel in the opening and tape the plate to the dowel. Dangle or dance

the puppet in front of the baby. You might also want to turn on some music; by three weeks the newborn has learned to kick rhythmically.

A TEXTURE BLANKET

MATERIALS

- [ ] a variety of fabric squares 4 inches by 4 inches, of different colors and textures, such as terry cloth, seersucker, corduroy, fake fur, lamé, velvet, burlap, wool, suede or leather, satin or taffeta
- [ ] fabric for backing
- [ ] needle and thread or sewing machine
- [ ] safety pins

Babies learn about the world through their senses. A texture blanket is interesting to both look at and feel. Simply sew the squares together to form a rectangle or square. Using this as a pattern, cut out a backing. Pin wrong sides together and sew along the edges. Be sure to leave an opening large enough so that you can turn the blanket right-side out. Slip-stitch the opening. You might want to pin the blanket to the baby's sheet so that it stays in place.

CRADLE GYM

MATERIALS

- [ ] cardboard tube somewhat shorter than width of crib or cradle
- [ ] 3 to 4 feet of clothesline (depending on width of crib or cradle)
- [ ] brightly colored Con-Tact paper or nontoxic paint
- [ ] sturdy string or cord
- [ ] variety of objects of different weights and textures that make different sounds, such as a sponge, measuring spoons, strings of spools or beads, curtain rings, brightly colored scraps of fabric, bells

Within two or three months the baby will not be content to look. She will want to reach out and touch things. A cradle gym hung with a variety of interesting objects puts the world of cause and effect within her reach. The simplest of all cradle gyms is a cord with objects securely tied to it and hung across the crib. But without much extra effort you can refine this toy by slipping the cord or clothesline through a cardboard tube. Decorate the tube with Con-Tact paper or nontoxic paint if you wish. The added rigidity that the tube provides will make it easier for the baby to bat and grasp the objects. Be sure to tie the objects very securely to the tube, and change them periodically. Once the baby is proficient at grabbing, you might want to hang some of the objects from quarter-inch sewing elastic so that they bounce more when she lets go.

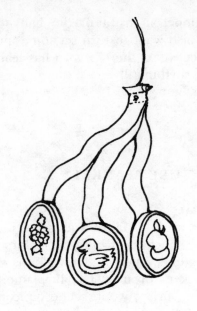

CLAPPER RATTLE

MATERIALS

- [ ] three 8-inch pieces of different colored grosgrain ribbon
- [ ] three jar lids
- [ ] nontoxic permanent glue
- [ ] brightly colored pictures of faces and objects
- [ ] clear Con-Tact paper
- [ ] needle and thread or sewing machine
- [ ] sturdy string or cord

A clapper rattle can be an additional object on a cradle gym or can be hung by itself, perhaps from the hood of a carriage. Cut out circular pictures for the tops and insides of each lid. Then set them aside for a moment. Next, sew the three ribbons together in two places; at one end and three-fourths of an inch from this. In the space between the two seams, make a hole through which you can thread a sturdy piece of string for hanging the finished product. Then glue each of the free ribbon ends onto the inside of a jar lid. Glue the circular pictures to the inside and outsides of the jar lids and cover with clear Con-Tact paper.

RATTLE

MATERIALS

- [ ] plastic pill bottle with lid (large enough so that it can't get lodged in the baby's throat)
- [ ] permanent glue
- [ ] bells, beads, paper clips, or pebbles

Rattles always provide interesting listening, but the baby will not be able to have fun with one on his own until about four months, when he can grasp well. Just fill the pill bottle with any of the above materials that rattle. Glue permanently shut. For added variety, partially fill the bottle with colored water.

BEAN BAGS

MATERIALS

- [ ] brightly colored fabric scraps
- [ ] fillers: dried beans, cellophane or tissue paper, marbles, bells, other packing
- [ ] materials such as Styrofoam or straw

Bean bags are fun for a baby to hold and mouth, but you can make them interesting to listen to as well. If you are feeling very artistic, you can cut out paper patterns in the shapes of animals and people. If you're not feeling so artistic, an abstract "amoeba" with several arms to hold onto and chew will do. In any case, be sure to cut out two identical shapes—one for the back and one for the front. With wrong sides together, sew back to front, leaving a small opening so that you can turn the shape right-side out; fill it; then close the opening. Before you do turn the shape, double-check to make sure your seams are foolproof and none of the filling can come out.

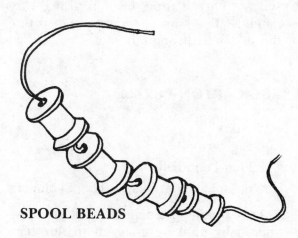

SPOOL BEADS

MATERIALS

- [ ] several wooden thread spools
- [ ] nontoxic, waterproof paint or Magic Markers
- [ ] strong, brightly colored shoelace

Decorate the spools and string them. Tie ends together securely. The baby will enjoy mouthing this toy and eventually wearing it as a necklace.

BLOCKS

MATERIALS

- [ ] 2 cream cartons for each block
- [ ] tape
- [ ] brightly colored Con-Tact paper or magazine pictures covered with clear Con-Tact paper

These lightweight blocks will not hurt the baby when she knocks them over on herself, and they are very simple to make. Cut the tops off two cream cartons (step 1). Fit one cream carton inside the other to form a cube (step 2). Snip off the pointed corners. Tape the cartons together (step 3) and cover with Con-Tact paper (step 4). If you wish you can put something that rattles inside before you tape the containers together.

PAPER-CUP NESTING TOY

MATERIALS

- [ ] paper cups
- [ ] Con-Tact paper or nontoxic Magic Marker (optional)

Just give the baby three or four cups. Decorated or not, they will be a hit.

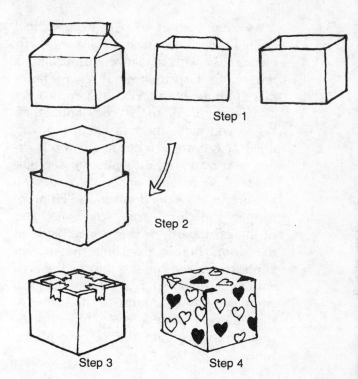

Step 1

Step 2

Step 3

Step 4

CARDBOARD HOUSE

MATERIALS

- [ ] large cardboard box, about the size of a washing machine
- [ ] razor blades or Exacto knife
- [ ] drawer knob with screw assembly
- [ ] fabric for curtains, and staple gun to secure fabric to windows (optional)

As soon as your baby can crawl, he'll enjoy having adventures on his own. His own house with a blanket inside and a few of his favorite toys is a wonderful place to hide, play peek-a-boo, or just get away from it all to be cozy and quiet. When you make the house, cut the windows at varying heights so that both sitting and standing, the baby can see out. Babies love to open and close doors, so be sure to leave the door intact. To make it open and close easily, score one layer of the cardboard, or the "hinge" side of the door. Before inserting the drawer knob for a door knob, reinforce the area with tape. If you are really ambitious, you can paste fabric curtains to the inside of the windows, paste a few pictures on the walls, and decorate the outside of the house.

POKE AND FEEL BOX

MATERIALS
- [ ] very shallow box, such as a shirt box
- [ ] tape
- [ ] glue
- [ ] variety of materials of different textures, such as fine-grade sandpaper, cotton, burlap, velvet, crinkly tissue paper

The life of a poke box may not be too long. The baby will soon want to pull out the materials her curious fingers are poking. Start by measuring the width of the box and drawing lines that divide it into four or five equal sections. Do the same to the outside of the box lid. Cut out four or five strips of different-textured materials, each the size of one of the sections, and glue them onto the bottom of the shirt box. Go back to the lid, and cut two or three holes in each section. The holes needn't all be round. Use your imagination. Tape the lid of the box to the bottom, and give it to the baby. She'll probably figure out what to do with it before you have a chance to show her.

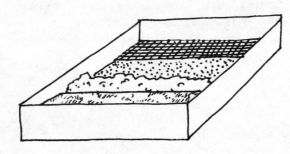

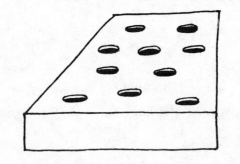

BATH AND SAND BUCKET

MATERIALS
- [ ] ½-gallon plastic food container
- [ ] thin rope
- [ ] Con-Tact paper (optional)

A plastic bucket makes a good bath toy or place for parents to store the baby's other small toys. Punch holes in the plastic container with an ice pick or sharp scissor. Thread rope through to make a handle. Tie knots, so that the rope doesn't slide through the holes.

EGG-CARTON PUZZLE

MATERIALS
- [ ] egg carton
- [ ] Ping-Pong balls
- [ ] nontoxic paint in a variety of colors

This simple puzzle may well occupy your baby until he goes off to nursery school. Ping-Pong balls are great toys in themselves—they go so far with so little effort and make such a wonderful sound as they travel. If you wish to make this toy more esthetically appealing, paint the balls and the depressions for the eggs different colors. If this toy lasts long enough, that is, until your child is over two, you can use it to teach about matching up colors.

WHAT'S IN THE BOX?

MATERIALS

- [ ] shoe box
- [ ] tape
- [ ] Con-Tact paper
- [ ] assorted objects of different textures, colors, and shapes, such as a small sponge, a ball, a paper cup, a block, a scrap of fabric

Babies love surprises, and they also love to empty containers. Simply cut a hole large enough for the object to fit through. Tape the top of the box closed, and cover with brightly colored Con-Tact paper. As the baby empties the box, you can talk about what comes out in terms of shape, color, texture, and weight.

SPINDLE TOY

MATERIALS

- [ ] small cardboard box with a lid, or a shoe box
- [ ] paper-towel roll
- [ ] assorted wooden curtain rings, screw-eyes removed; or inexpensive plastic bracelets; or rings made from pipe cleaners
- [ ] nontoxic paint, Magic Marker, or Con-Tact paper
- [ ] glue

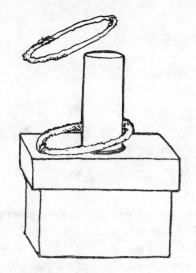

Decorate the box and the paper-towel roll. Then, using the end of the roll as a pattern, draw a circle on the lid of the box and cut out a round hole. Place glue in the bottom of the box and insert the towel roll. Show the baby how to place the rings on the spindle and how to take them off. By about nine months the baby is able to use thumb and finger to perform this skilled operation. Large rings made from pipe cleaners are good to start with. When this becomes easy, make the rings smaller.

SHOE-BOX PUZZLE

MATERIALS

- [ ] shoe box with lid
- [ ] 3 paper-towel rollers, cut to various

sizes but taller than the height of the shoe box

- [ ] magazine pictures and clear Con-Tact paper or brightly colored and patterned Con-Tact paper

As the baby nears his first birthday, simple puzzles will become more interesting. She may enjoy trying to fit the cardboard rolls from your paper towels into holes in a shoe box. Cut holes to the correct size by tracing around the roller. Cover the rolls and the box with pictures and/or Con-Tact paper.

NESTING AND STACKING CANS

MATERIALS

- [ ] tin cans of various sizes (no sharp rims)
- [ ] magazine pictures and clear Con-Tact paper or brightly colored Con-Tact paper
- [ ] glue

Glue the pictures or attach Con-Tact paper to the cans. When the baby can sit up well, he'll begin to enjoy knocking things down. These simple covered cans make wonderful clattering towers when they are stacked on top of each other. With them, the baby can also begin to learn about big and little, and how to fit one can into another.

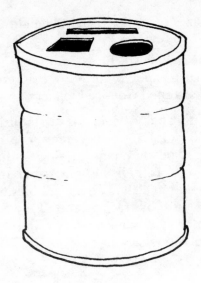

COFFEE CAN SHAPE SORTER

MATERIALS
- [ ] coffee can with plastic lid
- [ ] sharp knife or razor blade
- [ ] jar lids
- [ ] Con-Tact paper (optional)

Simply cut a slot in the plastic lid large enough for the biggest jar lid. You can modify this toy as the baby gets older. Add two more simple shapes—a square one for blocks, and a round one for a small ball. You can also use a coffee can for the clothespin game. Use the simple, old-fashioned one-piece wooden clothespins. Show the baby how to place them on the coffee can rim.

MATCHBOX TOY

MATERIALS
- [ ] a matchbox
- [ ] magazine pictures or your own creations
- [ ] nontoxic glue
- [ ] clear Con-Tact paper

Babies love to open things and find surprises inside. You can decorate a small matchbox with pictures. Cover with clear Con-Tact paper because four-color magazine print contains toxic lead dyes. Be sure to glue a picture on the bottom of the sliding drawer. When the baby discovers this, it will probably be his favorite.

THE SIMPLEST PULL-TOY

MATERIALS
- [ ] shoe box without the lid
- [ ] longish piece of thick, strong yarn
- [ ] wooden curtain ring
- [ ] pictures to decorate the box
- [ ] clear Con-Tact paper to cover and secure the pictures

As soon as the baby learns to walk, she'll enjoy pulling her favorite toys around in this primitive wagon. Simply make a hole in one end of the shoe box large enough to thread a piece of yarn through. Tie a large knot at the threaded end of the yarn so that it will not slip out of the hole. To the free end of the yarn, tie a curtain ring. This is so that the baby will be able to hold and pull easily. Decorate the box with pictures or your own designs. If you use four-colored magazine pictures, be sure to cover with clear Con-Tact paper.

PLAY GROUPS

When your child approaches two, you may want to start a play group with two or three of his contemporaries. Some early childhood experts maintain that children under the age of three don't benefit from a group experience, but many mothers disagree. A group that meets once or twice a week for no more than two hours at a stretch can be the basis for deep and lasting friendships, as well as an introduction to the joys as well as the trials of belonging to a group.

As the group rotates from house to house, it is an opportunity for your toddler to explore different environments, spend short periods of time away from you, learn to trust other caring adults, and realize that other people have different expectations and ways of dealing with situations. For mothers a play group can be a weekly break, albeit brief, and an opportunity to gain perspective on your own child. Who doesn't need to be reassured that you aren't the only mother in the world run ragged by death-defying physical feats, short temper, and the often unsharing nature as well as the imagination and charm of your two-year-old—especially in the depths of winter when places to go and things to do are limited?

Although a play group is unstructured playtime punctuated by a mid-morning snack, it does require some thought, careful supervision, and a few rules. If you have a group of four, at least two mothers should stay on duty to supervise. Make juice ahead of time; lock rooms where you don't want the children to go. In good weather a backyard sandbox or small wading pool is ideal. In bad weather, a balance between vigorous physical activities (dancing to records, hammock swinging, or bed bouncing) and quiet activities (play dough, fingerpainting, snack, books) will make the group run more smoothly. Our most successful bad weather mornings centered around a large cardboard box house. The children loved to run around it, dive inside with pillows, and surprise each other through the windows.

It's almost inevitable that the child hosting the group will demand the most

attention. As for sharing, one quickly learns that perfection or even halfway to perfection is far too much to expect from children this age. It is easier if toys are kept to a minimum, and if you can provide duplicates of some things—two pull toys, two balls, two hats, two pocketbooks or musical toys.

There are days when your efforts to mend and cajole, to sing and dance, may make you wonder why you're bothering to "socialize" your child so soon. But on days when the flow, for some mysterious reason, is right, and your presence is hardly noticed, you'll know it's all worthwhile. Here is the best play dough recipe.

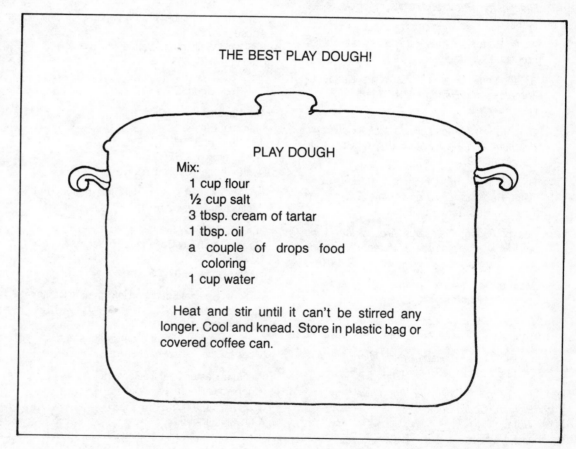

THE BEST PLAY DOUGH!

PLAY DOUGH

Mix:
    1 cup flour
    ½ cup salt
    3 tbsp. cream of tartar
    1 tbsp. oil
    a couple of drops food coloring
    1 cup water

Heat and stir until it can't be stirred any longer. Cool and knead. Store in plastic bag or covered coffee can.

RESOURCES

Learning and Play

Brazleton, T. Berry, *Infants and Mothers,* Dell Publishing, New York, 1964.

Koch, Jaroslov, *Total Baby Development,* Wyden, New York, 1976.

Prudden, Suzy and Jeffrey Sassman, *Creative Fitness for Baby and Child,* Morrow, New York, 1972.

White, Burton L., *The First Three Years of Life,* Prentice-Hall, Englewood Cliffs, N.J. 1975.

Broad, Laura P. and Butterworth, Nancy T., *The Playgroup Handbook,* St. Martin's Press, New York, 1974.

Dal Fabbro, Mario, *How to Make Children's Furniture and Play Equipment,* McGraw-Hill, New York, 1975.

Hartley, Ruth and Goldenson, Robert, *Complete Book of Children's Play,* Thomas Y. Crowell, New York, 1970.

Joseph, Joan, *Folk Toys Around the World and How to Make Them,* Parents Magazine Press, New York, 1972.

MacKenzie, Giselle, *Lullabye and Goodnight,* Pickwick Records.

Poston, Elizabeth, *The Baby's Song Book,* Thomas Y. Crowell, New York, 1972.

Rowen, Nancy, *Lullabies and Other Children's Songs,* Joan Love Recordings.

From Birth to One Year: The Nova University Play and Learn Book
Write to:

Institute for Child Centered Education
Nova University
Fort Lauderdale, Fla. 33314

Special Concerns

Child Abuse

Check phone book for toll free Child Abuse Hotline in your area.

National Committee for Prevention of Child Abuse
836 West Wellington Avenue
Chicago, Ill. 60657

The Exceptional Child

The National Foundation—
March of Dimes
1707 H Street, N.W.
Washington, D.C. 20006
(write for their publication list)

IMRID (Institute on Mental Retardation and Intellectual Development)

John F. Kennedy Center
George Peabody College for Teachers
Box 154
Nashville, Tenn. 37203

National Special Education Information Center
P.O. Box 1492
Washington, D.C. 20013
(write for list of parent organizations and services for the exceptional child)

National Easter Seal Society, Inc.
Crippled Children and Adults
2023 W. Ogden St.
Chicago, Ill. 60612

Single Parents

Parents Without Partners
7910 Woodmont Avenue
Suite 1000
Washington, D.C. 20014
(check your phone book first for local chapters)

Klein, Carole, *The Single Parent Experience,* Avon Books, New York, 1973.

Momma
P.O. Box 567
Venice, Calif. 90291
(a magazine for single mothers)

The Premature Baby

Galinsky, Ellen, *Beginnings,* Houghton Mifflin, Boston, 1976.

Breast-Feeding the Premature Baby

Info Sheet #13
La Leche League
9616 Minneapolis Avenue
Franklin Park, Ill. 60131

Twins

National Organization of Mothers of Twins Clubs
5402 Amberwood Lane
Rockville, Md. 20853

And Then There Were Two: A Handbook for Mothers and Fathers of Twins
The Twins' Mothers Club of Bergen County, New Jersey
Child Study Press
50 Madison Avenue
New York, N.Y. 10010

Part IX

THE QUESTIONNAIRE

Dear ———,

I am writing to ask for your help and participation in a practical and supportive book about babies. It deals with the mundáne but monumental details of living with and caring for an infant during, roughly, the first year of life, or until the time she/he learns to walk.

The idea for this book comes out of my own experience — which I do not think is unique. As a new mother (my daughter is now twelve months old), I had few friends with babies, and no relatives nearby. Many of the books I bought are interesting and authoritative. But most are also quite specialized and are written by experts who deal with matters such as behavior and development, health, nutrition, etc. What these books lack is the practical information and help we need to deal with the everyday complications of living with a baby. They also tend to be very "baby centered" with little support or information about parents (their adjustments, their needs, their feelings, etc.).

The enclosed questionnaire is the foundation for the book. Through it I hope to include your questions and solutions, your frustrations and rewards in a single, paperback book. You are an expert because you live with your baby twenty-four hours a day. This book will not be valid without you — without many contributors and points of view, because there is no single way to love and care for a baby.

For purely practical reasons I have addressed these questions primarily to the woman or mother in the family. If both parents have time to answer them together, this would be ideal. I have asked for your name so that I can acknowledge your contribution. However, I do want to stress that all you say will be held in strict confidence.

The questionnaire only partially reflects the information I will include. Even so it is overly long. Please do not feel you must answer every question. If you have a baby or a young child, your time is gold. Look over the index on the back of this page [index not included in book], and start with the section which interests you the most. Several of the questions will not apply if your baby is very young. (However, if you want to, feel free to speculate about what you might do or how you might feel.) If you have a small child, I welcome your hindsight and understand that you might have forgotten a lot. (I have already forgotten a lot myself.) Please feel free to write in the margins, or on additional pages of your own.

If you only answer one question and mail this back to me as soon as possible, you will be making a real contribution to a book I truly believe needs to be written. Thank you for sharing your experience and expertise with me. I look forward to hearing from you soon.

Sincerely,
Frances Wells Burck

SECTION ONE

INTRODUCTORY QUESTIONS

1. I want to thank you for your contribution to this book on an acknowledgment page. Please print the name you would like me to use and your correct mailing address.

2. Please use this space to describe your baby and yourself briefly (i.e., your baby's age, sex, what s/he is doing now—your own age, what you are doing now and have done before your baby was born, etc.).

3. Can you write down the first ten observations, thoughts, questions, etc. which come to mind about your baby or babies in general (I have given nine of my own as an example).
   She's drinking the bath water.
   He didn't sleep through the night for six months.
   I don't know anyone else with a baby.
   It's 11:00 a.m., and I'm still not dressed.
   We feel terrible when we fight in front of the baby.
   The baby smiled for the first time!
   My mother-in-law had only perfect babies.
   She fell off the changing table.
   How can we keep the floors clean enough for the baby?

4. Can you give me an example from your own experience to support or refute this statement? Taking care of a baby is a learned skill much more than a matter of "maternal instinct."

SECTION TWO

QUESTIONS ON FEEDING

1. Did you breast- or bottle-feed or both? Why? Did you feel any pressures to do either?

2. What questions did you have about feeding your newborn? What questions do you have now?

3. If you bottle-fed your baby, what kind of formula did you use? What equipment, if any (sterilizers, bottle warmers, etc.), was useful? How long did preparing formula take each day, and did you find any shortcuts?

4. If you breast-fed, what is the single most useful piece of information you can pass on to a mother who is nursing her first baby?

5. Did you have any problems nursing? If so, could you explain what they were and how you coped (or didn't cope, as the case may be).

6. When did you introduce solid foods and why? What did you start with and move on to? How did your baby react?

7. What is your idea of a good, well-balanced diet? Is there anything you avoid feeding your baby such as sweets, starches, or meat? Is there anything in particular which you try to make sure your baby does eat?

8. Did you buy baby food or make your own or both? Why?

9. If you made your own, I'm interested in your method of preparation and storage and any recipes, if possible.

10. If you used commercial baby food, did you have any questions about its contents or how to store it?

11. When did your baby start to feed him/herself? Which self-feeding foods does your baby like, and which are most convenient for you? If you have any special recipes, please include them.

12. Does it trouble you that your baby resists some foods that you think are good for him/her? If so, how do you manage to get the baby to eat those foods or do you feel this is unimportant?

13. Is your baby a vegetarian? What does s/he eat? What reactions have

you gotten from your pediatrician, friends, relatives, etc? What do you feed your baby instead of meat?

14. When did you wean your baby (from breast to bottle, breast to cup, or bottle to cup)? How did you do it, and how did you and your baby react? Were you aware of any signs of readiness on your baby's part? What?

15. When did you introduce a spoon? What signs of readiness did you observe? Can you describe the first time?

16. Have you taken your baby to eat in a restaurant? If so, please describe your experience.

17. What general questions do you have about feeding and nutrition?

SECTION THREE

QUESTIONS ON HEALTH

1. Did your baby have any minor health problems as a newborn? Did you feel confident in dealing with these?

2. Did your baby have any serious health problems at birth? Did you feel you had enough information?

What advice/support would be helpful for a new parent in a similar situation?

3. How did you find and evaluate a pediatrician or clinic? What kind of relationship do you have with your pediatrician or clinic?

4. Have you used any home remedies for illness or discomfort, such as cornstarch for diaper rash or herb teas for colic? Please be specific and if possible tell me where you found out about these remedies—and of course, whether or not they worked.

5. Did you have a colicky baby? What is colic, and how did you deal with it? What advice/support could you give to others in a similar situation?

6. Has your baby had a lot of colds? How do you treat colds? Do you take any preventative measures?

7. What was your baby's teething experience like (for you as well as the baby)?

8. How important is your baby's weight gain to you?

9. What first aid information would be useful to you (i.e., would you like to know how to deal with choking, or how to administer artificial respiration, etc.)?

10. Has your baby had any hospital emergencies? How did you handle

these, and is there any advice/support/information you would offer to others in a similar situation?

11. What areas or questions should be covered on health in a section of this book?

12. Are there any questions about your baby's health which you either have not had time to ask your pediatrician about or feel foolish asking your pediatrician about? If so, what?

SECTION FOUR

QUESTIONS ON CLOTHING AND BATHING

1. What was the most useful piece of clothing in the "layette"? The most useless?

2. What kind of diapers did you use? Why? If you used cloth diapers, how many and what kind did you buy? How did you wash them, store them, etc.?

3. What are your opinions about shoes for babies?

4. What clothing has been most useful for cold weather, warm weather?

5. Do you have any suggestions for diapering and dressing a wiggly baby?

6. How did you give your newborn a bath? Did you use any "equipment" such as bath seats, special tubs, etc.? How did you bathe the baby when he/she was older? Did your baby experience any fear of the bath?

SECTION FIVE

QUESTIONS ON SLEEP

1. When did your baby sleep through the night? Did you try to encourage your baby to sleep through the night in any way? Do you think this is possible?

2. What methods or rituals have you worked out for helping your baby to sleep?

3. If your baby is not a big sleeper, what advice would you offer to parents in a similar situation?

4. Has your baby gone through periods of night wakefulness during teething, motor spurts, etc? How have you handled them? Would you do the same thing again?

5. How have you scheduled and eliminated naps for your baby?

SECTION SIX

QUESTIONS ON THE FAMILY

1. Did you know anything about taking care of a baby before you had your own? Where did you get the experience? Were there any classes or discussion groups which you found helpful?

2. Did you have any preconceptions about living with and taking care of a baby based, for example, on friends' or relatives' accounts of their experiences? Did your own experience match up with the preconceptions? What were the major adjustments you had to make? What have the rewards been?

3. What was particularly pleasant and/or unpleasant about your return from the hospital? (If you had a home birth, please use this space to describe what it was like for the first couple of days after your baby was born.) Can you make any useful suggestions for new parents?

4. Can you describe the first day you spent truly alone in the house with your newborn?

5. Whom did you rely on for advice/support/information in the beginning? What questions and concerns did you have?

6. Did you suffer from postpartum symptoms? What were they and how long did they last? Do you feel you had enough information about the postpartum period? Did you feel that you needed support, and if so from whom did you receive it?

7. Do you feel that your body has permanently changed in any way due to the birth of your baby? If so, what is your attitude toward this change?

8. Have you felt a decrease or increase in your sexual desire since you had your baby? If so, has this been a source of conflict in your relationship with your husband?

9. Certainly you've suffered from fatigue. Have you found any practical way to deal with this?

10. Have you had any "destructive" fantasies toward your baby? Do these make you feel guilty?

11. Do you think that having a baby has given you a sense of "purpose"? What aspects of your character do you think having a baby has brought out? What aspects have been suppressed?

12. About how many hours do you spend taking care of your baby a day? What "work" do you associate

with taking care of a baby?

13. How much free time do you have a day? How do you use it—i.e., do you feel pressured to "use it well?"

14. Has your relationship changed with parents, in-laws and relatives since you had a baby?

15. Has your relationship with friends changed? If so, how?

16. When did you leave the baby in someone else's care? Who? How did you feel? How did the baby react? What child-care arrangements, if any, have you made?

17. Please react to this statement: "I can't reconcile motherhood with the women's liberation movement, but I feel very pressured to do so."

18. Do you work at a job, or have a career or a vocation? At what point did you resume your work? Did you experience any conflicts or guilt? What information/support would have been helpful to you? What practical problems were involved, and how did you solve them?

19. Do you feel that your relationship with your husband has changed since you had a baby? If so, how? (What has been positive, what has been negative?)

20. Do you feel your husband has changed since he became a father? How?

21. How much time does your husband spend with the baby? Is this ever a source of conflict in your family? If so, have you taken any steps together to resolve this?

SECTION SEVEN

QUESTIONS FOR FATHERS

(Please feel free to "interview" the baby's father, if this is easier for both of you.)

1. Were you present at your baby's birth? Please describe your experience and your feelings.

2. Do you feel that you experienced any type of postpartum symptoms? Do you feel that you received the information/support/advice which you needed? If so, where did it come from?

3. How much time do you spend with your baby? Have you altered your schedule to spend time with the baby, or has the baby's schedule been altered to accommodate you in any way?

4. Do you feel that you are as competent as your wife at taking care of your baby? Where do you feel most confident, most ill at ease?

5. Had you had any experience caring for a baby before yours was born? If so, where did you get it?

6. Describe the first time that you spent truly alone with your newborn. What did you do and how did you feel? What is the longest time period in which you have taken care of the baby?

7. React to this statement: "I cannot reconcile motherhood with the women's liberation movement."

8. Do you feel that your relationship with your wife has changed since you had a baby? How?

9. Would you be willing to participate in or run a taped discussion group for fathers or couples on a particular subject?

10. What questions do you have about living with and taking care of a baby in general?

SECTION EIGHT

QUESTIONS ON ENVIRONMENT AND LIFE STYLE

1. Do you live in the city, the suburbs, a small town, or the country? What

are the positive and negative aspects of where you live in terms of having a baby?

2. Have you simplified or reorganized your home since you have had a baby? How?

3. Have you created a special room or space for your baby? How is it planned? What further ideas do you have on a comfortable yet functional space for a baby?

4. How have you organized and stored your baby's possessions throughout the house?

5. Have you built, invented, or improvised anything for your baby to play in, sit in, sleep in, etc.? Can you tell me how you made this and include a rough sketch?

6. What is dangerous about your living space for a baby? What have you done to make the environment safe? Have any products in particular been useful to you? If so, what?

7. Has your attitude toward housework changed since you had a baby? If so, how?

8. Have you entertained differently since you had a baby?

9. What has been most useful to you in terms of taking the baby with you both as a newborn and later? When you go out with the baby, what in particular would you never be without no matter where you are going?

10. Have you traveled with your baby? If so, by car, plane, boat, bus, or train? Do you have any suggestions for making travel by any of these modes easier?

11. Have you traveled to a foreign country with your baby? I'm particularly interested in knowing what you needed and what you felt you could do without. What information would have been useful to you? Were any organizations such as Travelers Aid, American Express, travel agencies, hotels, and airlines helpful in any way?

SECTION NINE

QUESTIONS ABOUT YOUR BABY

1. Briefly describe how you think your baby sees the world. (If you feel comfortable with this technique, try to speak for your baby. You might start with, "I feel very small. Everything around me is large,"etc.)

2. What frustrates your baby right now? What frustrates you about your baby right now?

3. What delights your baby? What does your baby do that is funny?

4. Has your baby experienced "separation anxiety"? How did you feel about this and what did you do?

5. What are your feelings about playpens, walkers, Jolly Jumpers, swings, etc.? Which of these items have you used? For how long? Which baby products are worth having? Which are objectionable to you and why?

6. What toys does your baby like most? What "non-toys" such as household items does your baby like? Have you made any toys for your baby? If so, can you describe them and tell me how you made them?

7. Is your baby interested in books? Which ones does he/she like the best? Which do you like the best and think are the most appropriate?

8. Do you worry about "stimulating" your baby enough? If so, what triggers this concern? What do you do to "stimulate" your baby and what "stimulation" does the baby find on his/her own?

SECTION TEN

GENERAL QUESTIONS

1. If you had only one item to make life easier with a baby, what would it be? Why?

2. If you had one service to make life easier with a baby, what would it be? Why?

3. I would like to include a section in this book called "Resources," that is, books, records, films, plans for things to make, organizations, services, institutions, etc., that might be useful to people with a baby. What have your resources been?

4. Have you kept a record on your baby's development at any time or a journal about your own feelings and activities since you've had a child? Would you be willing to share any part of this with me at a later time?

5. Do you think a book dealing with the questions I have asked you (and more) will be useful to new parents? What have I left out? What have I included that strikes you as unnecessary or inappropriate?

6. What areas would you be interested in talking more about? Would you be interested in and/or willing to attend or run a taped discussion group on a particular subject? If so, what subject? (Here are a few possibilities: returning to work; being mobile with a baby; organizing your time and your environment; the postpartum period; fathers and babies.)

7. Do you have any friends with babies who might be willing to fill out this questionnaire? If so, please list their names and addresses.

Part X

A NOTE OF APPRECIATION

My thanks to the following parents, friends, and organizations for their help in putting together this book.

American Academy of Pediatrics

American Baby Magazine

Barbara Anderson

Jim Anderson

Tricia Clark Anderson

Ann Arensberg

Glenn Austin

Rosalie Hall Austin

Jonathan Ayres

Baby Talk Magazine

Jenny Wells Bealke

Lin Bealke

Walter Benoist

Florence Benson

Jay Benson

Amanda MacIntosh Berman

Louis Berman

Carl Bernstein

Elizabeth Bing

Marilyn Bittman

Sam Bittman

The Blessings Corporation

Evelyn Blatz

April Kingsberry Brookes

Brooklyn Botanical Garden

Mona Boyer

Judy Brown

Betty Bufano

Gilbert Burck

Mildred Burck

Esilda Buxbaum

Robert Buxbaum

Mrs. Mead Cherili

Diane Churchill

Marilyn Clayton

Cris Cory

Charlie Clagget

Katie Mullins Clagget

Dorothy Carpenter

Jessie Cochran

Columbia University, Institute of Human Nutrition

Terese Croft

Carolyn Curran

Brenda Daly

Jane Dickson

Anna Jo Dubow

Dick Dubow

Bobby Duffy

Sara Duffy

Mary Dunne

Tom Dunne

Lynn Eakin

Jerry Eisner

Marilyn Eisner

Carolyn Ennis

Mrs. Dart W. Everett

Dart W. Everett

The Family Center at Bank Street

Penny Feder

Dick Feinberg

Pamela Feinberg

Kathleen M. Fellin

Richard Flast

Ellen Galinsky

Norman Galinsky

Beverly Garsman

Jay Garsman

George Gill

Joyce Gluck

Ronnie Gluck

Robert Goell

Ethel Perry Good

Fred Good

Charlie Goodrich

Marian Goodrich

Joann Hughes Goodwin

Ridgeway Goodwin

Francine Gordon

Steve Gordon

Ann Dinsmore Gralnek

Judy Wells Gray

Bob Greenblatt

Prue Glass Greenblatt

Kate Grimes

Dick Grossman

Michael Gruen

Vanessa Gruen

Inez Grundy

Susan Harman

Carol A. Hayter

Isabel Heath

Harriette Heller

Annette Hollander

Cheryl Holtzman
Pud Houstoun
Meredith Hughes
Tom Hughes
Maria Huffman
Bob Ingram
Mary Lightburn Ingram
Good Housekeeping Institute
Judy Johnston
Peggy Jory
Terry Jory
Barbara Joseph
Steve Joseph
Murray Kiok
Susan Shapiro Kiok
Lisa Kirk
Jill Kneerim
Al Kramer
Doris Kreibich
Robbyn Kreigsman
Patricia Kruska
Adrian Leaf
La Leche League
Bette Lacina
Ivan Lacina
Marry Suzanne Lamont
Jane Lattes
Mel Layton
Mary Levine
Gail Levy
Janet L'Leurex
Ruby Ludwig
Eleanor Magid
Manhattan Maternity Center

Mary Jo Martin
Becky Wells Mattison
Peter Mattison
Kim McMullin
Lisa Mullins McMullin
Florence McCormack
Lorna McKay
Joan MacNamara
Elizabeth Metcalfe
James Metcalfe
Joanne Michaels
Gwenne Miorca
John Miorca
Ann Morrison
Carol Morse
David Morse
Eve Moser
Pat Murphy
National Organization for
Women (NOW)
Maudene Nelson
New York Lying-In Hospital
Carole Novick
Mary Roudebush Nowatny
Walter Nowatny
Annette Duffy Odell
Lois O'Brian
Diane O'Donovan
Cathy O'Gara
David Outerbridge
Lilias Outerbridge
Lila Pais
Esmeralda Party
Lionel Party

Jo Paul
Physicians for Automotive
Safety
Howard Posner
Janie Posner
Cathy Prendergast
Ann Russe Prewitt
Princeton Center on Infancy
Phillipa Quarrell
Marilyn Reynolds
Wade Robinson
Virginia Robinson
Nancy Rosenfeld
Alice Rouleau
Irwin Rappaport
Bobbie Rappaport
Margie Rivas
Pat St. Laurant
St. Louis Parent and Child
Association
Edith Gwathmy Sanderson
Doug Sanderson
Lucia Saradoff
Misha Saradoff
Rae Schapp
Glenda Schneider
Jason Schneider
Judi Schwartz
Leni Schwartz
Martin Schwartz
Brooke Sheaver
Phyllis Silverman
Nancy Sitrick
Mike Sitrick

Bill Smith
Genny Wilson Smith
Suzanne Smith-Freeland
Fifi Delacorte Spangler
Cris Steifel
Marilyn Stelzer
Steve Stelzer
N. Stoneman-Bell
Strobe Talbot
Arthur Tobier
Barbara Torney
Eleanor Tracy
Michael Trazov
Nancy Elliot Ulett
Pearl Watler
Judi Weber
Eugenia Wells
Frances Wells
George Wells
Carol Wend
Ann Werdel
Leslie Werther
Derinda Wines
Richard Wines
Shelia Weiss
Fran Weixel
Brenda Will
Harold Wise
June Wise
Jerry Zeidner
Margie Lewis Zeidner
Anita Zednik
Richard Zednik

Index

Temperature, taking baby's, 210–11
Tension, 114
Terminal sterilization method, 41–42
Thermometers, 210, 211
Tie-dyeing, 104–105
Toiletries, baby, 20
Toys, 225, 229–30, 232–39
Travel
  by bus, 177
  in car, 171–75
  clothing for, 182–83
  equipment for, 166, 167–71
  food during, 180–82
  medical care during, 177–80
  by plane, 176–77
  planning for, 175–76
  by train, 177

Urination, postpartum, 35, 110
Uterus, postpartum, 29, 109–10

Vagina, postpartum, 34, 111
Varicose veins, 113, 116
Vaporizers, 212
Vegetables, in baby food, 56, 57, 62
Vision, 219
Visual stimulation, 14, 20
Vitamins, 29, 38, 51, 113
  in cooking, 57
  in diet, 29, 50, 51, 52–54

Waking, night, 85–86
Waterproof pants, 98–99
Weaning, 64–67
Weight gain, baby, 35
Weight loss, postpartum, 112, 113

Well-baby examinations, 213–15
Wheat germ, 51
Whole-grain products, 51
Women's roles, modern, 14, 123
Work (employment outside)
  child care during, 157–62
  nursing and, 34
  part-time, 154
  returning to, 134, 153–56

Yogurt, 50

RECORD KEEPING

Name _____

Date of Birth _____

Time of Birth _____

Place of Birth _____

_____

(city)   (county)   (state)

Height _____

Weight _____

Length _____

picture of newborn baby

Birth Certificate
Paste a copy of the birth certificate here. It will be important later for establishing your child's right to attend school, to marry, obtain a passport, etc.

(paste here)

Birth Announcement

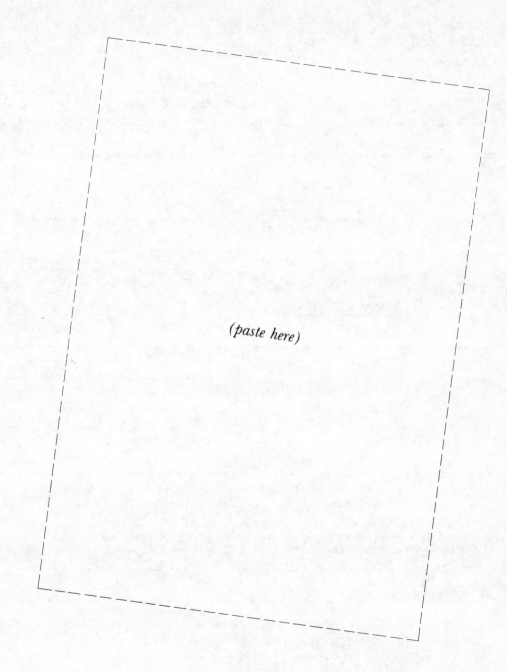

(*paste here*)

Labor and Birth Experience
Use this space to describe the birth.

Record of growth

AGE	WEIGHT	HEIGHT
birth		
1 month		
2 months		
3 months		
4 months		
5 months		
6 months		
7 months		
8 months		
9 months		
10 months		
11 months		
12 months		
13 months		
14 months		
15 months		
16 months		

Feeding
Interval between feedings as newborn

_____

_____

At three months

_____

_____

Introduction of solids   TYPE OF FOOD   DATE   REACTION (IF ANY)

_____

_____

Full or partial weaning

_____

_____

Fed from cup

_____

_____

Self feeding with fingers

_____

_____

Self feeding with spoon

_____

_____

Medical Record

Immunizations   Dates

Diphtheria, Pertussis, Tetanus (D.P.T.)   _____   _____   _____

Tuberculine Test   _____   _____   _____

Measles, Mumps, Rubella   _____   _____   _____

Trivalent Oral Polio   _____   _____   _____

Well-Baby Visits

Date: _____   Report: _____

_____

Date: _____   Report: _____

_____

Date: _____   Report: _____

_____

Accidents & Emergencies

Date: _____   Report: _____

Date: _____   Report: _____

Date: _____   Report: _____

Date: _____   Report: _____

DEVELOPMENT   *Age of Baby*

Lifts head briefly _____

Rolls part way to side from back _____

Follows objects with eyes _____

Smiles! _____

Can hold head up for a few minutes _____

Grasps and holds objects if placed in hand _____

Bats at objects _____

Sleeps through the night! _____

On stomach holds chest as well as head up _____

Enjoys being pulled to stand _____

Coos, and squeals _____

Explores face, eyes and mouth with hands _____

Vocalizes when talked to _____

Rocks like an airplane _____

DEVELOPMENT   *Age of Baby*

Rolls from stomach or side to back _____

Grabs objects _____

Babbles _____

Laughs! _____

Puts objects in mouth _____

Splashes in bath _____

Puts toes in mouth _____

Plays with rattle _____

Understands name _____

Vocalizes to get your attention
(interrupts conversations) _____

Rolls from back to stomach _____

Creeps _____

Sits with some support _____

_____

_____

_____

DEVELOPMENT

Age of Baby

Transfers object from one hand to other _____

Disturbed by strangers _____

Loves peek-a-boo _____

Tries to feed self _____

Crawls _____

Pulls self to stand _____

Sits alone _____

Imitates actions _____

Looks for hidden toy _____

Crawls upstairs _____

Stands alone briefly _____

Side steps or cruises along furniture _____

Seems to understand "no"
or a few other simple words _____

Plays pat-a-cake, so-big, waves bye-bye _____

_____

_____

_____

DEVELOPMENT

Age of Baby

Takes interest in books and pictures _____

Drinks from cup _____

Climbs on furniture _____

First words _____

Points to parts of the body when you name them _____

Forms attachment to security object
(a blanket, etc.) _____

Puts spoon in mouth _____

Teases parents _____

Walks! _____

Points _____

Tries to undress self (shoes and socks) _____

Gives up morning nap _____

Hugs you! _____

Notes, Observations, Questions, and Feelings During
The First Month

_____

_____

_____

_____

_____

_____

_____

_____

_____

_____

_____

_____

_____

picture

Notes, Observations, Questions, and Feelings During
The Second Month

_____

_____

_____

_____

_____

_____

_____

_____

_____

_____

_____

_____

_____

_____

picture

Notes, Observations, Questions, and Feelings During
The Third Month

_____

_____

_____

_____

_____

_____

_____

_____

_____

_____

_____

_____

picture

Notes, Observations, Questions, and Feelings During
The Fourth Month

_____

_____

_____

_____

_____

_____

_____

_____

_____

_____

_____

_____

_____

_____

picture

Notes, Observations, Questions, and Feelings During
The Fifth Month

_____

_____

_____

_____

_____

_____

_____

_____

_____

_____

_____

_____

_____

picture

Notes, Observations, Questions, and Feelings During
The Sixth Month

_____

_____

_____

_____

_____

_____

_____

_____

_____

_____

_____

_____

picture

Notes, Observations, Questions, and Feelings During
The Seventh Month

_____

_____

_____

_____

_____

_____

_____

_____

_____

_____

_____

_____

_____

_____

picture

Notes, Observations, Questions, and Feelings During
The Eighth Month

_____

_____

_____

_____

_____

_____

_____

_____

_____

_____

_____

_____

_____

_____

picture

Notes, Observations, Questions, and Feelings During
The Ninth Month

_____

_____

_____

_____

_____

_____

_____

_____

_____

_____

_____

_____

_____

picture

Notes, Observations, Questions, and Feelings During
The Tenth Month

_____

_____

_____

_____

_____

_____

_____

_____

_____

_____

_____

_____

picture

Notes, Observations, Questions, and Feelings During
The Eleventh Month

_____

_____

_____

_____

_____

_____

_____

_____

_____

_____

_____

_____

_____

_____

picture

Notes, Observations, Questions, and Feelings During
The Twelfth Month

_____

_____

_____

_____

_____

_____

_____

_____

_____

_____

_____

_____

_____

picture